Henley Park in Surrey

The History of a Royal Manor

by John Squier

Published 2012
by Normandy Historians
Quinta Cottage, Normandy Common Lane,
Normandy, Surrey   GU3 2AP

ISBN 978-0-9573822-0-6

With special thanks to HSH Dr. Prinz Donatus von Hohenzollern
for giving me advice and guidance from his extensive experience of publishing historical
reference books and for his very significant financial support for this publication.

Front cover photo collage by Jamie Squier.

Back cover: Conventual Seal of Chertsey Abbey
from Surrey Archaeological Society Collections Vol 1, 1858.

CONTENTS

PREFACE

It all started with my title deeds. I noticed that my house had been owned by a certain Henry Joseph Tenison Halsey of Henley Park and I wondered who he was. It was only part of his estate for 30 years but that connection lead me to research a thousand years of Henley Park's history.

History of any kind tends to sprawl, so we will make brief excursions to such far-flung places as Bengal and Western Australia and inevitably spend some time in London, but the majority of the action takes place in a couple of quiet Surrey villages. The historic mansion house of Henley Park lies some four miles north-west of Guildford in the civil parish of Normandy and occupies an imposing position on a ridge north of the village. As you round the bend of the road near the former Duke of Normandy pub you can see it over to the right above the trees in the distance. The influence of its proprietors extended much further, particularly into neighbouring Pirbright, although their estates at different times also included parts of Worplesdon, Bisley and Chobham and even Woking and Farnham.

The owners and occupiers of Henley Park included colourful and abrasive characters such as the peer of the realm whose bitter feud with the vicar changed the landscape of Pirbright village, the widely respected country squire whose eldest son had a penchant for marrying young and even under-age girls, and the king who liked Henley so much that he moved the tenants out and turned it into his own private park.

As a keen local historian Henley Park with its important historical associations has been a source of interest and fascination to me for much of the 38 years that I have lived in Normandy. With my young son I used to spend many a weekend exploring the grounds and former gardens which had declined into an overgrown wilderness. These were unhappy years for Henley Park when despite its Grade II listed building status, its future became increasingly uncertain as a succession of plans for redevelopment all met with opposition. The house was systematically looted and became more and more derelict, so much so that when John Baker, the artist and local historian, came to look at it in 1992 for one of his articles in the *Surrey Advertiser*, he was almost moved to tears by what he saw.

Now after so many years of uncertainty, the mansion house has been restored to its former splendour and has become home for another generation of owners. It is therefore an ideal time to publish an updated history of Henley Park which has long been overdue.

NOTES

Names

There was no consistent spelling of the names of people or places until the 19th century, and even then variations were common. In the earlier years names would often be spelled differently even within a single document. I have ignored these differences and tried to use consistent names throughout, choosing the most common variant at the time or the accepted form of the name now, except when quoting directly from source documents. Where there are examples of a person's own signature (for example Solomon Dayrolle) I have used his spelling rather than the more widely used variant (e.g. Dayrolles).

Dates

Dates are rendered in the New Style (Gregorian calendar), meaning years before 1752 have been adjusted to start on the first of January.

Money

Decimal currency was introduced in Great Britain in 1971. For readers unfamiliar with earlier systems the following explanation is offered. Until the late 13th century the only coin actually minted was the silver penny; 240 of these coins weighed one pound.

1 old penny (d, for denarius, a Roman coin) = 0.42 new pence.

1 shilling (s, for solidus, a medieval silver coin) = 12d = 5 new pence.

1 pound or sovereign (£, for libra, a Roman pound) = 240d = 20 shillings.

A guinea; originally worth one pound, its value fluctuated until it was fixed in 1717 at £1 1s.

A mark was ⅔ of a pound sterling, so 13s 4d. It was a unit used in financial calculations and agreements in the 12th - 13th centuries, but not issued as a coin.

Measurements

For readers unfamiliar with Imperial (pre-metric) measurements, the following explanation is offered.

Distance:

1 inch = 25.4 mm

1 foot = 12 inches = 30.48 cm

1 yard = 3 feet = 0.91 metres.

Capacity:

1 pint = 0.57 litres

1 gallon = 8 pints = 4.55 litres.

Land area:

5½ x 5½ yards or 30¼ square yards = 1 [square] rod, pole or perch

40 perches = 1 rood = 1210 square yards

4 roods = 1 acre = 4840 square yards

1 acre = 0.4 hectares.

Virgate - an old unit of land area equal to a quarter of an acre.

Landholding

A Husbandman was a tenant of the land.

A Yeoman worked the land he owned.

A Gentleman directed work on his land without engaging in the labour.

Some archaic terms and concepts

Advowson - the right to nominate to a benefice (a church living, e.g. the vicar). In prosperous parishes, the advowsons had substantial resale value. They provided the entry-ticket to a secure, well-paid and not too onerous job for life.

Copyhold - a form of land tenure under the manorial system. Ownership was recorded by copying the grant into the manorial roll. If a copyhold tenant died and no heir could be found, the land reverted to the lord of the manor.

Entail - a settlement of succession of landed estate so that it cannot be bequeathed at pleasure.

Escheat - reversion of lands to the lord of the manor (or the crown) upon failure of heirs capable of inheriting.

Glebe lands - land belonging or yielding revenue to a parish church or ecclesiastical benefice.

Heriot - a feudal duty or tribute (tax) due to a lord of the manor upon the death of a tenant or transfer of manorial property. Often in the form of 'best of live goods', meaning the lord could seize the best animal on the property.

Honour - a seigniory (see below) of several manors held under one baron or lord paramount.

Knight's fee - an obligation accepted by the tenant of an estate to provide an armed knight for the king's service. In time of war the king could demand from his tenants in chief (barons) the free provision of knights for a period of two months, in time of peace they might be called up for 40 days' service or for the duty of guarding castles. The king, if he preferred, could instead levy a tax for every enfeoffed knight on their books. In the middle 12th century there were about 300 barons and 7,000 knights out of a total population of say two million.

Lay Impropriator - a person entitled to receive the tithes, out of which he paid the curate or vicar's stipend.

Moiety - one of two equal shares, typically in an estate.

Patron - the holder of an Advowson (see above).

Seigniory - the territory under the dominion of a lord, esp. a feudal domain.

Toft - land once occupied by a homestead (e.g. before the Black Death).

LIST OF FIGURES AND TABLES

LIST OF ILLUSTRATIONS

1. AN ANCIENT MANOR

Modern English history conventionally begins with the Norman Conquest in 1066, but Henley Park is much older than that. The settlement names are Saxon - Hen-lea meaning the high clearing, reflecting the Saxon practice of cultivating strips of land up the hill behind their settlement - and Fremlesworth, the former name of this part of Normandy, probably meaning the enclosed homestead of a Saxon called Frem or Fremel. The southern part of Henley Park and the area around Tickner's Bridge lie on a strip of alluvium which is more fertile than the sandy wastes of the Surrey Heath to the north and more easily worked than the heavy clays to the south. It is known that the Saxons had a good eye for the type of vegetation that indicated a good location in which to settle and the geology of the area gives rise to numerous springs and streams issuing from the lower slopes of the Hog's Back and the Fox Hills. A bonus would have been an abundance of wild animals to hunt and a supply of oak timber for building.

The Saxons began, or continued, systematically clearing the wooded lands of southern England and placed their imprint indelibly on the shape of the English countryside - by the year 1000 most of the towns and villages of modern England had been settled by the sea-farers. But as Fremel and his extended family came up the river valleys from the Thames looking for a good place to live, they may possibly have adopted an even older Roman settlement, because evidence of Roman domestic habitation has been found in the fields just to the south of Henley Park. A Roman coin hoard and several other individual coins have been found in the vicinity, as well as a Saxon coin of around 700 AD and other possibly Saxon artefacts.

The name of Henley had many different spellings in medieval times until spelling became standardised in the 18th and 19th centuries, but these have no significance. The first recorded reference to Henley is in a charter of Chertsey Abbey dated 727AD, but this may well be a forgery for reasons that will become clear.

Edward the Confessor was almost the last Saxon king of England but he had no obvious heir. His indecisive handling of the succession, apparently promising the throne to both Harold of the powerful house of Godwin and to William of Normandy, subsequently known as the Conqueror, contributed to what one historian described as 'one of the greatest catastrophes to which the English have ever succumbed'. William invaded England and took the throne by force, imposing Norman rule on the country. The Norman forces inflicted considerable damage throughout the countryside. In 1066 two sections of the 'plundering horde' proceeded towards Winchester 'laying waste on their way the manors of Wanborough and Farnham amongst others', but it is not known how badly Henley was affected. England was one of the wealthiest countries in Europe at the time, which is why it was so attractive to the Normans.

Domesday

The Domesday Book is often believed to be an attempt to update King William's tax 'database' but it is not organised well for that purpose, being laid out by owner not by location. In fact Domesday gave William new power and control and confirmed him as England's rightful heir. It completely ignores the short reign of King Harold whom the Normans regarded as an 'illegal usurper'; establishing William as undisputed owner of the kingdom, it completed the conquest begun in 1066.

There was a revolution in land ownership after the Norman conquest and Domesday records the impact the conquest had on the English people. After the conquest there was confusion over who the legal land owners were, but once ownership was recorded in the Book it was final - it established who owned what in England. It recorded the biggest transfer of land ownership England has ever seen, and the dispossession of the English elite. Many English landholders lost everything and many freeholders were downgraded to rent-paying peasants (villeins).

Domesday was the largest bureaucratic exercise which had ever been attempted in Europe. 60,000 people gave testimony to the inquest and it spread suspicion and fear throughout the country. All sorts of dubious documents were produced to the inquests but once entered into the Book they became irrefutable evidence - entry in Domesday was the final word, there was no appeal.

Each entry contains information on land ownership at the time King Edward died in 1066 and at the time of the survey 20 years later. Henley (see Plate 1) in Woking hundred (a subdivision of a county with its own court) was held by a Saxon called Azor in 1066. At that time it was rated (assessed) for eight hides and it was valued at £6. Originally a hide was a portion of land which could be cultivated in a year by a full plough team of eight oxen; the area depended on the type of soil but was typically 120 acres. By the time of Domesday it had become a unit of assessment with no fixed relationship to an area of land, but it suggests that Henley had a possible size of 800 to 900 cultivated acres. At this early stage it is probable that the manor of Henley included all the later manors of Ash and Cleygate, and thus much of the current parishes of Ash and Normandy; there is no separate reference to Ash in Domesday. Azor is said to have been one of Edward the Confessor's personal guards and was one of the few Saxon leaders who kept some of their land after the Conquest. He held several manors, some of which he lost to the Normans, but he retained Henley until he died.

Domesday records that Azor bequeathed Henley to Chertsey Abbey 'for the good of his soul', although he may have had in mind that if it passed to another Saxon owner it could have been taken forcibly by a Norman. Many of the early charters recording the land-holdings of Chertsey Abbey are now viewed with some suspicion and one can imagine that the Abbots of Chertsey, eager to substantiate their claim to the lands they held, created them retrospectively and presented them to the inquisition to confirm their claims. Once accepted and recorded in the Book, they became 'fact' along with the Abbey's ownership of the land.

In 1086 Henley, one of the Abbey's many holdings, was rated for 5½ hides and was valued at £5, indicating a significant reduction in agricultural yield from pre-conquest times, possibly because rents skyrocketed after the conquest. There was arable land for five ploughs (five carucates). Unlike a hide, a carucate still indicated a specific area of land, the amount that could be cultivated in a year by a full plough team of eight oxen, while again the area depended on the type of soil but was typically 120 acres, so suggesting an area of around 600 acres of cultivated land. There was one plough owned by the manorial lord and there were ten villeins (serfs or villagers) and six bordars (smallholders who rendered menial service for a cottage held at the will of the lord) with five ploughs. There were two bondmen (slaves) - it is known that there was slave labour in pre-Conquest England but apparently people often felt uneasy enough about it to free their slaves as a charitable act in their wills. There were four acres of meadow and woodland for pannage (pasturage) of 50 hogs, a very necessary source of meat protein for the villagers. There was a church in the manor which has been identified as the predecessor of St Peter's Church in Ash village.

The wheeled plough was the foundation of life for English people - it looks slow and primitive to us now, but compared to farming techniques in most other parts of the world at the time it was supercharged. One man held the plough while the other walked with the oxen, coaxing and goading them forward. It was the reason why England at the turn of the millennium was able to support a population of at least a million. "The ploughman feeds us all" declared Aelfric, the contemporary Wessex schoolmaster.

Only 1% of the population of England was Norman but Domesday gave the Normans security of title, becoming legitimate owners of the land they had taken. King William owned all the land in England and the nobles held their land from him. Nevertheless, under the Normans England became largely peaceful and remained stable for many years, only being troubled by the necessity to raise knights and mercenaries to engage in foreign wars as the English kings went to fight in the crusades and struggled to retain their possessions in France.

Chertsey Abbey

Chertsey Abbey was founded in 666AD by Saint Erkenwald who became the first Abbot. The earliest mention of Henley is in a charter of 727AD which appears to be a grant from Frithuwald, sub-king of Surrey under King Wulfhere of Mercia, to Chertsey Minster of land at several places including Henley, which is described as having five mansas (farmsteads). A charter of 1062 from King Edward confirms the Abbey's privileges and land and mentions six mansas at Henley. While experts now doubt the authenticity of these early charters, they claim to establish the Abbey's ownership of Henley from an early date, but this conflicts with Azor's tenure in 1066, and whether Azor had a grant for life from the Abbey or whether the charters are spurious is an open question. Certainly the Abbey retained ownership of Henley for three centuries after Domesday and later documents record their attempts to claim the rent rightfully due to them, as we shall see in due course.

In a bull (edict) dated 18 February 1176, Pope Alexander III gave the patronage of a chapel at Henley to the Abbey, perhaps the first hint of a process that was to divide Ash and Henley into separate manors. In 1537 Chertsey Abbey was dissolved and its manor of Ash became the property of Henry VIII, but by then Henley had already been in royal hands for 200 years.

The Forest, 13th century

In Anglo-Saxon times there were no restrictive land laws and anyone wishing to hunt could do so, but after the Conquest William claimed the monopoly of hunting in England. King

Henry II (1154-89) declared the entire county of Surrey to be part of the Royal Forest of Windsor, which was very unpopular with the landholders and tenants. Within the royal forest as well as the stringent protection of game, no landowner could improve his land by ditching, hedging or draining, nor could he build houses or cut down trees and underwood to make land fit for cultivation except by express permission of the Forest Court, and he would be expected to pay for the privilege. This period of forest law contributed to the backward and underdeveloped state of this part of Surrey at the time.

While other parts of Surrey were deforested in Richard I's reign the north-west part including Henley and Guildford remained subject to forest laws despite several attempts by the barons to deforest them. One of the terms of Magna Carta, first issued in 1215, was that this area of Surrey was to be deforested, but Henry III soon tried to reclaim it. He finally gave up his claim in 1226 in return for a large subsidy, but for the next 300 years it was still treated as a purlieu of the Forest of Windsor and the king retained a right over deer straying, employing a ranger to drive them back. The hierarchy of Forest officials was headed by the Bailiff. Under him were officials for each ward, with specific duties including verderers and foresters who were responsible for looking after the deer and presenting offenders at Forest Courts. Woodwards were responsible for the timber and Agisters collected rents for the feeding of cattle or pigs in the demesne lands of the Forest. Rangers were responsible for the observance of forest laws in outlying areas of the Forest and for reclaiming any deer straying from the forest proper.

Henley and Guildford parks, being held by the Crown at that time, remained part of the forest after the rest of Surrey had been deforested, up to the 17th century when both parks were sold. Forest Courts held at Bagshot in the 1500s include reports from the park keepers of Henley but these are just a bland 'all is well' and give little information about the state of the park.

Owners and Tenants, 14th century

The monks of Chertsey Abbey were renowned for their proficiency in estate management and farming but this part of north-west Surrey with its poor soil was amongst the least profitable of the Abbey's possessions and by the 14th century it had sublet the manor and some lands at Fremlesworth to a family of some importance who assumed the name 'of Henley'. Deeds refer to John de Henley and in 1306 to William de Henley. William was Sheriff of Surrey until 1313 after which date he sat in parliament as one of the knights of the shire. The tenant paid an annual 'service' or rent to the Abbey of 22s 8d (in 'old money' there were 20 shillings in £1 and 12 pence in a shilling) and 12 gallons of honey at Michaelmas, and suit of court at the Abbot's manor of Ash every three weeks. The inhabitants of the village of Henley were required to come to the Abbot's annual court leet at Ash, which looked after the administrative matters of the manor and judged less serious crimes, on the feast of St Matthew (21st September). 12 gallons of honey would be the produce of about 24 skeps (straw bee-hives used in the middle ages).

In September 1324 William de Henley sold the lease of the manor to King Edward II. As well as the purchase money, the king undertook to provide William with the marriage of an eligible male heir for one of his daughters 'to the value of 100 marks' before next Christmas, or to pay the 100 marks in money (a mark was ⅔ of a pound sterling). This concept seems alien to us now but presumably in medieval times arranged marriages were the norm, and so when a father died with underage children, under the wardship system the king assumed the right to arrange the marriage for the children. This right apparently became a commodity that the king could sell, so that purchasers could buy a 'landed' son-in-law for their daughter to marry. In fact William settled for the money instead and acknowledged receipt of it on 'the Thursday before the feast of St Nicholas' (5th December) the next year.

The king directed John de Hildesle to take possession of the manor in his name and to depute a trusty bailiff to receive and account for the rents. Royal account books show that Edward II stayed at Henley with his entourage several times in 1325-26. From March to July 1325 he commissioned his carpenters managed by Jack Cressing to build a new timber-framed chapel on stone foundations. To have a chapel within the house would require a dispensation from the Pope so the edict of 1176 must have remained in force. At the same time diggers worked on the ditches round the manor and its park, indicating that there was already a house and some form of emparkment here.

In November he granted custody of the manor of Henley and lands in Ash, Worplesdon and Henley to Walter Bishop of Exeter, but then revoked the grant and in the following March granted custody to one Walter Ladd. In exchequer accounts Walter Ladd is described as bailiff of Henley. An account of the profits of the manor from Michaelmas 1325 to 1326 was given to Ladd. Among the receipts are a heifer for a heriot (a feudal tax due to a lord of the manor upon the death of a tenant or transfer of manorial property), a gown sold for 1s 1d for another heriot, and the milk of 15 cows and 45 goats let to farm, the former at 4s 6d the latter at 4d. The whole receipts amount to £34 0s 4d. Amongst the payments are two bushels of salt for the potage of the servants 6d, tithe paid for four calves 4d, mowing, gathering and binding corn at 5d per acre except barley which was 6d, wages of a plough-boy in harvest 2s 4d, mowing, making and carrying hay was 8d an acre, thrashing and winnowing 196 quarters and a half of various sorts of corn 12s 5¼d (but at three farthings a quarter it would come to 12s 3½d so that there seems to be a small mistake in the calculations), two ploughmen, two carters, one plough-boy and one mower had one halfpenny a week allowed for potage, according to the custom of the manor making 13s, the wages of these six with one keeper of the goats, one hog-driver and one cowherd came to £2 7s being, if paid equally, around 5s 2½d each. The bailiff who superintended and accounted for it all had 2d a day. The clear profit was £17 11s 10d (roughly £6,000 at today's values).

In 1327 the Abbot of Chertsey petitioned the new king Edward III because he had not been paid his rent since Edward II bought the manor, whereupon an instruction was issued on 12th March to Hugh de Bury and William Husee, and another one to the sheriff, to enquire into it. An inquisition into the matter at Harpersford in Egham found the allegations to be true and that William de Henley and his ancestors as lords of the manor had 'from time immemorial' paid this rent to the Abbey and the Abbot had never released his right to receive it. In September 1327 the king granted Henley to Sir William de Clinton but he too apparently did not pay the rent to the Abbot who petitioned the king again. This time, however, the king directed him to sue de Clinton at Common Law. The Abbot was forced to petition again in 1335 but no follow-up action is recorded.

Events of national significance came to Henley in 1328. During a rebellion in the 1320s against Edward II by his cousin Thomas Earl of Lancaster, Lancaster's most trusted retainer Robert de Holland defected to the king during a decisive campaign. Many of the rebels were executed and de Holland was imprisoned until 1327, but on his release was pursued by Lancastrian partisans and is said to have been captured in a wood near Henley. He was subsequently beheaded.

In the 14th century Henley was part of the 'villata' of Ash, roughly translated as village. The king levied a national tax called the fifteenths and tenths, whereby rural areas paid one fifteenth of the value of the goods on the land. In the first assessment of 1332 William de Clinton was taxed by far the largest amount and there were 24 other taxpayers in Ash, paying a total of 39s 5d, something like £700 at today's values. In addition there were eight further taxpayers in 'the Abbot of Chertsey's villani (small village?) in the recent ownership of the king', assessed for a total of 6s 6d (see Figure 1). From the later assessments it is evident that this refers to Henley. The eight tenants in Henley were assessed for less tax than many of those in Ash and seem to have had smaller holdings. However, those resident in the king's domains were exempted by a special writ and the collectors for Ash were allowed exemption from collecting the 6s 6d. From this tax return it seems clear that the main area of settlement was in the western 'Ash' end of the manor with a smaller settlement or a few scattered farmsteads at Henley. William de Clinton himself seems to have had land in Ash rather than in the part of Henley 'in the ownership of the king'.

William de Clinton, described as a 'soldier and magnate', was a friend of King Edward III and as well as engaging in active military service held several important appointments including warden of the Cinque Ports where he was heavily involved in defence of the south coast from projected French and Flemish attacks. He was created Earl of Huntingdon in 1337. The king having previously granted Henley to him for life, in August 1337 granted it to him 'in fee simple' (freehold), but apparently this was so that de Clinton could convey it to Sir John de Molyns which he did two days later. The same year John de Molyns obtained a licence from the king to empark woods called West Grove and Goddard's Grove in 'his manor of Henley' and 300 adjoining acres of land, meadow and pasture, even though these lay within the royal forest. In 1338 and 1339 the grant was extended several times to include further privileges such as the right to hold a court leet at Henley and the right of Return of Writs 'with Infangthef, Outfangthef (the right to hold trials of those within and outside the manor), goods and chattels of felons and fugitives, waifs, strays and the right to erect gallows'. A similar form of wording was used in deeds transferring ownership of Henley Park until as late as the 19th century, long after they had ceased to have any significance.

John de Molyns was active in public life and was a senior administrator for the Crown. As the king's personal friend he advanced rapidly in the royal household and exploited his position to become a significant landowner, holding over 30 manors by 1340. Unfortunately he became involved in a financial dispute with the king who owed him a considerable amount of money, and he failed to remit money that Edward demanded to support the siege of Tournay in 1340. The king had to abandon the siege and return to England where he imprisoned de Molyns and, regarding the breach as nothing less than rebellion, seized all his estates and so took possession of Henley again.

Figure 1: The 1332 Tax Assessment.
Hundred of Woking, Villata de Asshe
Landholders paid a fifteenth of the value of the goods on the land.

Willelmo de Clynton 8s 4d qa *[quarter]*

Ricardo le Rede 16d ob *[has died]*

Jordano le Vannar 24d qa

Phillipo ate Brug 10d ob qa

Roberto le Sutre 11d ob qa

Willelmo Spotte 10d ob qa

Johanne Wyn 3s ob qa

Johanne at Brug 20d qa

Gilberto Wysdom 8d

Waltero le Longe 8d

Ricardo de Asshesham 12d ob qa

Willelmo Farman 17d ob

Johanne le Marsh 8d

Summa 39s 5d probatur (added later)

Thoma South 14d qa

Henrico ate Mulle 8d

Waltero Cobat 20d

Sayer' Est 19d qa

Johanne Est 2s 1d ob

Johanne Carpenter 23d ob

Jordano Waryn 18d ob

Roberto Spurie 8d

Roberto Farman 8d

Henrico Gale 8d

Galfrido Lacer 17d qa

Thoma le Reue 19d qa

Villani Abbatis de Certes' in Villa de Asshe deductis redditibus et serviciis eorundem Villanorum per breve domini Regis
[Reductions in rents and services to the village of the Abbey of Chertsey in the villages of Ash in the same village during the short ownership of the king]

Johanne de Fokelbrok 12d

Willelmo de Fokelbrok 6d ob qa

Willelmo le Skynner 14d ob

Galfrido le Reve 14d ob

Summa 6s 6d ob probatu

Johanne le Vannar' 11d ob qa

Roberto Robelot 6d ob

Jordano Serle 8d qa

Willelmo Haluelord 3d qa

2. A ROYAL RESIDENCE (1340-1400)

Royal residence and Building works, 1340-45

King Edward III maintained a ring of satellite houses and hunting lodges round his castle at Windsor, so that in whatever part of the forest he chose to hunt there was a house where he could eat and sleep. He often resided at Henley from 1340 to 45, 'reserving it to the Chamber' (meaning keeping it for his own use as a place of royal business) as his father Edward II had done. He hunted, entertained and conducted the business of the realm, as evidenced by the many letters patent and other royal decrees issued from Henley. In this period it was usually referred to as 'South Henley' or 'Henley on the Heath', probably to distinguish it from Henley in Oxfordshire which was another of John de Molyns' former manors.

Edward III continued to make improvements and additions to the manor house, creating a complex of buildings of some considerable size worthy of a royal residence equipped for royal visits and entertaining guests. In 1343 he had building work carried out at Henley at a cost of some £40 (something like £16,000 to us). Another timber-framed chapel was built in the outer court of the manor and was fitted with five windows painted with religious themes. The 'chapel of the king and queen', presumably the chapel built by Edward II, was retiled and next to it a new 'oriel', also called an oratory, was constructed for the king and queen to hear mass in. This was roofed with lead, stood at first floor level over a chamber, contained its own altar and had seven stained-glass windows with the arms of the royal family. It was built principally by master carpenter Richard Bledlawe and his team, who also made two new chambers in the manor house. There were repairs to the chambers of the king and queen, 'a little chamber towards the garden', the kitchen, the larder and the great cellar. Evidently distinct from these there was also a new 'house' of four chambers equipped with two double fireplaces. Wall paintings were commissioned under the Edwards but are rarely referred to in later accounts probably because tapestry hangings were becoming the fashionable form of wall covering. A fragment of highly-decorated 14th century floor tile, discovered in the fields of Henley Park, was described by the curator of Guildford Museum as a well-made example 'presumably from the medieval manor house' (see Plate 4).

While these rooms sound normal to us, they were still a novel concept in the 14th century. The invention of fireplaces with chimneys, based on the development of good bricks that can deal with heat, radically changed the way people lived. Suddenly it was possible to lay boards across the beams and create a whole new world upstairs; a host of new room types appeared in the 13th and 14th centuries that had not existed before - bed chamber, oratory, parlour, library, etc. Gone was the ancient custom of the whole household living by day and night in the great hall.

Outdoor works at Henley at this time included heightening and levelling the inner courtyard, which was provided with a stone drain to take away rainwater, heightening the outer gate of the manor and repairs to the drawbridge between the hall and garden. There was work on a lookout or viewing tower and the garden was dug and sown ready for 'the coming of the king and queen', which suggests adequate notice to get annuals into flower. The fish-pond was stocked with fish for the royal visits. Even had land-based meat been freely available it was forbidden by religious rules for nearly half the days of the year, so fishponds probably contained a wide variety of fish including many that we seldom eat now such as pike, lamprey and gudgeon. 'Fish days' were abandoned after the break with Rome but were reinstated by Elizabeth I to support the fishing industry.

The evidence of later buildings on the site, as we shall see in more detail in the next two chapters, suggests the likelihood that the medieval manor complex was sited in an upland position where part of the Vokes factory was until recently. The drawbridge mentioned in the records of building work has been taken as evidence of a moat or ditch and a later building in this position had a moat-like feature. The only known well at Henley Park was just to the south of this feature, a little way north-east of the present-day mansion. The name of the manor, meaning 'high clearing' indicates the importance of this area and three practical considerations would have also made it a prime choice. The first was that there would have been no risk of flooding which might have been the case had the manor house been built on the lower land to the south. The second was the proximity of the road which runs along the ridge from Pirbright to Ash, which is believed to be an ancient route giving direct access to the western reaches of the manor and the church at Ash. The third was the existence nearby of land suitable for cultivation.

The royal household would have been relatively self-contained and followed the king when he moved, but a core of retainers would have remained at each residence to ensure the maintenance and upkeep of the buildings. The retainers probably included local people and at least one of them apparently went on to hold an important position in the royal retinue. William of Fremelsworth, whose name suggests a local origin, became keeper of the king's stud and was responsible for the horses at Henley. John de Molyns had kept horses there and the king took them over with the property, for breeding and for hunting. He issued orders to pay William of Fremelsworth for expenses incurred in maintenance of the horses and when John de Molyns later returned to favour and most of his property was restored, the king apparently retained the horses at Henley.

Manors and lands

With John de Molyns in disgrace, the Abbot of Chertsey renewed his demands to the king for payment of rent due, asserting grandly that the Abbey had held Henley 'since the time of its foundation'. As a result in 1343 the king ordered a Commission to enquire into the matter and produce a valuation of the manor, based on which he issued a writ to Henry de Greystoke, keeper of the manor, to pay the arrears of rent due since the manor came into the king's hands.

William de North, Escheator of Surrey, produced the following valuation: Income: A capital messuage and curtilage, of no value beyond reprises (a yearly deduction or charge); 256 acres of arable land at 4d per acre making £4 5s 4d; 30 acres of meadow at 2s making £3; 10 acres of meadow in the park, £1; the customary rents of free tenants and one villein, £5 6s 8d; 60 acres of separate pasture at 2d making 10s; an enclosed Park of 120 acres at 3d for pasture making £1 10s; a wood in the same park, value for pannage 10s; 200 acres of heath on the waste, 2s; harvest works of the free tenants and villein, fed by the lord twice a day, 3s; pleas and perquisites of courts, nothing; Total £16 7s 0d. Expenditure: £1 2s 8d and 12 gallons of honey at Michaelmas at 6d making 6s, paid to the Abbot of Chertsey, lord of the manor of Ash. Total £1 8s 8d. Clear (profit) £14 18s 4d (a reduction of over £2½ since the last valuation 17 years earlier). Tenants dwelling at Henley owe three-weekly suit of court at Ash manor and attendance at the annual court leet there on St Matthew's day.

The area of cultivated land described in the valuation is about half that implied by the assessment in the Domesday Book (see Figure 4), suggesting that the manors of Ash and Henley had split by this time. This is supported by a 1344 tax assessment which refers to the manor of Henley in the village of Ash, although both were still under the ownership of Chertsey Abbey. The earliest surviving Ash manorial roll dates from 1382. As the population increased in the 12th and 13th centuries a lot of the manors mentioned in Domesday were divided, either as subfeudary manors under the same lord or under different lords. At this time Henley probably contained all of the eastern end including what later became the manor of Cleygate and eventually the village of Normandy.

The early decades of the 14th century were a period of famine, plague (in people and animals), soil exhaustion and social unrest. At this time, even before the effects of the Black Death, the manorial system was undergoing a fundamental change. Commutation of villein services for money payments was increasing rapidly, allowing the lord to hire labour when he wanted it and giving the villein the freedom to work his own fields when he wished. He still had to abide by manorial restrictions such as the lord's right of heriot, wardship and escheat, but farming for profit was to supersede farming for subsistence and the villein with initiative would try to buy his land and become a yeoman (a farmer who worked his own land). Those who did not succeed would become landless agricultural workers. In the 15th century the change from agriculture in common to agriculture in severalty continued and the tenant farmer had become a man of substance enjoying a higher standard of life, but this was outside Henley Park because by then there were no tenant farmers left.

The Black Death, 1348-49

Estimates of the population of England at the eve of the Black Death range from 3 to 7 million, with around 6 million being the most likely, a significant increase from the time of the Norman Conquest. If you were to meet a pre-Conquest Englishman the first thing that would strike you would be how tall he was, very much the size of anyone alive today. It was during the centuries that followed that population growth, overcrowding, climate change and rapidly inflating prices leading to harvest failures, malnutrition and famine, aggravated by wars and restrictive government practices such as export embargos, affected the stature and well-being of western Europeans. Europe in the mid-14th century was ripe for tragedy and archaeologists who have studied these centuries say that they can almost see the devastation of the Black Death looming in the evidence of the increasingly frail and unhealthy skeletal remains. The Black Death peaked in England in 1348-49 and latest research suggests that up to half of the population died.

It seems that the more affluent suffered less mortality than the peasantry and indeed only one member of the royal family, a daughter of Edward III, is known to have died from the plague. A consequence of the Black Death was an extreme shortage of labour causing a rise in wages which the government and landowners tried to control by repressive laws, which led to resentment and ultimately the 'Peasant's Revolt' of 1381. Despite the violence and social unrest, the crisis was handled much better in England than in France which descended into chaos and total collapse. When the worst of the epidemic had subsided leaving depopulated villages and a severe labour shortage, the surviving landowners set out to increase and consolidate their holdings. In the case of Henley, the king decided to buy out some of the tenants and turn part of the manor into a royal hunting park.

Royal Purchase and Emparkment, 1351-55

John de Molyns had returned to favour in the mid-1340s, joining Edward in the 1346 Crècy campaign, and the king restored Henley to him and confirmed his liberty to empark the land and woods granted in 1337. A Henry de Stoughton who perhaps obtained some interest in the manor while it was in possession of the Crown, released all his rights to John de Molyns and his family. However, in June 1351 de Molyns sold the manor back to the king for £550 and the rents from some manors in Buckinghamshire (see Plate 3). William, de Molyns' son, confirmed this and released all his and his heir's rights in Henley in 1359.

In the meantime, in a series of land transactions in May 1355 the king had bought or exchanged lands or rights in the manor from some 20 different tenants and landholders, and the lands were transformed into a royal park. Figure 2 lists these transactions and shows that some were purchases, some were exchanges and some involved paying off a mortgage. Some reveal details of the landscape, describing plots of meadow, pasture and moor, and mentioning features such as a new lane, an old park and John the miller's water-mill. Others hint at family relationships, so we can speculate that Isabella wife of William Millicent and Emma wife of William Stedman were sisters who inherited equal shares of Hewersmead and Hewersmoor from their father, and were probably related to John Hewer who released his rights in the property. Some of the property names are familiar even now; Cobbettsmoor is still adjacent to Cobbett Hill while Heathers and Clements survived for centuries in the Cleygate manorial records.

None of the tenants who were taxed just over 20 years earlier appears in the deeds so it seems that the Black Death caused a complete turnover in the landholdings, and may have left some plots unoccupied and unclaimed, making it easier for the king to acquire the land he needed for his park, and to offer plots in exchange to the people he was removing.

Figure 4 shows some estimates of the population and extent of Henley derived from the various valuations and other sources. It is clear that in the 14th century the main centre of population was the village of Ash, centred around the church which has been identified as the church mentioned in Domesday. The Henley end of the manor was probably sparsely populated with scattered small farms, a pattern of settlement which was to remain virtually unchanged right up to the late 19th century.

In 1357 the king compensated the rector of Ash for the loss of his tithes from the former tenants in Henley by securing a prebend (revenue from a church estate) of 30 marks a year for the church of Ash 'for ever', and granted him £10 compensation for the two years since the enclosure of the lands. In return, the rector and his successors were required to provide a chaplain to perform divine service daily within the manor house at Henley. This grant was reconfirmed by subsequent monarchs including Richard II, Henry VI and Edward IV.

Although the watermill that John att Mull granted to the king in 1355 is long gone, there are some curious features of the watercourses in Henley Park that may give us a clue to its whereabouts. The stream that enters the park from the south at Tickners Bridge and runs in an arc to exit in the east at Cobbett Hill, formerly ran in two separate courses. In the earliest Ordnance Survey maps the eastern branch runs through a channel (which has been slowly 'drying out' in later editions) to two long ponds at different levels with a thin strip of land separating them. The ponds have now become isolated and the channel has been obliterated by ploughing. Both ponds remain and the level of the southern, upstream pond is about five feet above the level of the downstream one, and they are connected by a sluice through some old brick constructions. At some time, considerable effort went into creating the two ponds and the diversion of the Tickners stream, and it is tempting to suggest the junction of the two ponds with the drop in water level as the location of the Henley Park watermill, but there is no firm evidence to support it. An alternative explanation is that the whole feature was created in the 19th century when the Halsey owners made their boating lake by broadening the stream, but of course both theories may be correct. In a fairly flat and featureless landscape, perhaps the Halseys made use of the remains of a much earlier irregularity when they were modifying the waterways.

Another strange feature of the landscape within the park is 'Drove Lane'. This is listed in the 1844 tithe apportionment of Normandy and is still described as a lane in 1922, but it leads from nowhere to nowhere, starting at the edge of a field and ending at the stream. Adjacent plots on the tithe survey are named Drove Lane Field, Drove Lane Moor and Drove Lane Coppice. It is clearly a substantial way with well-defined banks and ditches. It is positioned to be a continuation of the Flexford - Bailes Lane route which may have been pushed to the east by the emparkment, but it is impossible to know how old it actually is.

The boundary of the park that Edward III enclosed is an elongated hexagon roughly delineated by the A323 Guildford Road to the south, the A324 Pirbright Road to the north and Cobbett Hill to the east (see Plate 120). In several places the boundary embankments and ditches can clearly be seen today. The area emparked is about 420 acres, leaving about 250 acres of the manor outside the park. The manor of Cleygate, comprising much of modern Normandy and parts of Wood Street, came into being after this time and included the properties on all sides of the enclosed royal park, so it would appear that it eventually 'replaced' the manor of Henley and included all the residual lands not enclosed by the king. From the 1380s the king appointed keepers for 'Cleygate and Whetersh' in the manor of Henley and rented 'lands called Cleygate lying at Henley' to various tenants. From the 1460s it became the 'manor of Cleygate' which was owned by the Crown until Elizabeth I sold it in 1560 to Edward Fynes, Lord Clinton and Saye. When Lord Clinton sold the manor on a few years later, the deed specifically excluded 'lands within Henley Park'.

Manorial roll, 1357

Only one manorial roll is known to have survived for Henley (see Plate 5). The manor must have continued to function after the emparkment to manage the remaining tenants outside the park, until it was 'reincarnated' as the manor of Cleygate, but the only surviving court record is dated 12 June 1357. The business of the court included two property transactions and 16 tenants who trespassed on the king's crops (see Figure 3).

The king gave John and Joan Fletcher, who had granted 'Heathers' to him in 1355, a piece of land 'which was formerly emparked', so possibly there was some adjustment to the boundary of the royal park still happening. The holding known as Heathers included the field later called Dairymead which occupies an anomalous position on the other side of the road beside the park boundary, suggesting the possibility that it was taken out of the park by this transaction. Four hundred years later it was purchased by Solomon Dayrolle, the then owner, and thus brought back into Henley Park. The king also granted William Allan, who was not mentioned in 1355, a parcel of land 'by the new lane which formerly was in the old park', and it is tempting to assume that this refers to the original emparkment granted to John de Molyns, which therefore may not have been entirely within the king's new park.

The trespassers ranged from William and Thomas East, each fined one penny for trespassing with two pigs in the king's pasture, to Ralph Swift the servant of Robert de Wykeford who was fined a total of 15s for not only trespassing with a whole variety of animals on many occasions 'by day and night and against the inclosure of the bailiff', but also for apparently stealing the king's colts from the royal stud. Only two of the trespassers took part in the 1355 land transactions, but presumably they all inhabited the area surrounding the park which later became Cleygate.

Ongoing taxation

The fifteenths and tenths tax continued to be collected throughout the 14th century and Henley continued to be exempted as it was in 1332. The amounts 'for the property of the king in the manor of Henley' varied from 8s 4d to 14s 4d. There was a much later assessment carried out in 1586 and surprisingly it mentions 'villani abbatis de Certes', because Chertsey Abbey had been dissolved some 50 years earlier. In the tax assessment of 1379 there is specific reference to 'the property of the king in the manors of Worplesdon and Henley', and the amount exempted was 28s 8d. This might indicate a separate property entirely but it could refer to the part of Henley south of the stream that runs through the park. Worplesdon and Ash parishes were disputing the ownership of this area for several hundred years and elderly inhabitants in the 16th century reported 'beating the bounds' along the stream, rather than following the later parish boundary along the road to the south of the park.

More building works, 1350s-1399

After the king bought the manor back from John de Molyns, further building work was carried out in the early 1350s although no details are available. In May 1356 the 'rapidly rising clerk' William of Wykeham was appointed clerk of works at Henley on the Heath and Easthampstead (near Bracknell, Berkshire). In October he was appointed 'surveyor' of works at these manors and also Windsor, then in 1359 'the king's beloved clerk' William of Wykeham was appointed 'Chief Keeper and Surveyor' of four castles including Windsor and 12 manors including Guildford and Henley on the Heath, with full power to 'ordain and dispose' covering all works in those places and cause all dilapidations in them to be made good. In a five-year period he handled over £9,000 of the king's money and disposed of immense quantities of building materials. He remained a favourite of the king with very wide-ranging and increasing power and control, becoming Royal Chancellor in 1367 and Bishop of Winchester in 1368, but nemesis followed hubris and he was disgraced some years later for mismanagement of royal policy and administrative abuse. Between 1356 and 1361 William spent the very considerable sum of £785 on Henley (say £200,000 at today's values) and while no details survive to describe what was done, there are references to the construction of new buildings as well as the repair of existing ones. The whole of Merrist Wood was purchased to provide timber for the works.

The clerk of works was empowered to appoint a deputy for purchasing materials and labour who was known as the purveyor. From at least 1359 to 1362 John Alkeshull was purveyor for works at many places including Henley, and he received a wage of 6d a day, while the usual wage for a purveyor was 4d or 3d. In 1361 William of Wykeham's group of royal works was broken up and put in charge of lesser clerks of works. At Henley his place was taken by John Henaud. Smaller sums were spent in the 1360s by the bailiff of the manor then in 1368 the fabric was put into the charge of Adam of Hartington, clerk of the works at Windsor Castle and its 'attendant manors', which henceforth included Henley. Richard Bledlawe built a new house 'next to the gate' in 1368 but apart from that there was little beyond maintenance for the rest of Edward III's reign.

As well as those responsible for the building works many different officials had responsibilities at Henley and the other parks attached to Windsor, such as stewards, bailiffs, wardens and even the king's purveyor of brushwood. The king's clerks were the civil service of the age, and able administrators established public records which survive to this day to throw light on these distant times.

Richard II and his household occasionally visited Henley and the accounts show it was adequately maintained and kept tidy ready for his arrival, with references to the king's (great) chamber which had a tiled floor, to the queen's chamber, two chambers at the north end of the hall and nine chambers on the east side of the manor, as well as to the king's wardrobe and cellar, to the chambers of the chief butler and the treasurer, the kitchen and buttery, the great chapel and the inner gate. There are also frequent references to a lodge in the park.

At the manor house itself new works were undertaken between 1394 and 1396 when John Boweman, a layer, laid the foundations of new 'houses', for which Stapleton and Reigate stone, originally purchased for repairs at St George's Chapel, was brought from Windsor Castle for the works at Henley. Henry IV only dated letters patent at Henley during one visit in May 1403 and after this the records go quiet, Henley Park was put into the hands of park-keepers and there is no sign of royal owners visiting it again.

Figure 2: The Emparkment of Henley.
Transactions took place in May 1355 unless otherwise noted.
Lands are 'in Henley' unless otherwise noted.

Name of Tenant	Land granted or released
Alayn, William	At the 1357 manorial court the king granted him a parcel of land 'by the new lane' which was formerly in 'the old park', rent 1d.
Aynolf, John	Granted a cottage and toft (land once occupied by a homestead, e.g. before the black death) called Aynolfsthyng to the king, in exchange for a plot called 'Le Hethers' which the king acquired from John and Joan Fletcher, Philip and Juliana Rickford and Emma, Juliana's sister.
Clement, Henry	Granted a plot of moor called Clementsmoor, 6 acres, and a yearly rent of 12d and 'two works in autumn' worth 6d which he used to receive from the tenement Aynolfesthyng, to the king, in exchange for a croft called Putridescroft, 2½ acres 7 perches, and for a wood at 'La Hook' 1 acre 1 rood 7 perches. (He was fined for trespass at the 1357 manorial court.)
Edward, John	Granted a plot of meadow called Porsmead 5½ acres 14¼ perches, and a plot of moor 3 acres 19¾ perches, to the king (see also Isabel Pors below).
Finch, William	Before 1355 apparently mortgaged plots of meadow and moor in Henley to William att Gate for £3. In 1355 granted two parcels of Hewersmead and Hewersmoor to the king (see also William Stedman below).
Fletcher, John and Joan his wife	In 1355, granted a plot of land called Heathers to the king. At the 1357 manorial court the king granted them a piece of land 'which was formerly emparked', rent 2d.
Gate, William att	In 1352, was given power of attorney from Robert de Wykford to deliver lands in Worplesdon to the king. In 1355 acknowledged receipt of 60s in settlement of 'mortgage' for plots of meadow and moor that William Finch sold to the king. In 1355 granted a messuage and a virgate (quarter acre) of land with 18d yearly rent of John att Mull's lands to the king, in exchange for a virgate of land called Hallersland in Worplesdon (which the king acquired from Richard de Rokeslee), and 2½ acres 18 perches of meadow called Westsmead and an acre 35 perches of moor called Westmoor in Worplesdon (which the king acquired from Robert de Wykford), and 3 acres 31¾ perches of pasture called Cobbetsmoor in Henley.
Hewer, John	Released all his rights in a parcel of meadow called Hewersmead, ½ acre 29 perches, and in a parcel of moor called Hewersmoor, 3 roods 25½ perches, which the king has 'of the gift of' William Stedman and Emma his wife.
Millicent, William and Isabel or Isabella, his wife	Granted a parcel of meadow called Hewersmead, ½ acre 29 perches, and a parcel of moor called Hewersmoor, 3 roods 25½ perches, which they hold in Isabel's right, to the king (see also William Stedman below).

Figure 2: The Emparkment of Henley (continued).

Name of Tenant	Land granted or released
Molyns, John de, Knight	Attorney for the king in payment to William att Gate.
Mull, John Att	Granted a messuage and curtilage, a water-mill, 1½ acres 1 perch of land, 2 acres 3 roods 5½ perches of pasture and moor and 1 acre 13½ perches of meadow to the king.
Norwico, Richard de, clerk	Attorney for the king in payment to William att Gate.
Pors, Isabel or Isabella	Released all her rights in a plot of meadow called Porsmead, 5½ acres 14¼ perches, and in a plot of moor containing 3 acres 19¾ perches, which John Edward gave to the king. Also released all her rights in the cottage and curtilage which Richard and Juliana Pors gave to the king.
Pors, Richard and Juliana his wife	By 1355 had apparently granted land to the king (but no documentation recorded).
Rickford, Philip de and Juliana his wife, and Emma, Juliana's sister, the daughter of Robert atte Hethe	Released all their rights in a plot of land called Hethers, which the king holds 'of the gift of' John and Joan Fletcher. (They were fined for trespass at the 1357 manorial court.)
Rokeslee, Richard de	By 1355 sold a virgate of land called Hallersland in Worplesdon to the king (see William att Gate above).
Stedeman, William and Emma his wife	Granted a parcel of a meadow called Hewersmead, ½ acre 29 perches, and a parcel of a moor called Hewersmoor, 3 roods 25½ perches, which they hold in Emma's right, to the king.
Stoughton, John de	Granted a plot of moor called Stoughtonsmoor, 8 acres 1 rood 19½ perches to the king.
Threle, Gilbert	Granted a moiety (half share) of a plot of meadow called Smallmead containing 1 acre 33¼ perches to the king.
Withewell, George de	In 1352 was given power of attorney from Robert de Wykford to deliver lands in Worplesdon to the king. (At the 1357 manorial court a George de Wychewelle gave excuses for not attending.)
Withewell, John de	Granted a moor called Pilmoor, 7 acres 20 perches, to the king. (At the 1357 manorial court a John Wychewelle, clerk, was fined for default of suit of court.)
Wykford, Robert de, clerk	In 1352 granted Westsmead, 2½ acres 18 perches of mowable meadow and Westsmoor, 2 acres 15 perches of moor with wood growing on it, in the town of Worplesdon near Southhenley, to the king. Power of attorney to George de Withewell and William att Gate to deliver seisin of the said lands to the king.

Figure 3: Manor of South Henley Court Roll
12 June 1357.

Name of Tenant	Court Proceeding
Alayn, William	The king granted him a parcel of land 'by the New lane' which was formerly in 'the old park', rent 1d at the feast of St Michael.
Blakeman, Richard	Vouched for R Smith.
Chouter, John	Did not appear at court.
Clement, Henry	(Granted land to the king in 1355.) Trespassed with 4 pigs in the king's oats, fine 4d.
Duk, Richard	Vouched for W Maydeman.
East, Thomas	Assessor; trespassed with 2 pigs in the king's pasture, fine 1d; pledged for W East & R Swyft.
East, William	Trespassed with 2 pigs in the king's pasture, fine 1d; pledged for Thomas East.
Fletcher, John and Joan his wife	(Granted land to the king in 1355.) The king granted them a piece of land 'which was formerly emparked', rent 2d at the feast of St Michael.
Forster, John	Trespassed with 3 bullocks in the king's pasture, fine 2d.
Goldyng, P	Assessor.
Hen, William the	Trespassed with 4 oxen in the king's pasture, fine 3d.
Kember, Ralph	Fined 1d for default of suit of court.
Lovelond, John	Vouched for W Milcent.
Martyn, John	Trespassed with his 4 sheep in the king's crops, fine 4d.
Maydeman, William	Did not appear at court.
Meledon, John	Pledged for R Parker; trespassed with 2 cows in the king's crops, fine 2d.
Meledon, Ralph	Trespassed with one draught animal and one bullock in the king's crops, fine 2d.
Milcent, Walter	Did not appear at court.
Neel, Robert	Trespassed with 2 cows in the king's crops, fine 2d; pledged for J Meledon.
Parker, Richard [the]	Vouched for J Chouter; trespassed with 2 pigs in the king's meadow, fine 2d; pledged for J Martyn.
Rede, Richard the	Assessor; trespassed with 2 oxen in the king's crops, fine 2d; pledged for P Rickford.

Figure 3: Manor of South Henley Court Roll (continued).

Name of Tenant	Court Proceeding
Rickford, Philip de	(Granted land to the king in 1355.) Pledged for several trespassers; trespassed himself with 3 cows in the kings crops in a field called Etistowe, fine 3d.
Roger, Richard, bailiff of William Fremelesworth	Trespassed with 6 oxen in the king's meadow, fine 2s.
Russell, Ralph	Trespassed with his 4 pigs and his geese in the king's oats, fine 8d.
Shephurd, Peter [the]	Vouched for G de Wychewelle; pledged for several trespassers.
Shephurd, Walter the	Trespassed with one cow in the king's crops, fine 2d.
Smith, Richard the	Did not appear at court.
Swift, Ralph, servant of Robert de Wicford	Many trespasses in the king's pasture and king's meadow with different animals 'by day and night and against the inclosure of the bailiff', fined 5s; and removed 12 of the king's oxen and 2 colts, fined 10s.
Worshep, Ralph	Pledged for R Swyft.
Wychewelle, George of	Did not appear at court. (A George de Withewell was given power of attorney for lands in Worplesdon in 1352.)
Wychewell, John, clerk	Fined 2d for default of suit of court of 3 tenements. (A John de Withewell granted land to the king in 1355.)

The tenants itemised the loss of animals through murrain (disease) in the year 1355: one cow before calving, one ram before shearing, 24 male sheep before shearing (besides 12 presented in the roll of the last court), 9 ewes before lambing, 4 ewes after lambing and before shearing, one ewe after shearing, 2 hoggets (yearling sheep) before shearing, 21 lambs before marking, 2 lambs after shearing, 2 pigs (besides 2 pigs presented in the roll of the last court), 3 piglets and one small piglet.

They then itemised the loss of animals through disease between September 1356 and June 1357: one cow before calving, 8 calves from the extraordinary coldness of the weather and for lack of buildings, 2 rams before shearing, 36 male sheep before shearing, 2 male sheep after shearing, 12 ewes before lambing, 5 ewes before shearing and after lambing, 24 hoggets before shearing and marking and 3 pigs of which one was a sow.

Figure 4: Estimates of Population and Extent.

Date	Context	Extent and Value	Population estimate
Pre-Domesday (early charters)	All of Ash & Normandy	5 or 6 farmsteads.	At least 25 or 30, but probably other smaller households.
1066 Domesday	All of Ash & Normandy	Value £6. 8 hides, say 800 acres.	
1086 Domesday	All of Ash & Normandy	Value £5. Arable 600 acres, meadow 4 acres, woodland for 50 hogs.	10 serfs, 6 smallholders, 2 slaves; estimated total 80 to 100?
1325-26 account	All of Ash & Normandy?	Receipts £34 0s 4d, clear profit £17 11s 0d.	
1332 tax assessment	All of Ash & Normandy		38 taxpayers in total, of which 8 in Henley only (so 8 taxable households).
1343 valuation	Henley & Cleygate only?	Income £16 7s 0d, clear profit £14 18s 4d. 256 acres arable, 30 acres meadow, 10 acres meadow in a park, (so total cultivated 296 acres); 60 acres of separate pasture, 120 acres enclosed park, 200 acres of heath on the waste.	Say 24 households (average 20 acres each), with 120 people (average 5 per house).
1355 emparkment	Henley only	420 acres enclosed including woodland; deeds mention 10 acres of meadow, 30 acres of moor and 2 acres of 'land'.	20 tenants inside the park, unknown outside.
1357 court roll	Henley & Cleygate		16 tenants trespassed, plus 2 property transactions.
1840s tithe & census	Normandy	1,159 acres of cultivated & residential land	59 households with 304 people.

3. KEEPERS OF THE ROYAL PARK (1400-1632)

Guildford Park

Guildford royal park was in some ways Henley's 'bigger brother'. At its nearest point it was only two miles from Henley Park and during this period there were many parallels between the two. They shared several of the park-keepers and extensive repairs to the buildings were carried out in consecutive years. Guildford was much bigger than Henley, having about 1,620 acres. Guildford Park was apparently in royal possession from a very early date and when Henry III's Queen Eleanor of Provence established the Dominican Friary in Guildford in about 1259, they were given the part of the park nearest to the town, which is now occupied by the bus station, police station, etc. The rest of the park was eventually sold in three separate transactions from 1620 to 1650.

The Keepers

The office of park-keeper seems to have been a much sought-after sinecure and reward for services rendered to the monarch. Originally the keeper was granted the park for a farm, out of which he could make profit, but Guildford Park had become unprofitable by the middle of the 14th century due to overgrazing and the keeper was granted a daily payment instead. The first known grant of the keepership of Henley Park, to John de Henaud in 1356, includes instruction to the bailiff of the manor to pay him 'wages of 6d a day out of the issues of the manor', which equates to about £3,000 a year in modern values and represented about a third of the income from the manor at that time. Although 6d a day was a typical craftsman's wage, in most of the grants Henley was just one in a list of keeperships and other offices which amounted to a substantial financial package. This remuneration remained unchanged during the following low-inflation century and a half, although later grants also included the herbage and pannage of the parks and later still, other unspecified fees and profits.

The keeper was responsible for land management and the maintenance of timber, and also the management of livestock although there are references to other officers with specific responsibilities such as the keeper of the king's stud. When commanded he had to provide deer (often for royal gifts) and timber for building works elsewhere. In the earlier years while there was still a frequent royal presence the keeper would have been responsible for the repair and maintenance of the fences, ponds, bridges and buildings which are mentioned in the records. He was responsible for the administration of the park and for keeping accounts. Earlier park-keepers were court officials such as the yeoman of the cellar or cofferer of the household, but later favourites of the court, landowners and statesmen of greater importance were appointed (see Figure 5). Very few of the keepers were resident locally. Day-to-day administration of Guildford Park was in the hands of two subordinate officials called the Parker and the Paliser (the enclosureman) but there is no mention of these roles at Henley, although some of Henley's appointed keepers appear to have 'subcontracted' the office for a fee and at a reduced wage of 2d a day. The early keepers were Constables of Windsor Castle and had custody of many of the king's parks so no doubt they employed local keepers to manage the day to day affairs of each park but these people are generally invisible in the records. Other court officials also had interests that extended to Henley, for example in 1445 Richard Jordan was 'keeper of the cellars within Windsor Castle, Easthampsted Park and Henley on the Heath'.

Sir John Stanley, appointed keeper of Henley Park in 1409, was a soldier and administrator who achieved eminence as Lieutenant of Ireland and steward of the household of Henry IV. Outlawed in his 20s for a murder he committed with his elder brother, he was pardoned and set out on a military career and became a soldier of some standing in the French wars. He was rewarded for his support to the Lancastrian regime with manorial lordships and official posts within the royal household, culminating in his appointment as Constable of Windsor Castle and the keepership of its associated parks including Henley. During his service in Ireland he had a reputation as a ruthless and grasping soldier who hated and was hated by the Gaels and he died in Louth in 1414.

Thomas St Leger was knighted by Edward IV in 1478 a few months after he was appointed to the keepership of Henley Park and some years after his appointment to Guildford Park. He apparently fought against the Lancastrians at the decisive battle at Towton in 1461 and was a loyal supporter and friend of King Edward throughout his life. Official appointments came thick and fast and he held a variety of posts in south-east and south-west England including Controller of the Mint. In Surrey he was a Justice of the Peace, joint Sheriff of Surrey and Sussex and a Knight of the Shire in several parliaments. Much prestige was attached to these offices and he was clearly a well known and respected figure. He had family lands in Kent and received many grants of lands and fees from the Crown, including in Surrey such places as Clandon, Cleygate in Ash and Field Place in Compton. By his marriage to the king's sister he acquired interests in considerable properties in the south-west and close relationships with men of influence and substance. These lands and appointments carried significant financial rewards and although he originally came from a family of lesser gentry he rose to be among the 'greater knights' of the land. After the unexpected death of Edward IV he remained loyal to the king's family and actively opposed Richard's coup, which ultimately led to his execution in November 1483.

Sir Reginald Bray also took part in the 1483 rebellion against Richard III but he was able to obtain a pardon for his offences including treason, and went on to become a conspirator and fund-raiser for the successful invasion by Henry Tudor in 1485 when he is said to have pulled the crown of England from under a Hawthorn bush on Bosworth field. He received immediate preferment from the new king; he was knighted at the coronation and appointed to a series of high offices including Treasurer of England, and received grants of stewardships, parkerships and other estate offices in many parts of the country including Henley Park in 1486 and the lordship of the manor of Cleygate. He was returned as MP for Hampshire on three occasions and was appointed to the bench in Surrey and other counties. At their greatest extent he had estates in 18 counties and one of his three main properties was at Shere near Guildford. His long and loyal service to Henry VII and the king's mother Margaret Beaufort made him one of the most powerful of the king's councillors. His influence with the king was widely recognised and sometimes feared. Although there is no evidence to support his reputation as an architect he was directly engaged in at least three major building projects including St George's Chapel at Windsor and the chapel of Henry VII at Westminster, as well as many lesser works. He was elected a Knight of the Garter in 1501 and died in 1503 aged about 63. After his death the next person appointed keeper of Henley was William Cope who had been Bray's servant in earlier years and rose to become Cofferer of the royal household.

Sir William Compton was another courtier who rose to eminence through a deep and lasting friendship with the king, having originally been a page to the prince before his accession to the throne as Henry VIII. He did enormously well out of the king's service, holding many offices and lands and taking what Wolsey described after his death as 'excessive fees'. He does not appear to have played much part in the government of the realm or the administration of his properties and was described as 'more attentive to his profit than public affairs'.

During Compton's keepership some major repairs were carried out at Henley Park. Surviving accounts (see Plate 6) show that 17 workmen; carpenters, sawyers, bricklayers, tilers and labourers, worked under the supervision of Richard Wade the overseer from August to December 1515 (see Figure 6), suggesting that the buildings were timber-framed with tiled roofs. The two sawyers probably worked in a saw-pit and the top man and bottom man were paid the same amount. About 18 oak trees were felled for timber and supplies of bricks, tiles, stone lime, laths, nails and 400 white oak boards were procured and carted into the park. Four pairs of hooks and hinges and some window clamps were purchased from a blacksmith in Guildford and four locks and keys from Robert Smith 'of the castle'. The work cost a total of £41 11s 4d which was authorised by Henry Smyth, Clerk of the King's Works. Similar work carried out at Guildford Park the year before at a cost of about £74 has been described as 'roughly equivalent to building two shire houses'. It has been estimated that four-fifths of the work at Guildford was carried out on the manor house and the rest on a lodge house, but at Henley the repairs were to the lodge and the great barn, there is no reference to the manor house at all, so the work on the lodge at Henley must have been quite extensive.

Like most keeperships Compton's appointment to Henley in 1513 was for life, but in 1516 this was replaced by a joint appointment 'in survivorship' to Compton and Sir William Fitzwilliam who had been appointed to Guildford Park two years earlier. Compton died in 1528 leaving Fitzwilliam as the surviving keeper of Henley Park. Sir William Fitzwilliam (see Plate 7) was a courtier and naval administrator from a comparatively insignificant gentry family, and his paternal inheritance in Yorkshire formed only a small part of what became his vast estate. He and his half-brother Sir Anthony Browne became two of Henry VIII's closest friends during a reign in which many fell from grace. During an active military career he also began acquiring lands and offices in Surrey, doubtless aided by the Browne family's prominence in the shire. Among many others he acquired the keepership of Guildford Park in 1511, the manors of Cleygate and Worplesdon in 1513, the keepership of Henley Park in 1516 and the manor of Pirbright in 1537. During this time he assumed a larger role in the central government and found it difficult to balance national and local responsibilities. He became vice-admiral in which capacity he outfitted the ships that carried Henry's entourage to the Field of the Cloth of Gold and he accompanied the king there. He subsequently spent much time on embassies abroad, all the while acquiring more lands and offices at home including an estate at Cowdray near Midhurst in Sussex which he purchased in 1528 for £2,193 6s 8d. Ever loyal to Henry VIII he played an active role in the dissolution of the monasteries and was one of the principal beneficiaries of the redistribution of ecclesiastical lands, so that his estates ultimately included over 16,000 acres in Surrey, Sussex and Hampshire alone, not to mention additional lands in at least nine other counties. In 1537 he was created Earl of Southampton and although elevated to the House of Lords he played an important part in the election of members of the Commons in 1539, including arranging the election of Sir Anthony Browne for Surrey. He praised the beauty of Anne of Cleves to Henry, compounding the false impression earlier conveyed by Hans Holbein the younger's portrait, which incurred the king's anger but he possibly redeemed himself by helping to get the marriage nullified. He continued to collect offices until his death in 1542 in Newcastle upon Tyne aged about 52. His will requested burial in a chapel to be constructed at Midhurst if he should die within 100 miles of there but although the chapel exists his tomb is not in it.

The careers of these keepers illustrate the importance of personal relationships in the Tudor political structure, where personal recommendation was the sole route to promotion. The aristocracy and landed gentry were well known to one another at court and often related by marriage. It is clear that they were busy and influential men and while being appointed keeper of a royal park was an honour, it probably did not feature very high amongst all their other honours so it is doubtful whether any of them had any direct involvement with or ever visited Henley Park. Even their deputies had deputies, for example in 1555 Michael Simson, deputy of Walter Cresswell, retainer to Viscount Montague the current keeper, was fined by Cleygate manorial court for letting cattle he was being paid to feed graze on the common. When Viscount Montague was required to report to the 'Swainmote' Forest Courts in the 1570s he sent Thomas Lush as his deputy for Henley and William Luff for Guildford Park. Nevertheless when Sir Anthony Browne (see Plate 8) was appointed keeper in April 1543 this began a close association between the Browne family and Henley Park which lasted for nearly a hundred years, and with Pirbright for even longer.

The keepership was formerly held by Browne's half-brother the Earl of Southampton, who bequeathed him many of his lands including Cowdray. Despite being a staunch and outspoken traditional Catholic, Browne was also regarded as a 'dissolution profiteer' and had supported and profited from the appropriation of church properties. As he sat banqueting in the hall of his newly-acquired Battle Abbey, one of the dispossessed monks is supposed to have come up and foretold the ruin of his family 'by fire and water', which has become famous as the curse of Cowdray. The Brownes became Viscounts Montague until in 1793 the eighth Viscount, the 24-year old last male heir, was drowned while attempting to 'shoot' the falls of the Rhine at Laufenburg and the male line of the Brownes of Cowdray became extinct. Just after he left his hotel for the fateful trip to the falls a letter arrived announcing the destruction of Cowdray House by a fire caused by a careless workman. Cowdray was described as 'a treasure house full of rare and priceless things' but everything was destroyed by the fire and now the roofless ruin still stands in its park.

However, all this was in the future and Sir Anthony Browne prospered. He probably grew up in the royal household and was regularly at court when not engaged in diplomatic, military or other official duties for the king. In 1520, at the age of about twenty, he demonstrated his prowess in a tournament at the Field of the Cloth of Gold and he was knighted in 1532 after playing a notable part in the successful siege of Morlaix in Brittany. He held many high official posts and acted for the king on embassies abroad. The Browne family had a significant estate at West

Horsley Place and he was JP for Surrey where he and Fitzwilliam headed a locally powerful faction. He was elected as Knight of the Shire for Surrey on several occasions and arranged for his son Anthony to be returned as a burgess for Guildford. He remained close to Henry VIII throughout his life and the king made him an executor of his will and guardian of his children Edward and Elizabeth. By the time of his death at Byfleet in April 1548 Browne owned about 8,500 acres of land in Surrey and 11,000 acres in Sussex.

A glimpse inside Henley Park at this time is provided by a document preserved in the Loseley manuscripts which lists counts of deer in various royal parks. Henley had 30 'deer of antler', huntable stags of six years or more, and 140 'rascalls' meaning all the rest, while Guildford Park had 40 deer of antler and 500 rascalls.

It appears that Sir Michael Stanhope became the next keeper of Guildford and Henley Parks, but he was removed in 1551 and subsequently executed. In his place William Parr, Marquis of Northampton and brother of Henry VIII's sixth and last wife, was appointed but he too was stripped of his possessions in 1553 for supporting the wrong side in the dynastic struggles following the death of Edward VI. His cousin 'Queen Jane' (Lady Jane Gray) wrote to him that 'she makes her entry into the Tower of London as rightful queen of this realm and is confident that he will do all he can', but clearly he could not do enough.

Now Browne's son, also Sir Anthony Browne (see Plate 9), was appointed to the keeperships. He was created the first Viscount Montague the next year and unlike his two predecessors he retained the offices until his death. A nobleman and courtier, among other appointments he was Sheriff of Surrey and Sussex and was elected to the Commons several times before his elevation to the House of Lords which he attended regularly. He travelled widely in his official capacities, at one time being Master of the Horse to Philip of Spain and later going via Venice to visit the Pope to discuss restoring Catholicism to England. His most prominent position was appointment to the Privy Council but he was always a patron of the Catholic restoration and was dropped from the Privy Council when he spoke against Queen Elizabeth's religious policies. Despite his staunch Catholic convictions he retained not only the queen's esteem but also many of his other offices and continuing liberty to both enjoy his inheritance and practice Catholicism. That his loyalty to the Crown was above suspicion was confirmed when he sat as one of the commissioners on the trial of Mary Queen of Scots which led to her execution for treason in 1587, and actively aided the defence against the Spanish Armada the next year. In August 1591 the queen spent six days at Cowdray where he entertained her lavishly and she rewarded him by knighting his second son George. He died in 1592 and was buried at Midhurst under a splendid tomb of marble and alabaster, surmounted by a kneeling figure of himself and recumbent effigies of his two wives. The tomb was moved in 1851 to the nearby church of St Mary Easebourne and memorials on the tomb and the wall record details of his family and his services and embassies for the Crown.

Elizabeth I and Recusancy, 1570s-90s

Queen Elizabeth I stayed at the manor house in Guildford Park on several occasions but there is no record that she ever visited Henley Park, apparently preferring mostly to stay at other people's houses rather than her own. She was a terrific visitor and the annual royal progresses which lasted eight to twelve weeks were greeted with a mixture of excitement and dread. The royal household numbered about 1,500 people and 150 or so travelled with the royal personage. Hosts had not only the huge expenditure of feeding, housing and entertaining an army of spoiled and privileged people, but could expect quite a lot of pilfering and property damage too and some were bankrupted for their pains.

Although the prayer book was now in English rather than Latin, in the 16th century the Church of England was not that different from the Catholic Church, the main point of contention being the role of the Pope. The interiors of churches were still furnished and decorated in the same way that they had always been, the more austere form of Protestantism not becoming dominant until a century later.

The early years of Elizabeth's reign saw religious tolerance with the emphasis on 'outward conformity rather than inward conviction', but the arrival on English soil in 1568 of the Catholic Queen of Scots with her claim to the throne, followed by increasing threats from extremists abroad with schemes for invasion, massacres in France and papal edicts that any person who assassinated Elizabeth 'would have treasure laid up for him in heaven', heightened tension and forced her to clamp down. The Dutch leader William the Silent was assassinated in 1584 and there were fears for Elizabeth's safety. The original 1559 Act of Uniformity had imposed a fine of a shilling a week for not attending Anglican services, but in the climate of rising suspicion and fear harsher laws such as the 1593 'Act for restraining Popish Recusants to some certain place of abode' increased the fine to a massive £20 a month.

The earldom of Southampton had become extinct when William Fitzwilliam died without issue but Edward VI recreated the title and bestowed it on another royal favourite Thomas Wriothesley, who is generally considered to be one of the least scrupulous time servers in an admittedly dangerous era. His son Henry, second Earl of Southampton married Mary, daughter of the first Viscount Montague (see Figure 7) and he too remained faithful to Catholicism so that he was placed under house arrest when suspected of treason for involvement in one of the papist plots. The relationship between captor and jailor was ambiguous; in 1570 while another wave of plague ravaged London, the Privy Council ordered 'the prisoner' Southampton to be removed to the custody of Sir William More at Loseley, yet three years later Southampton accepted a social invitation from More to come and visit him at Loseley while on his way to London. More was later to become custodian of one of the Brownes of Henley Park and he, More, also acquired church property appropriated by the government.

Sir William More opposed Catholicism and withdrew from political activity during the reign of Queen Mary and the change of religion enforced by that regime, but after the succession of Queen Elizabeth he received several high appointments including Sheriff of Surrey and Sussex. He began building a magnificent new house at Loseley and entertained the queen there in 1569 even before the house was fully completed, the first of several royal visits. Viscount Montague, his friend and neighbour at Cowdray, assisted in the building of Loseley by donating building materials, including about 90 loads of stone from the demolished Waverley Abbey, a third given freely and the rest purchased at a reduced rate, and lending More the use of his own master carpenter.

Viscount Montague is said to have visited Henley Park on several occasions, probably to visit his younger brother Francis Browne who lived there from at least 1576 to 1588. When the Bishop of Winchester was enquiring into the conformity of laity and clergy to the Act of

Supremacy and Viscount Montague (although his own sympathies were really Romanist) asked William More for his report of his 'neighbours' opinions' to lay before the bishop, Francis Browne was included in the return listing recusants (someone who refused to attend services of the Church of England) in Surrey who made a regular payment in lieu of attending church.

In a Surrey muster around this time Francis Browne was responsible for providing one archer, one corslet (full body armour) and one 'haquebut'. Nevertheless, in May 1585 under a royal warrant his armaments were seized and delivered into Sir William More's custody. The inventory of his arms at Henley Park mentions two old brigandines (a form of cloth body armour lined with steel plates) decorated with fustian, two light houseman's staves, two swords and several other items, while his armourer in Guildford delivered two pykes (long thrusting spears) and other pieces 'all broken and disorder'. Browne himself was apparently not taken into custody at this time although in 1586 his house at Henley Park was searched for hidden priests, but "other men's harms make Mr Browne wary" and nothing suspicious was found, as the letter of thanks to More and Laurence Stoughton for performing the search indicated. However, by November 1588 he too had been taken into honourable protective custody at Loseley mainly for his own safety. His detention under the care of his family's friend was fairly lenient and at one point he was released on bail to attend to some lawsuits 'of great weight'.

Henley Park gained a reputation as 'notoriously the refuge of recusants and suspected priests' and in 1592 a warrant was issued to the High Constables of the hundred of Woking for the arrest of Roger Borrowe, Thomas Thorpe, George Maybanke and Rose Foster, recusants dwelling in the lodge at Henley Park. There is no further note of their fate except for Thomas Thorpe, a yeoman who was buried at Ash in July 1597 and whose probate inventory lists the livestock on his farm at Henley Park.

Sir William More's extensive correspondence preserved in the Loseley manuscripts gives us occasional glimpses of the day to day matters that concerned the occupants of Henley Park. In response to a royal proclamation compelling owners of parks more than a mile in circumference to keep brood mares, in 1585 Francis Browne notified Sir William More, presumably in his role of sheriff, that he had always had two mares of his own in Henley Park. On another occasion Browne writes requesting that William Harding be granted a licence to have an alehouse in Ash 'very necessary for the parish'. In 1573 Viscount Montague wrote from Cowdray to More that he would make his way to visit him via Henley Park, so that he could see two recently repaired ponds in Pirbright. These may be the two ponds that fed the stream down to the lord of the manor's mill pond in the heart of Pirbright village. In another letter Montague explains to More why he had to dismiss More's kinsman George Elliott for his 'insufferable pride and incorrigible insolency', and there are many other letters from him to More in his capacities as JP, sheriff and forest official dealing with actions against deer poachers in the parks. Although the first great wave of the Black Death had not been repeated the plague remained endemic and frequent infections swept the country for hundreds of years thereafter. In a letter at around this time Montague's cousin Sir Henry Neville mentioned to Sir William More that "people are still dying at Henley".

There is a curious story which has never been confirmed, that Queen Elizabeth presented Henley Park to Robert Devereux the Earl of Essex. In the late 1580s he was high in the queen's favours and she might have intended to honour him with Henley Park but the only known grant at this time is a grant in reversion to Sir Henry Browne, a younger son of Viscount Montague. Montague never fell out of favour and held the keepership until his death, by which time the queen may have changed her mind and confirmed the grant to Browne, who thus became keeper on the death of his father in 1592. Sir Henry Browne was living at Henley Park during the early 1600s and two of his children were baptised at Ash, although his uncle Francis Browne did not die until 1615 so they may have resided there together.

Sir Henry Browne, while not involved himself, was associated by marriage with the most famous of the Catholic plots. He married Anne Catesby whose nephew Robert Catesby was the charismatic instigator and chief actor of the 1605 Gunpowder Plot, an assassination attempt against King James I which we celebrate to this day thanks to the 1606 Observance of 5th November Act of Parliament which enforced an annual public day of thanksgiving for the plot's failure. It was only in the 1850s that the anti-Catholic rhetoric associated with the celebrations was toned down.

Brownes and the manor of Pirbright

Pirbright had been part of the marriage portion to Henry VIII's first wife Catherine of Aragon and was subsequently granted to the original Earl of Southampton after her death. Following his death in 1542 the manor was granted for life to his half-brother Sir Anthony Browne, then in 1555 to Browne's son, later to be Viscount Montague, outright 'for himself and his heirs for ever'. In the 1620s King James wanted to reclaim Viscount Montague's land at Pirbright because it lay in the midst of his hunting country. Montague chose some of the king's estates in Hampshire that he was willing to exchange for Pirbright but the king rejected the offer and apparently nothing came of it. During the Civil War while Francis the third Viscount Montague was abroad on the king's service and his property was in danger of being sequestrated by the Parliamentarians, his cousin Stanislaus Browne was acting lord of the manor and apparently resident in the parish, where four of his children were baptised. The lordship of Pirbright was inherited by the Browne heirs until the third Viscount Montague sold it in 1677 to the then owner of Henley Park, after which the ownerships went hand in hand for nearly 250 years. During the third Viscount Montague's lordship a dispute over peat digging on Pirbright common arose and he sued his tenants in court for trespass but lost the case, although this dispute was to flare up again later with a subsequent lord of the manor and owner of Henley Park.

Demise of the medieval manor complex

Over the course of two centuries the impressive medieval manor complex at Henley Park with its chapels and chambers which had been occupied by kings in the 14th century completely disappeared. In 1459 there were grants to Richard Ludlowe, the keeper, for the repair and rebuilding of the manor of Henley on the Heath 'now in decay' and the pales (fencing) of the park thereof. The money was allocated from eight prisoners who escaped from Oxford jail and thus forfeited their property. However, there is no record of any work being done and in the 15th century only minor repairs are recorded. In 1515 significant repairs were made to the lodge and barn, but not the manor complex. During this time all references to people living at Henley Park or to work on the fabric refer only to the lodge. By the time Henley Park was surveyed in 1607 there was no sign of the manor house at all; the only buildings in the park were the lodge and barn that were repaired 92 years earlier and one smaller house just below the lodge.

Norden's survey

In 1607 while Sir Henry Browne was keeper, John Norden produced a 'Description of the Honor of Windesor' mapping and describing 'the castle, forest, walks, parks, rayles, lodges and all other things memorable within the honour' (a walk was a division of the forest regularly perambulated by a ranger or keeper and a rayle typically a holding pen for deer). Two copies are preserved, one dedicated to King James and the other to Henry Prince of Wales.

The map of Henley Park (see Plate 10) is the 12th of 17 beautifully hand drawn and coloured maps in his survey and is the earliest accurate map of Henley Park and its immediate surroundings. The most noticeable feature is the building called 'Henley Parke lodge' which is situated on an upland ridge near to the northern boundary and has been drawn in more detail than the other little houses which are shown in a uniform style. It comprises a central section with wings at each end which project to the west to form an open-ended court accessed through an archway in the north wing. The building has a pitched roof and is at least two storeys high but there are variations in detail between the two copies of the map; one has more windows and shows chimneys which are missing from the other copy. The lodge is surrounded on the east, south and west by a paling coloured brown. Despite the slight differences in the appearance of the lodge in the two versions of the map it is clear that the building was a half-H-shaped house with a pitched roof and gables. A detailed comparison with modern maps confirms the accuracy of the

Figure 8: The Lodge on Norden's survey

main features of the survey and shows that the lodge occupies exactly the same site as the restored Georgian-style mansion house which stands in Henley Park today. An architectural survey of the mansion house carried out in 1986 found that the original 'pre-Georgian' structure had eaves not a parapet and when they stripped out the guttering in the roof gully at the front of the mansion they found sprockets which were part of the structure. Therefore the mansion that was remodelled in 1751 and still retains its former Georgian appearance not only stands on the site of the medieval Henley Park lodge but may even still have parts of it incorporated within its structure.

The lodge, originally built towards the end of the 14th century or early 15th century to provide additional accommodation, is likely to have been sited close to the royal manor complex. After the manor ceased to be a royal residence, the large complex of main buildings may have quickly fallen into disuse and disrepair and so disappeared by the time of the survey, while the people responsible for the upkeep of the park took up residence in the smaller and relatively newer lodge so ensuring its survival.

Within the park the map shows the approximate location of the 'Garden Barne' although there is no pictorial representation of it, which could mean that it was no longer in use or even standing at that time. A large part of the park appears wooded although Norden's brief introductory description states that 'the timber decays'. Two areas of woodland, or possibly individual great oaks, are named; Bedills oake in the south-east corner and Bane oake on the higher land to the north-west. According to the description the park contained about 120 (presumably fallow) deer, 70 males 'of antler' of which 40 were mature, and 50 females, which Norden commented was 'very many in respect of the general sum', meaning too many males in proportion to the females. Antlered deer were prestigious and park owners liked to show many of them in their parks, but this imbalance would have led to unrest and fighting.

The park contained about 420 acres of 'good ground' and was surrounded by a boundary just over three miles long marked by timber palings and an embankment. It is still possible to follow the boundary embankment along much of its length today. Four park gates are named on the map and various other features shown outside the park. Ashe gate is in the north-west corner, which is now occupied by the house and grounds of Henley Park Farm, and Heath gate is shown in the position of the Pirbright Road entrance which survived right up to Vokes' time until it was closed off in the 1990s. A roadway or track leads directly from this gate to the arched entrance into the lodge. Nothing is shown on the map but a copyhold cottage had been established just outside this gate by 1620 and later a gate lodge house which was demolished about 1980. In the middle of the east side is another gate called Purses gate and another track is shown leading from here across the park to the south side of the lodge. A footpath still leads from this point on Cobbett Hill into the park. None of the cottages depicted on the map has been named, but the two cottages shown outside this gate were known as Cobbett Hill Cottages in the manor of Cleygate records and were owned by the Purse family from at least 1546 to 1649 so giving their name to the gate, but the buildings no longer exist and the land is now incorporated into a golf course. Cobbotts bridges are named where the stream exits the park and a triangular junction called Playstreete is shown at the junction with the present Guildford to Aldershot road. The shape of this junction survives to this day but not the place name. Halfway along the stretch of road west from Playstreete two cottages are shown, one with two end gables, on the site of Whipley Farm which dates back to the 1540s. Bedills gate which no longer survives, is shown opposite the present-day Chapel Farm which was a smallholding known as Heathers as early as the 14th century and was occupied by the Bedill family in the 16th century, although its buildings are not shown on the map. On the western boundary of the park, the only side that does not follow the line of a road, a feature called 'Costoll stile' is marked approximately where the present day footpath exits the park and as its name suggests, it may have led to Costalls, a freehold tenement which appears several times in the manor of Cleygate records. Between the stile and Ashe gate another cottage is shown close to the boundary but there seems to be no trace of it in the manorial records and there is no building there today.

On later maps there is a significant track named Badger Walk that used to lead north from the entrance to the park at Heath gate directly to Rails Farm in Pirbright, until part of its length was closed off to create the firing ranges. This track is not shown on Norden's survey of Henley Park but in his map of Pirbright Walk an enclosure named 'Le Rayles' is shown in the position of Rails Farm. It seems likely that the track from Henley Park to Le Rayles existed at that time even though it is not shown on the map.

Final assignments and Sale to private owner

In July 1609 while Sir Henry Browne was still at Henley an estimate of £26 18s 8d 'for the repair of Henley Park' was approved and the woodward of Windsor Forest was ordered to deliver 25 loads of wood. This work was possibly instigated with a view to making the property more attractive to a potential assignee. By 1613 Browne had bought the manor of Kiddington in Oxfordshire and apparently moved there. The accession of James I brought a new generation of courtiers looking for land and houses within reach of Westminster and Browne assigned the keepership of Henley Park to others, so setting in motion a curious chain of transactions whereby the benefits of the park were sold by one courtier to another, all of whom appear to have been favourites of the king. It is not clear whether the king 'persuaded' Browne to assign his rights or whether he was happy to get rid of them and devote his attention to his new estate in Oxfordshire.

Sir Alexander Hay was Secretary of State for Scotland, but Browne's grant of Henley Park to him in September 1609 was short-lived because in December Browne sold the privileges and rights of the keepership for £800 to Philip Herbert, Earl of Montgomery. In both cases the assignment was for the duration of Browne's life because the park still ultimately belonged to the Crown and would revert back on Browne's death. Montgomery was a court favourite and was granted many honours. He was passionately interested in both hunting and gambling and the king's favour was evident in James' reported willingness to pay his extensive debts. He maintained a household with 80 staff in London and twice as many at his country seat at Wilton House, where he entertained the king every summer. Presumably like most other keepers his interest in Henley Park was financial rather than as a residence but perhaps it was not as profitable as he hoped because in 1620 Montgomery assigned it to Robert Ratcliffe, fifth Earl of Sussex during the lives of Browne and himself, and the next year Sussex assigned it to Robert Tyrwhitt Esq during the lives of Browne and Montgomery.

The family of Tyrwhitt was long-established with many excellent connections and influence at court, and Robert may have been the son of William Tyrwhitt who inherited the family estate of Kettleby, Lincolnshire, and married Katherine, daughter of Anthony Browne the second Lord Montague. There were other family connections because a Mary Tyrwhitt married George Browne, a son of the first Lord Montague. Robert Tyrwhitt presumably had some position of influence because of the events he was subsequently able to arrange.

In 1623 Tyrwhitt appointed brothers Arthur Squibb and Stephen Squibb keepers for 12 years provided Browne and Montgomery lived that long, for an annual rent of £100, two years of which they had to pay in advance. Tyrwhitt probably regarded the keepership as a useful sinecure and source of income like his predecessors but when neighbouring Guildford Park was sold he may have seen an opportunity for some property speculation, or possibly Arthur Squibb saw an opportunity for his own advancement and persuaded Tyrwhitt to use his influence to procure Henley Park outright.

The English monarch was almost always short of funds with which to raise armies or equip navies and while the situation was not critical it was a time of economic transformation and the Crown was ill-equipped to keep pace with its wealthier subjects and was forced to part with much of its land. So while no particular event caused Charles I to look around for things to sell, when he was approached by a potential buyer for one of his parks it must have seemed like a good idea. In June 1631 Tyrwhitt covenanted with Arthur Squibb that for £2,500 he would arrange the sale of Henley Park to Squibb. Both Browne and Montgomery were still alive at this time but the king must have revoked their grants of keepership because a year later Charles I indeed sold Henley Park to Tyrwhitt for £850 by Letter Patent on condition that he grant half to Arthur Squibb (see Plate 11). The grant included liberty to dispark or assart (convert the land to arable use) and free warren (the right to hunt game, with the specific replacement of forest law by common law), but the Crown retained a 'ground rent' of £10 per annum and a quarter of a knight's fee (an obligation to provide an armed knight for the king's service in time of war). This rent was apparently sold in the 1650s by the 'Commissioners for selling Fee Farm Rents belonging to the Commonwealth of England formerly payable to the Crown of England' thus finally terminating the royal connection which had lasted for 300 years, and by the 19th century the rent was payable by the owners of Henley Park to the Earls of Sandwich.

Although mentioned many times in the Patent document, Squibb was apparently not a party to the deed and presumably was not aware of the financial details. Tyrwhitt duly sold his share on to Squibb as agreed and at a handsome profit.

Figure 5: Keepers of Henley Park.

Appointed	Keeper	Notes
by 1343	Henry de Graystoke	
1356 March	John de Henaud (or Henand) (for life)	Wages 6d a day.
1384 May	Simon de Burley (for life)	Constable of Windsor Castle, also Keeper of Guildford and several other parks.
1384 May	Thomas Tyle (for life of Simon de Burley)	Constable of Windsor Castle, etc.
1388 July	Grant by Thomas Tyle to Nicholas Churchill	Parker of Henley (only).
1390 Jan	Peter de Courtenay (for life)	Constable of Windsor Castle, etc.
1397 June	Nicholas Churchill, one of the Yeomen of the Cellar	Henley only. Wages 2d a day.
1405 Feb	Hugh de Waterdon (for life)	Constable of Windsor Castle, etc.
1409 July	John de Stanley (for life)	Constable of Windsor Castle, etc. Died 1414.
1414 Jan	John Waterton (for life)	Constable of Windsor Castle, etc. subject to the interest of Thomas Earl of Arundel in Guildford Park.
1427 March	Richard Ludlowe, with assent of Nicholas Churchill ('during [the king's] pleasure')	Wages 2d a day.
1437 Nov	Richard Ludlowe, one of the Yeomen of the Cellar (for life)	
1448 Oct	Richard Ludlowe and his son (in survivorship)	Later also of Guildford Park.
1462 Oct	Richard Hunte (for life)	
1465 March	Richard Hunte and Geoffrey Springe (for life)	
1478 June	Thomas Seintleger (St Leger) and Richard Hunte (for life)	Earlier also of Guildford Park. St Leger executed 1483.
1484 June	William Norton (for life)	
1486 Oct	Reynold (Reginald) Bray (for life)	Also of Guildford Park and manor of Cleygate. 6d a day plus herbage and pannage. Died 1503.
1503 Oct	William Cope, Cofferer of the Household (for life)	Also of Guildford Park.
1510 March	Grant renewed by Henry VIII	
1513 June	William Compton (for life)	Also manors of Cleygate and Worplesdon. Died 1528.
1516 Sept	Sir William Compton and Sir William Fitzwilliam, subsequently Earl of Southampton (in survivorship)	Also manors of Cleygate, Worplesdon and later Pirbright. Fitzwilliam also of Guildford Park.
1522	Grant renewed	Fitzwilliam died 1542.

Figure 5: Keepers of Henley Park (continued).

Appointed	Keeper	Notes
1543 April	Sir Anthony Browne (for life?)	Also of Guildford Park. Died 1548.
	Sir Michael Stanhope?	Also of Guildford Park. Executed 1552.
	William Parr, Marquis of Northampton?	Also of Guildford Park. Attainted 1553. Many of his estates and titles were restored by Elizabeth I. Died 1571.
1553 Oct	Sir Anthony Browne, subsequently Viscount Montague (for life?)	Also of Guildford Park. Died 1592.
1592	Sir Henry Browne (had been granted it in reversion in 1590)	Died 1638/39.
1609	Sir Henry Browne assigned it during his life to Sir Alexander Hay	but of short duration because -
1609	Sir Henry Browne sold the keepership with all its privileges and rights for £800 during his life to Philip Herbert, Earl of Montgomery	Montgomery died in 1650.
1620	Montgomery assigned it to Robert Ratcliffe fifth Earl of Sussex during the lives of Henry Browne and Earl of Montgomery	Sussex died in 1629.
1621	Sussex assigned it to Robert Tyrwhitt during the lives of Browne and Montgomery	
1623	Robert Tyrwhitt appointed Arthur Squibb and Stephen Squibb keepers for 12 years provided Browne and Montgomery lived that long	He charged them annual rent of £100, two years of which they had to pay in advance.
1632	The king sold the manor and park outright to Robert Tyrwhitt for £850 for the use of him and Arthur Squibb	
1632/33	Robert Tyrwhitt sold his share to Arthur Squibb for £2,500.	

Figure 6: Repairs to the Lodge and Great Barn, 1515.

Workmen

Four carpenters throughout the 18-week period: 362 days @ 6d per day = £9 1s

Two sawyers from weeks 2 to 16: 146 days @ 6d per day = £3 13s

Two bricklayers from weeks 8 to 16 and one more from weeks 13 to 16: 116 days @ 6d per day = £2 18s

One tiler throughout the period and two more from week 3 to the end: 252 days @ 6d per day = £6 6s

One labourer from week 1, three more from week 3 and one more from week 7, to the end: 390 days @ 4d per day = £6 10s

Total workmen: £28 8s

Purchases and external work

John Goring for making 10,000 laths @ 20d the thousand = 16s 8d

Richard Goring 6 days & John Cherlen 3 days for digging loam & sand @ 4d = 3s

John Cherlen & Richard Goring for felling & cutting timber, 6 days each @ 5d = 5s

William Pullen for carriage in his cart of timber, 11 days @ 1s = 11s

Thomas Goring for carriage in his cart of timber, loam & sand, 16 days @ 1s = 16s

John Plonket, tilemaker, for 6,000 plain tiles brought to the lodge @ 3s 8d per 1000 = 22s

Same John Plonket for 3,000 bricks brought to the lodge @ 4s 4d per 1000 = 13s

Same John Plonket for 100 hollow ? = 3s 8d

Same John Plonket for 5 loads of stone lime brought to the lodge @ 4s 10d a load = 24s 2d

John Parvis, tilemaker, for 3,000 bricks brought to the lodge @ 4s 8d per 1000 = 14s

Philip Foster for 1,000 bricks, 4s 4d and 600 plain tiles, 2s 3d = 6s 7d

Edward Maybank, 500 plain tiles, 22d and 250? ridge tiles, 11d, brought to the lodge = 2s 9d

Nicholas Maybank, 700 plain tiles for 2s 6d

John Chuter for 5 loads of stone lime brought to the lodge @ 5s a load = 25s

Thomas Maybank the tiler for 8 bushels of tilepins at 8d a bushel = 4s 8d

Richard Milward for ? of tile pins = 2d

Thomas Blank of Guildford for
- 13,000 lath nails @ 9d/1000 = 9s 9d,   - 19,000 sprigs @ 8d/1000 = 12s 8d,
- 1,200 5d nails @ 4d/100 = 4s,   - 1,800 4d nails @ 3d/100 = 4s 6d,
- 500 3d nails @ 2d/100 = 10d and   - 400 6d nails @ 5d/100 = 20d; total 33s 5d

Robert Faggotter of Guildford, blacksmith, for 4 couple hooks & 4 couple hinges, 2 pairs of squares for windows and 3 clamps for windows, in all weighing 66 lb @ 1½d per lb = 8s 3d

Robert Smith of the Castle for 4 locks that were bestowed at the lodge @ 7d a lock = 2s 4d

Robert Exfold for 400 white boards of oak @ 2s per hundred = 8s

Symond to mend a chimney mantle of firestone 4d and for ochre to colour with 2d = 6d

Paid for a tub to bear water in, 4d, and for a ? to sift the lime with, 2d = 6d

Richard Wade to purvey all necessaries for the repairs as needed and to oversee the workmen for 17 weeks @ 2s 4d a week = 39s 8d

Robert Faggoter the smith for the masons' tools = 6d

Total purchases: £13 3s 4d

Grand total: £41 11s 4d

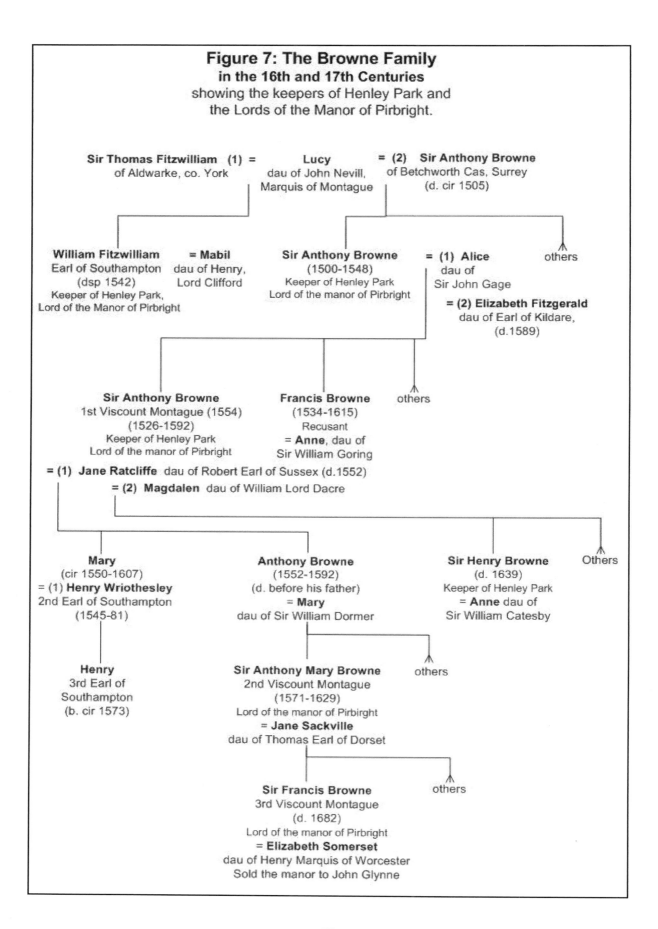

Figure 7: The Browne Family
in the 16th and 17th Centuries
showing the keepers of Henley Park and
the Lords of the Manor of Pirbright.

Sir Thomas Fitzwilliam (1) =
of Aldwarke, co. York

Lucy
dau of John Nevill,
Marquis of Montague

= (2) Sir Anthony Browne
of Betchworth Cas, Surrey
(d. cir 1505)

William Fitzwilliam
Earl of Southampton
(dsp 1542)
Keeper of Henley Park,
Lord of the Manor of Pirbright

= **Mabil**
dau of Henry,
Lord Clifford

Sir Anthony Browne
(1500-1548)
Keeper of Henley Park
Lord of the manor of Pirbright

= (1) **Alice**
dau of
Sir John Gage

others

= (2) **Elizabeth Fitzgerald**
dau of Earl of Kildare,
(d.1589)

Sir Anthony Browne
1st Viscount Montague (1554)
(1526-1592)
Keeper of Henley Park
Lord of the manor of Pirbright

Francis Browne
(1534-1615)
Recusant
= **Anne**, dau of
Sir William Goring

others

= (1) **Jane Ratcliffe** dau of Robert Earl of Sussex (d.1552)

= (2) **Magdalen** dau of William Lord Dacre

Mary
(cir 1550-1607)
= (1) **Henry Wriothesley**
2nd Earl of Southampton
(1545-81)

Anthony Browne
(1552-1592)
(d. before his father)
= **Mary**
dau of Sir William Dormer

Sir Henry Browne
(d. 1639)
Keeper of Henley Park
= **Anne** dau of
Sir William Catesby

Others

Henry
3rd Earl of
Southampton
(b. cir 1573)

Sir Anthony Mary Browne
2nd Viscount Montague
(1571-1629)
Lord of the manor of Pirbirght
= **Jane Sackville**
dau of Thomas Earl of Dorset

others

Sir Francis Browne
3rd Viscount Montague
(d. 1682)
Lord of the manor of Pirbright
= **Elizabeth Somerset**
dau of Henry Marquis of Worcester
Sold the manor to John Glynne

others

50

4. IN PRIVATE OWNERSHIP (1632-1739)

Squibb

Arthur Squibb was descended from an armorial family of Winterbourne Whitechurch, Dorset. He was probably born in Dorset in 1578 and married Joan, daughter of John Seymer of Hanford in Dorset (also an armorial family) and they had 12 children. They were living in Westminster by 1604, where their children were baptised. Arthur owed his advancement to his father's sister Alice Pitt who found him an appointment in the Department of the Exchequer where he spent much of his working life, advancing to the important position of Teller by 1626. In his late 60s, thanks to the influence of his son-in-law John Glynne, he was appointed Clarenceux King of Arms, a senior herald in the office of the College of Arms, a position said to be worth £400 a year. He appears to have always had an interest in genealogy and heraldry and during his time as Clarenceux he was responsible for four grants of arms, which have been described as well designed, suggesting the grantor was a sound herald.

It is not clear who actually lived at Henley Park after Sir Henry Browne left until the Squibbs took up residence. After the brothers were appointed to the keepership by Tyrwhitt, Stephen may have lived there while Arthur lived in London. Stephen's elder children were baptised at Ash up to the time Arthur bought the property outright, after which it appears that Stephen moved to a farm in Pirbright while Arthur took up residence as a country gentleman at Henley Park. He settled there for the rest of his life, although he continued to have a house in Westminster called the Black Spread Eagle Tavern in the 'New Palace' next door to John Glynne's residence, and he also had land in Somerset and Dorset.

Two years after his purchase Squibb wrote to Tyrwhitt from Henley Park complaining of 'many things amiss in the forest'. A large number of trees had been felled at the Holt and people had been invited to come and buy the 'lops and tops' but a multitude of 'disorderly people' came and stole many of the deer, so he recommended that the next sale should be limited to freeholders and keepers who would have more respect.

He seems to have been a rather arrogant and 'prickly' character and was not slow to claim special privileges. Around this time the Lord Lieutenants of Surrey complained to the King's Council that Squibb 'contemptuously refused' to find arms at the musters despite having sufficient arms in his house, claiming he was exempt as an 'Exchequer man'. He was also in dispute and litigation with the lord of the manor of Cleygate regarding peat digging and non-payment of rent, although the outcome of this dispute is not recorded.

As became clear later in his life, Arthur Squibb might have had more desire for self-aggrandisement than financial sense, as he apparently bought Henley Park from Tyrwhitt at a very inflated price and then spent a considerable sum building a suitably ostentatious new mansion to reflect his social aspirations. The mansion (see Plate 12) is very grand and its style Elizabethan or Jacobean. Its façade rises three storeys to a parapet which hides the roof and the central grand entrance porch rises to the full height of the house. It has large rectangular mullioned windows, some of which are in bays two storeys high; elaborate stone carvings over the doors; two imposing towers surmounted by cupolas and groups of tall, possibly ornate, chimneys. It had 21 hearths according to a later hearth tax assessment. There are some curious features of the building such as the yawning aperture on the left-hand side which could be a single storey bay window but with no glazing, surmounted by two smaller windows and a very elaborately decorated stone canopy. Based on the evidence of similar houses that have survived virtually unchanged, it is likely that the house extended to the rear round a single central courtyard. In particular the mansion at Chastleton in Oxfordshire (now National Trust) has similar dimensions and style to the Henley Park mansion, and coincidentally before the house was built the Chastleton estate was owned by the Robert Catesby of Gunpowder Plot infamy and nephew-in-law of Sir Henry Browne.

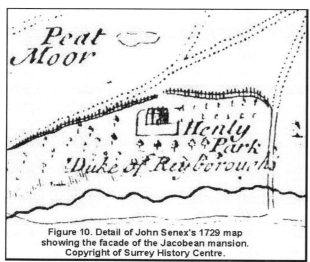

Figure 10. Detail of John Senex's 1729 map showing the facade of the Jacobean mansion. Copyright of Surrey History Centre.

Knowledge of this mansion at Henley Park had been lost and when it was revealed in a portrait of John Glynne and his family (Plate 13) it came as quite a surprise. An enlargement from John Senex's 1729 map of Surrey (Figure 10) shows a house which resembles that in the painting as opposed to the house as it appears on John Rocque's 1768 map of Surrey (Figure 14), a fact which had previously escaped attention. Two more modest buildings of an earlier style than the mansion, two storeys high with steep pitched roofs, are shown in the painting to the left of the mansion. The furthermost building to the left has at least one dormer window indicating a third storey and it would appear to be the central portion of the lodge as shown on Norden's map (Figure 8) which was left standing when the new mansion was built. This and the contours of the land confirm that the Jacobean-style mansion was sited slightly north-west of the present restored mansion, on land subsequently occupied by the factory buildings of Vokes Ltd, and that it is shown in the painting from the east across a stretch of water that no longer exists.

This stretch of water is deep enough on which to row a boat as depicted in the painting and its existence indicates that a similar feature could have existed on the upland ridge in medieval times, suggesting that the medieval manor could have been situated here with the lodge to its south. It is tempting to speculate that if Arthur Squibb knew that the foundations of an earlier medieval manor complex existed at the site, it would be advantageous to re-utilise them by building a new house on top, and if there was already a moat or ditch such as the one shown in the painting, it would lend itself to being re-used in his grand creation. Squibb had a keen sense of his own importance so the idea that he was building his 'palace' on top of a former royal residence might have appealed to him.

Squibb might already have been in financial difficulty as early as 1639 because he is reported to have felled and sold all the timber in the park. At a Forest Court at Windsor that year he claimed to have the right to dispark and cut down all the timber under the 1632 Patent and the court accepted his claim. Then by 1649 he lost his Tellership in unexplained circumstances and thus lost most of his livelihood. This increased his financial difficulties considerably and he initially mortgaged and then sold his main asset, Henley Park, to John Glynne and he died impoverished without sufficient funds to pay his debts.

Arthur Squibb died on 22 May 1650 and was buried at Ash on the 27th. He made his will less than a month before his death and in it he set up an annuity for his eldest surviving son William, who had been serving as a soldier in Holland for nearly 20 years, but appointed his four sons-in-law as executors; John Glynne, William Lister, Griffith Bodurda and John Crathorne. Arthur bequeathed a tenement called Marlins or Marvines in the tithing of Normandy in Ash (subsequently Halsey Cottage and its surrounding land) to his son Stephen, but Stephen sold it to John Glynne even before the will was proved. He bequeathed his properties in London to two of his daughters 'in satisfaction of their marriage portions' and his land in Dorset to his son Arthur. He did not specifically bequeath Henley Park to anyone, apparently because he had already sold it to John Glynne. The will is not well laid out and appears unfinished, with 'gaps' where the actual sums given to named servants and friends are missing, and he may have drawn it up himself in a hurry when he knew he was dying, although he made sure the will was witnessed. At first the executors did not bother to have the will proved and there may simply not have been enough money to execute it, so possibly they were trying to solve the problems themselves when they were presented with a lawsuit that forced their hand.

Arthur's eldest son William came home three years after his father's death and tried to recover all his father's property. He commenced a suit in Chancery against the executors, which prompted them finally to have the will proved a fortnight later. William claimed that he was the heir and administrator of his father, who had been persuaded to make a will disinheriting William by 'the conspirators' John Glynne, the other executors and Arthur's younger sons, who had alleged that William was 'dead beyond the seas'. He asserted that his father had an estate worth £7,000 and all his properties should have descended by right to him as heir at law, but instead had come into the hands of the conspirators. Each of the executors responded to the court that Arthur had conveyed Henley Park in his lifetime to John Glynne 'for good and valuable consideration' and conveyed his other properties to his executors and sons by his will. They denied that Arthur was in any way induced to make his will or was 'a lunatic or of an undisposing memory as is scandalously and disgracefully alleged'. Arthur did not have enough estate even to satisfy his debts, and they denied all the other claims in William's complaint.

John Glynne in particular went further in his response, finding 'much matter of infamy and fraud falsely laid on his reputation' and stating that he had lent Arthur £2,000 and then he agreed to buy the reversion of Henley Park (so that it became his property after Arthur's death) to discharge the debt and for £1,000 more, allowing Arthur and subsequently his widow to remain there for life and have the benefit of the rental value of about £190 per annum. Glynne felt it was 'a very dear bargain which he would not have made had it not been for the great affection he did bear for Arthur', who at that time was much indebted and driven to great extremity having lost his place as one of the tellers and being 'much pressed by his creditors'. Glynne also bought the tenement 'called Normandy' from Arthur's son Stephen for £200 which was 'dear enough', and bought some household effects from Arthur's widow for more than they were worth, so that she could pay Arthur's creditors who 'earnestly called upon her for their money'.

One curious allegation that Glynne denied was that Glynne or others paid Arthur Squibb for 'diet or horsemeat', and they had not 'dieted' with Arthur except sometimes to visit and stay with him as a friend, whereas Arthur and his family often dined with Glynne at Glynne's expense and he did not expect any payment for the same.

There is no record of the outcome of the case, but John Glynne retained ownership of Henley Park and there is no further mention of William Squibb. Joan, Arthur's widow continued to live at Henley Park until she died and was buried at Ash on 7 February 1652 and Glynne took full possession of the estate.

Glynne

John Glynne was born in 1603 into a long-established and prominent family at the ancestral home of Glynllifon, Caernarvonshire, which by chance is just a few miles south of Plâs Dinas which was the family home of Sir Owen Roberts who lived at Henley Park at the beginning of the 20th century. As a younger son Glynne was destined for a career in the law and he was admitted a member of Lincoln's Inn in 1621 and called to the bar in 1628. He soon entered public office and was returned to Parliament in 1640 for both Westminster, his residence, and Caernarfon. He quickly assumed a prominent role and gained national recognition as a lawyer and politician, serving tirelessly on as many as 800 parliamentary committees. He was a staunch supporter of the parliamentary system and played a significant role in the turbulent years of the mid 17th century. He was one of the MP's who led the offensive against Charles I's personal rule, culminating in the Civil War where he occupied the middle ground looking for a negotiated settlement. He became Cromwell's Serjeant-at-law and in June 1655 he was promoted to Chief Justice of the Upper Bench. It was probably on this occasion that he commissioned the portrait of himself wearing the robes of Chief Justice with his family, using Henley Park as the backdrop (Plate 13). Although a strong supporter of the parliamentary cause, Glynne advocated that Cromwell should assume the title of king rather than lord protector, because kingship was known to the law and had parliamentary sanction. His pro-monarchial views were conveniently published at the restoration and he continued his political work under Charles II. At the coronation he rode in the procession and was thrown from his horse and all but killed by the animal falling on him and Pepys the diarist, who regarded him as a rogue and a turncoat, saw the hand of God in the event. He was a great political survivor who prospered during both the Commonwealth and after the restoration of the monarchy, so that he was reputed to have made £100,000 in the last 19 years of his life.

John Glynne's first wife was Frances, daughter of Arthur Squibb, and two of their children were baptised at Ash in 1636 and 1640, long before he acquired Henley Park. Although he apparently bought Henley Park at an inflated price from his father-in-law as a favour to help Squibb out when he was in financial difficulties, Glynne evidently came to regard it as his favourite residence. Despite having other properties in Oxfordshire, North Wales and London, when he was knighted in 1660 he chose as his title Sir John Glynne of Henley Park. It was in an attractive position and much nearer to London than his other country properties. He was a rich man so it probably did not matter to him if Henley Park did not pay its way, but it may have become a millstone for later generations until they were eventually forced to sell.

Sir John Glynne died in 1666 at his house in Lincoln's Inn Fields in St Giles in the Fields parish and was 'carried to Westminster' to be buried in the chancel of St Margaret's Church. He had married twice and had a large family and his will divided his estates among his three sons; Sir William, the eldest, inherited estates at Bicester in Oxfordshire and the castle of Hawarden in Flintshire (later the house of the prime minister William Gladstone when he married Catherine, a descendant of Sir William), Thomas received other properties in north Wales and the house in Lincoln's Inn Fields, while Henley Park was to go to his youngest son John after his wife's death. His second wife, Ann, died two years later and John inherited Henley Park while still a minor.

John Glynne the younger was admitted to Hart Hall, University of Oxford in 1666. In 1679 he married Dorothy, daughter of Francis Tylney of Rotherwick, Hampshire. Possibly as part of the marriage settlement he 'sold' Henley Park and Marlins in trust to her brother Frederick Tylney for five shillings. At this time the Henley Park estate supposedly included not only the mansion and 500 acres of land with houses, cottages, mills, barns, stables and dovehouses but also the rights to leisure pursuits including fishing, hawking, hunting and fowling, as well as such manorial privileges as heriots, courts leet, views of frankpledge (a system where each member of a tithing is responsible for the good behaviour of others), courts baron and inquests. The lord of the manor had the right to the goods and chattels of felons, fugitives, clerics, convicts, condemned persons and of persons put in exigent (a writ for outlawry) as well as fairs, markets, tolls, stallage (rent for stalls in a market) and waifs and strays! Although the 1632 Patent specifically granted the manor of Henley along with all these supposed manorial privileges as well as the park and the buildings within it, there was in fact no functioning manor. For two centuries these imaginary manorial rights were transferred from owner to owner as the pro forma wording continued to be included in the deeds.

John and Dorothy had three daughters, two of whom were baptised at Ash and one who died in infancy. Then John Glynne died young in 1682 leaving his two surviving infant daughters co-heiresses under the terms of his will, the trustees of which were their uncles Sir William Glynne and Frederick Tylney. Dorothy his widow remarried the next year to George Woodroffe of nearby Poyle and anecdotal records speak of 'the late great wedding at Henley Park'. The family continued to live at Henley Park for a while, probably until George inherited the family estate at Poyle and with it the manor of Cleygate, in 1688.

By the time Glynne's middle daughter Dorothy married Richard Child in 1703 her elder sister Anne had died and Dorothy was in sole possession of Henley Park. At the time of the marriage Frederick Tylney took out a mortgage of £20,000 to provide his niece Dorothy with a dowry in addition to Henley Park, suggesting that Henley Park was not considered sufficiently valuable or financially viable. The marriage had advantages for both parties; Dorothy was marrying into one of the new class of wealthy landowners whose fortune had been built up by trade and while she was not wealthy she was the granddaughter of the famous Sir John Glynne and represented the landed gentry, so a desirable alliance for the ambitious younger son of a former merchant who was not expected to succeed to his father's estates.

Tylney

Richard Child was the son of Sir Josiah Child, a former East India merchant who amassed a vast fortune, was granted a baronetcy and set himself up buying the estate of Wanstead in Essex in the late 17th century. Richard was an ambitious man and was prominent in politics. Both Richard and Dorothy unexpectedly inherited large estates on the death of relatives. In 1704 Richard succeeded to the baronetcy and inherited the estate of Wanstead on the death of his elder half-brother, and was subsequently created Viscount Castlemaine in 1718 and Earl Tylney in 1731. He took the surname of Tylney by act of parliament in 1733 in recognition of Dorothy inheriting the Tylney Rotherwick estates on the death of a cousin.

The Squibbs and Glynnes had to a large extent made Henley Park their home, although of course they had other properties elsewhere. The Tylneys however had much grander aspirations and the premises to go with them and it is unlikely that they resided at Henley Park for long, if at all. The estate at Wanstead was about 10,000 acres and Rotherwick was also substantial. Richard and Dorothy chose to live at Wanstead where he built a magnificent new house in Palladian style which rivalled that of Blenheim in size and splendour (see Plate 14). Unfortunately when a later descendant Catherine Tylney-Long inherited the estates and became briefly the richest woman in England outside the royal family, she made a disastrous marriage to 'a well-known scoundrel' William Wellesly-Pole who managed to spend the entire fortune and more, until just a hundred years after its completion the house was demolished and sold piecemeal even down to the bricks, to pay his debts.

By 1710 the tenant in residence at Henley Park was Lord Charles Bruce, fourth Earl of Elgin and third Earl of Aylesbury, and his wife Anne the daughter of the second Marquis of Halifax. The Earls of Elgin were descended from a cousin of Robert the Bruce, King of Scotland. Charles was MP for Marlborough in 1710-11 and was called to the House of Lords in 1711. They had one daughter baptised at Ash and the registers also record their servants' marriages and childrens' baptisms, but after his wife Anne died in 1717 Bruce may have moved away. The Earldom eventually passed to a cousin and his descendant the seventh Earl collected the works of art from Greece commonly known as the 'Elgin Marbles'.

By 1723 Henley Park was the country seat of the first Duke of Roxburghe. He had been instrumental in the Scottish government's vote for the union with England in 1707 and in addition to his dukedom, he was created Marquis of Bowmont and Cessford, Earl of Kelso, Viscount of Broxmouth and Lord Ker of Cessford and Caverton, the last title ever created in the peerage of Scotland. A remarkable man, he was described in his younger days as 'a young gentleman of great learning and virtue, the best accomplished man of quality in Europe'. A Fellow of the Royal Society, he was a pallbearer at the funeral of Sir Isaac Newton in Westminster Abbey in 1727. He was still resident in 1729 but may have become dissatisfied with Henley Park for some reason because in 1730 it was advertised to let furnished or unfurnished and had pleasant gardens, large fish ponds and walls well stocked with fruit trees, and would be let with 200 acres of land. Maybe this was just a bluff on the Duke's part to try to get the rent reduced, because by 1731 it was again described as his country seat. Nevertheless in 1734 the mansion at Henley Park was occupied by Charles Freewood at £80 per annum rent and the other lands let to various tenants for £135 per annum.

The Squibbs and Glynnes had made some attempt to extend their estates around Henley Park (see Figure 11). Arthur Squibb purchased 428 acres of royal park, comprising a mixture of wooded cover, coppice and farmland ('plowed lands' as described by Norden some years earlier). Over the next seven years he felled the timber and apparently converted much of the park back to farmland. He may have intended to increase the size of his Surrey estate, because in 1637 he bought the 13-acre smallholding called 'Marlins' situated alongside Glaziers Lane in the manor of Cleygate, from Thomas West. However, he was soon in financial difficulties and made no further property purchases in the area. Marlins was not mortgaged to Sir John Glynne with the rest of the property and Arthur bequeathed it to his son Stephen Squibb, but Stephen soon sold it to John Glynne and it remained in the same ownership as Henley Park for more than 250 years.

John Glynne's first local property purchase was the copyhold cottage with half an acre of land called 'Canters', which a villager called Richard Canter had enclosed from the waste (uncultivated land) some years earlier. This property was right alongside the northern gate to Henley Park so Glynne probably decided that it would be tidier to incorporate it into the park and it subsequently became the 'Lower Lodge'. Unfortunately he did not follow the correct manorial procedure when he purchased it from William Cheesman in the early 1660s and in 1668 he was posthumously fined 5s by the Cleygate manorial court. The Glynnes also bought 11 acres of land near the 'Marlins' holding from a Nathaniel Purse, which they or their successors apparently used as coppice, and as late as the 1930s this plot was still called 'Pussey's (or Purse's) Copse'. The Glynne family's most significant purchase in the area during their ownership of Henley Park was in 1677 when John Glynne the younger bought the manor of Pirbright from the Brownes, thus beginning the long association between the 'lords' of Henley and the villagers of Pirbright. This purchase included the Manor Farm with 120 acres and the Manor Mill with its millpond in the heart of the village, and Rails Farm with 86 acres, a fenced enclosure in the heath which had been shown as 'Pirbright Rayles' on Norden's 1607 map. The Tylneys, however, do not seem to have had any ambitions to extend their Surrey estate and made no local purchases during their ownership.

If the rent from tenants and the land did not meet the expenses of keeping up the property, Henley Park may have become a drain on its owners' resources. Although he could afford to maintain it apparently Richard Earl Tylney saw no reason to do so any longer and so he mortgaged Henley Park, possibly to offset its costs. He was a wealthy man and did not need to raise what for him was a small sum, but in 1734 he mortgaged it to Millicent Fuller, widow, for £2,500 and the next year both Henley Park and the manor of Pirbright to James Martin for £6,000.

However these may only have been temporary measures. For four generations Henley Park had passed from family to family by inheritance or marriage (see Figure 9) but now it was transferred by an outright sale for the first time since the king sold it a hundred years earlier. In 1739 Earl Tylney sold it to Solomon Dayrolle, a Huguenot refugee who was prepared to put money into Henley Park and its estate for the advantages it would bring him.

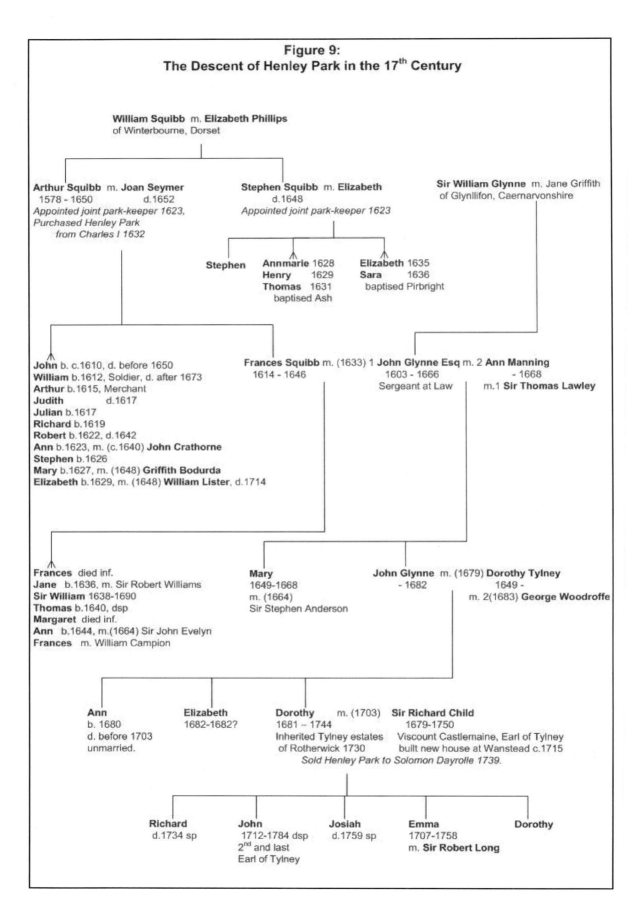

Figure 9:
The Descent of Henley Park in the 17th Century

William Squibb m. Elizabeth Phillips
of Winterbourne, Dorset

Arthur Squibb m. Joan Seymer
1578 - 1650   d.1652
Appointed joint park-keeper 1623,
Purchased Henley Park
from Charles I 1632

Stephen Squibb m. Elizabeth
d.1648
Appointed joint park-keeper 1623

Sir William Glynne m. Jane Griffith
of Glynllifon, Caernarvonshire

Stephen

Annmarie 1628
Henry   1629
Thomas   1631
baptised Ash

Elizabeth 1635
Sara   1636
baptised Pirbright

John b. c.1610, d. before 1650
William b.1612, Soldier, d. after 1673
Arthur b.1615, Merchant
Judith   d.1617
Julian b.1617
Richard b.1619
Robert b.1622, d.1642
Ann b.1623, m. (c.1640) **John Crathorne**
Stephen b.1626
Mary b.1627, m. (1648) **Griffith Bodurda**
Elizabeth b.1629, m. (1648) **William Lister**, d.1714

Frances Squibb m. (1633) 1 John Glynne Esq m. 2 Ann Manning
1614 - 1646   1603 - 1666   - 1668
                                        Sergeant at Law   m.1 Sir Thomas Lawley

Frances died inf.
Jane b.1636, m. Sir Robert Williams
Sir William 1638-1690
Thomas b.1640, dsp
Margaret died inf.
Ann b.1644, m.(1664) Sir John Evelyn
Frances m. William Campion

Mary
1649-1668
m. (1664)
Sir Stephen Anderson

John Glynne m. (1679) Dorothy Tylney
- 1682   1649 -
                  m. 2(1683) George Woodroffe

Ann
b. 1680
d. before 1703
unmarried.

Elizabeth
1682-1682?

Dorothy   m. (1703)
1681 – 1744
Inherited Tylney estates
of Rotherwick 1730

Sir Richard Child
1679-1750
Viscount Castlemaine, Earl of Tylney
built new house at Wanstead c.1715
Sold Henley Park to Solomon Dayrolle 1739.

Richard
d.1734 sp

John
1712-1784 dsp
2nd and last
Earl of Tylney

Josiah
d.1759 sp

Emma
1707-1758
m. **Sir Robert Long**

Dorothy

Figure 11: Private Owners' Property Purchases before the 'Halsey Explosion!'

Property	Purchased by
Henley Park, 428 acres	Arthur Squibb in 1632
'Marlins', 13-acre smallholding in Normandy	Arthur Squibb from Thomas West in 1637
(sub-total 441 acres)	
'Canters', copyhold cottage and ½ acre by Heath gate of Henley Park	Sir John Glynne from William Cheesman, by 1664
'Glaziers otherwise Barretts', subsequently Pussey's Copse, 11 acres of land in Normandy	Glynne family from Nathaniel Purse between 1668 and 1682
The Manor of Pirbright, with Manor Farm, about 100 acres, Manor Mill with 20 acres, Rails Farm about 86 acres	John Glynne from Francis Browne, third Lord Montague, in 1677
(sub-total: 658 acres)	
'Dairymead', 2-acre field in Worplesdon parish	Solomon Dayrolle from John Westbrook, by 1750
Cowshot Farm, 103 acres in Pirbright, Bisley and Chobham	Solomon Dayrolle from John Kidder for £380 on 4 October 1750
Whipley Farm, 152 acres in Worplesdon and Normandy	Solomon Dayrolle from William Bray Esq about 1775
(sub-total: 915 acres)	

5. SOLOMON DAYROLLE (1739-1784)

The contrast in the social backgrounds of Solomon Dayrolle and Earl Tylney and their attitude towards Henley Park could have hardly been greater. The lands which Dayrolle purchased in 1739 comprised the former royal park with the mansion and grounds and Henley Park Farm plus three small holdings in Normandy, making about 452 acres in the parish of Ash. In Pirbright he owned the lordship of the manor with two farms and the mill, making 206 acres. These totalled over 650 acres and formed an estate of considerable size and significance in the locality. The Earl of Tylney on the other hand also owned the far greater estates of Wanstead in Essex and Rotherwick in Hampshire. Henley Park had probably ranked very low in his esteem, especially if it had proved to be an unwelcome drain on his resources. However for Dayrolle, who was descended from a family of French refugees and had recently come into a fortune, it represented the means by which he could establish himself not simply as a landed gentleman but more importantly, as an English landed gentleman.

Solomon Dayrolle was probably born around 1710 but very little is known about his early life. His uncle James Teissoniere alias D'Ayrolles was born at St Germain in France and was a Protestant refugee granted English residence in 1696 and citizenship by act of parliament in 1700. His diplomatic career began at The Hague where he replaced Alexander Stanhope as the English Resident (Ambassador) to the United Provinces in 1706. One of his diplomatic duties was to organise transport and issue passes for 'the Palatines', the thousands of refugees from harsh conditions in the Palatinate (now southern Germany) who were encouraged by the English government to settle in the new American colonies. Except for a three-year period when he was Resident with the Republic of Geneva, James remained at The Hague until his death there on 13 January 1739 in his 83rd year, while still serving in his official capacity. In his will he left monetary bequests to 'the poor French refugees of the City of London' and to various of his kinsmen who were also described as refugees. He directed that no inventory need be made of his household goods, as they were listed in his journal which contains 'the state of my affairs'. He bequeathed the bulk of his considerable estates in France, Holland and England to his nephew Solomon and within months, Solomon had purchased Henley Park.

Every change of regime in France was accompanied by a Terror from the right or left, and French refugees were a permanent feature of London society. Travel, intellect and curiosity led the Whigs, a loosely grouped political party and ideological tendency, to admire other cultures and predominantly that of France, so maybe it was natural that the Dayrolle family should be drawn into the Whig social circle. Solomon's godfather and mentor was Philip Dormer Stanhope, fourth Earl of Chesterfield, a prominent Whig, and it was through his help that Solomon obtained some of his court positions and diplomatic postings.

Whiggery was far more than politics, Whigs dominated the activities that filled the leisure hours of London's social elite. Whigs were metropolitan and cosmopolitan; they were rich and were landed, but with a dislike for the country and a strong preference for the metropolis; the London season from October to May or June, was their home. The Whigs' great palaces were not houses in which families expected to live, rather they were power statements in stone. For the whole of the 18th century the ownership of property was thought to be the main qualification that fitted a man for political life. It entitled a man to vote, to consideration, to influence and respect, so it was natural that Solomon should acquire a substantial property as soon as he could. Whigs believed passionately that men resisted tyrants in order to defend their property; they saw themselves as defenders of parliament against the tyranny of kings and the church.

Solomon apparently aspired to be a diplomat and courtier like his uncle. He first appears in 1730 when he sent reports with details of military numbers and strengths from a military camp at Mühlberg near Leipzig, to his uncle in The Hague. Perhaps as a young man in his teens or twenties he was able to pass unnoticed while he engaged in this espionage activity. Ten years later Solomon was involved with Court life and London society; he was admitted as Gentleman of His Majesty George II's Privy Chamber in 1740 and quickly became a favourite of the king, then in 1744 he was admitted as Master of the Revels, a petty sinecure which ceased to exist when he died.

Accounts of travellers and archaeologists provided source material and proofs of the Whig world view of a political system that linked liberty and order. Thanks to the Whigs' defence of the parliamentary tradition in crisis after crisis England had attained that lucky goal and this gave Whigs the right to lecture their own countrymen on how to preserve freedom and foreigners on how to achieve it. In 1742 Solomon was proposed and elected as a member of the Egyptian Exploration Society, a group of gentlemen dedicated to research into Egyptian antiquities. Solomon had not been to Egypt himself but was admitted under the clause that allowed 'Gentlemen who had been in the Levant or distinguished themselves by their knowledge and curiosity'. In 1743 he was also elected, as a 'gentleman of merit and learning', to the Fellowship of the Royal Society (see Figure 12), which had been at the forefront of scientific progress since its foundation in London 80 years earlier. At the time of his election to the Royal Society Solomon described himself as 'of Henley Park in Surrey' but by 1745 his diplomatic career had begun and he spent most of the next 12 years abroad.

He began as Secretary to his friend and patron Lord Chesterfield in his postings at The Hague and as Lord Lieutenant of Ireland, where Solomon was appointed Gentleman Usher of the Black Rod in 1745. Then in 1747 his persistent patron finally secured him the much-coveted diplomatic post when he was appointed to his uncle's former position as British Resident at The Hague. In 1752 when he was moved to the Residency at the Court of Brussels, the States General sent a letter of commendation for his time at The Hague.

Soon after the outbreak of the Seven Years' War, sometimes referred to as the first World War because of its global nature, for reasons unknown Solomon lost his position as British Resident in 1757 'to his distress', and thereafter had some difficulty finding another position. The Whig-Tory two-party system disintegrated in the 1760s into a number of essentially personal political groups and the end of the old-corps Whig cohesion was an important aspect of the instability of the 1760s, which apparently disadvantaged Solomon. His friend and mentor Lord Chesterfield tried to assist, but feared he was useless 'in his retirement and with his deafness and other infirmities'. In 1758 Lord Chesterfield recommended Solomon in his application to be

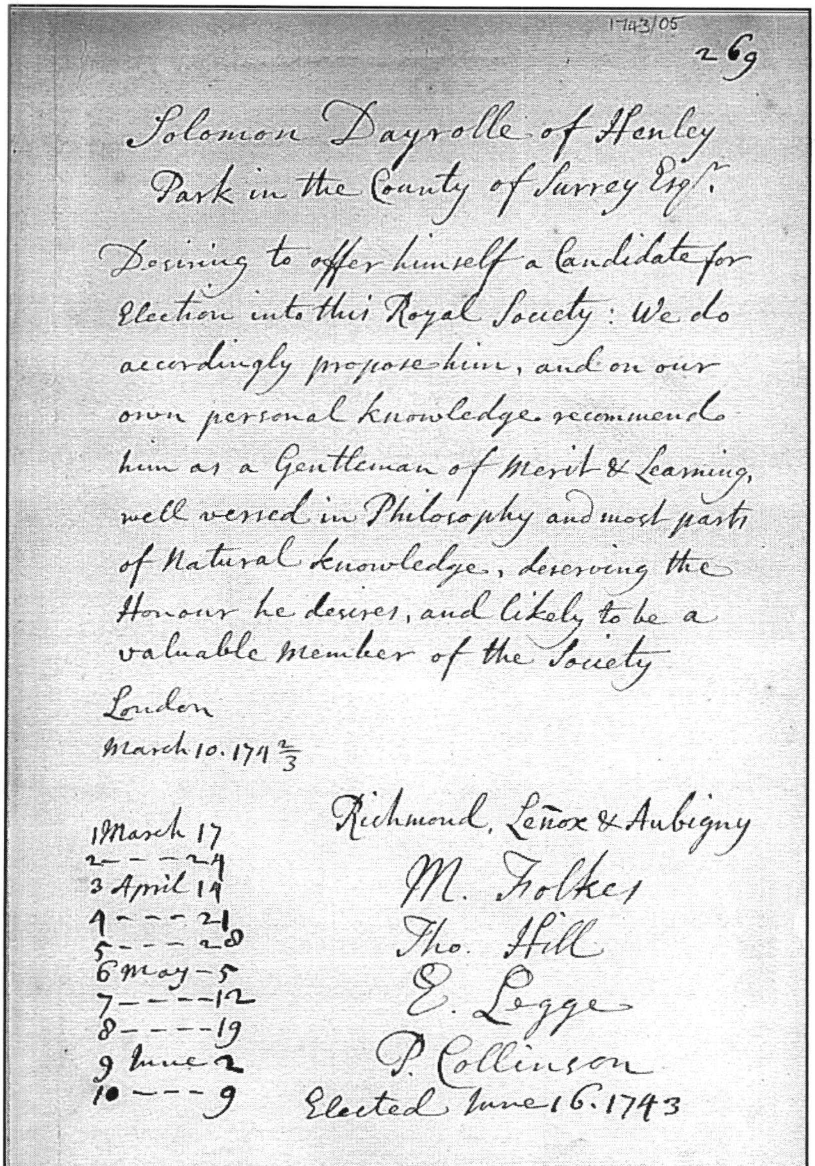

Commissioner of the Excise in London, saying 'you must be unlucky if you do not get it when everybody likes you', and in 1765 an L Stanhope offered to secure the Ambassadorship of Constantinople worth £3,000 a year for him, but nothing seems to have come of these efforts and Solomon is not mentioned as having any official capacity again.

The Earl of Chesterfield is remembered for his wise and witty letters to his son, in which he twice recommends that his son 'go to the court of Brussels and stay a month or two there with Dayrolles'. Solomon and the Earl became lifelong friends and when Chesterfield died in 1773 Solomon was with him, and ever thoughtful of his friend's comfort, the Earl of Chesterfield's 'famous last words' are recorded to have been "Give Dayrolles a chair".

On 4 July 1751 Solomon married Christabella, the 18-year old daughter of a Colonel Ludovick Peterson, at Somerset House Chapel. She was a lady of accomplished manners and dignified appearance, well known in the fashionable circles of London and still more admired at the court of Brussels, even though she was still only a teenager when Solomon took up his post there. The Earl of Chesterfield wrote many letters to her which are preserved in his 'Miscellaneous Works'. It is possible that Christabella assisted the Earl by writing the 'Letters of Junius' for him. These were a series of anonymous and vitriolic letters attacking leading public figures of the day, which were published in the London Public Advertiser between 1768 and 1772. Whoever wrote them could not have risked that their handwriting would be recognised and would have needed a trusted assistant, and later students have shown that the handwriting of the 'letters' appears to match that of Mrs Dayrolle, but the identity of the author and their amanuensis has never been finally proved.

Figure 12: Solomon Dayrolle's application to the Royal Society, 1743.
© The Royal Society

Although he was still resident abroad, Solomon was obviously keen to create an impressive and fitting home for his bride because he undertook extensive work at Henley Park prior to their wedding. Instead of attempting to improve the now-unfashionable Jacobean-style mansion, which might already have deteriorated into a poor condition, he turned to the nearby older lodge house to form the core of his redevelopments. Although it would have been nearly 400 years old by this time, it could have survived as a farmhouse or tenanted dwelling and it was this house that was remodelled in the more restrained country-house style of the Georgian period. Much of the older structure was retained internally and a complete new outer layer was built onto it. The whole of the exterior was faced in a smooth two-inch red brick skin and the windows sashed with thick oak glazing bars. The roof structure was retained but the former eaves on the east face was replaced with a parapet. The principal façade was made symmetrical and the front door given an architectural character with a pediment supported on scroll brackets. Certainly he spared no expense, because the workmanship of the facing brickwork was fine quality, especially the voussoirs of the window heads which were formed of rubbed bricks with extremely fine joints. The workmanship compares very favourably with the contemporary developments at nearby Westwood. Inside there were three storeys connected by a 'best' staircase and a 'back' staircase, with eight or nine main rooms on each floor. This work was probably undertaken by a competent local builder using published architectural sources, producing the appearance and shape of the mansion that we see today. Some chalk blocks of well-moulded door and window openings mortared together which derive from an earlier building were re-used in the footings of the south end wall and these may have been from the Jacobean mansion, which was probably removed at this time and it completely disappeared from maps and popular memory.

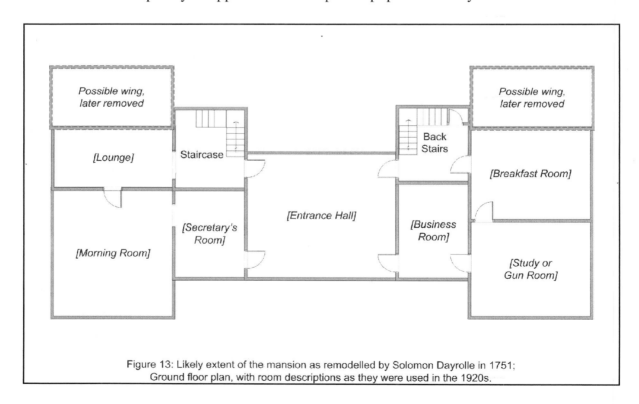

Figure 13: Likely extent of the mansion as remodelled by Solomon Dayrolle in 1751;
Ground floor plan, with room descriptions as they were used in the 1920s.

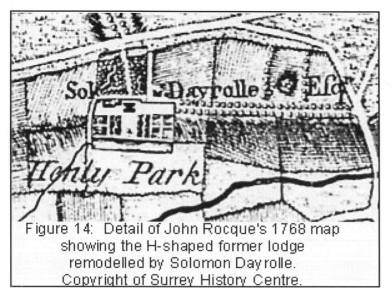

Figure 14: Detail of John Rocque's 1768 map
showing the H-shaped former lodge
remodelled by Solomon Dayrolle.
Copyright of Surrey History Centre.

John Rocque's detailed map of Surrey in 1768 (see Figure 14) shows an H-shaped house with north and south ranges connected by a central portion. There are outbuildings to the north-west and extensive gardens to the south-east and south-west around a central lawn. The mansion, outbuildings and gardens seem to be surrounded by a wall or fence. The north approach is through wooded parkland and the east approach is along an avenue of trees leading directly towards the mansion.

Solomon made three further land purchases to supplement his Surrey estates during his ownership, and they were very different in nature. A few years after buying the property, he purchased a two-acre field called Dairymead from John Westbrook. Dairymead was part of a seven-acre freehold smallholding called Heathers alias Beadles in the manor of Cleygate. It appears that Solomon was tidying up his boundaries because Dairymead adjoined the fields of his Henley Park Farm, but it was separated from the rest of the holding, subsequently known as Chapel Farm, by the Ash - Wood Street road and the Bailes Lane - Whipley Lane road which cross at Willey Green. The former annual rent of 2s 6d payable to the lord of Cleygate Manor was apportioned as 1s for Dairymead, 1s 6d for the rest of the holding.

On 4 October 1750 he bought Cowshot Farm, 103 acres in Pirbright, Bisley and Chobham, from John Kidder a brickmaker of Worplesdon for £380. He made his final purchase about 1775 when he bought the whole of Whipley Farm, 152 acres mostly in the parish of Worplesdon but including one field called Cobbetts Bridge Mead in the parish of Ash, from William Bray Esq. Thus during his tenure, Solomon increased the size of the estates from about 658 acres to over 900 acres (see Plate 15).

Apart from Cowshot Farm his purchases were to the south and east of the estate, and unlike later holders, Solomon showed little interest in Pirbright. He held his first court baron as lord of the manor of Pirbright on 13 July 1739 and the manor purchased a large new leather-bound court book to record the proceedings. But in fact, again unlike his successors, he did not have a harmonious relationship with his tenants in Pirbright and he was in dispute and litigation with them over turf cutting rights for more than 30 years.

When Solomon bought the manor of Pirbright from Earl Tylney he believed he was also receiving a long lease to dig peat on a section of the peat moor there, but this was news to the tenants. Solomon assigned the lease to Thomas Chilton who stepped up the peat-digging activity significantly, which alarmed then angered the tenants to the point where they brought a court action against Solomon and Thomas demanding the restoration of their rights of common pasture on the land. They complained of large holes and five-foot deep trenches being dug, and peat stacked on the grass. This dispute dragged on for most of the time that Solomon was lord of the manor - in 1739, the very year he took over, the tenants pledged to share the costs of the legal action against him for loss of common pasture, which was to be led by John Collins, one of their number. The case came to court in 1743 and again in 1744 but the result was inconclusive, although the lawyers benefited to the tune of £6 10s 9d. By 1762 the tenants had taken some sort of direct action which prompted Solomon to commence legal action himself against another tenant, John Howard of Cowshot Farm, who had apparently asserted his right to use the land for pasture. Pirbright was estimated to have 1,175 acres of which 200 were pasture, with 157 horses, 275 bullocks and 1,197 sheep which had the right to graze there. In 1763 the tenants claimed that 58 acres of the surface of the common had been dug up, 50 more acres were covered with turfs for over a year and 500 cartloads of turfs and 1,000 cartloads of peat had been carried away. The case was taken to Croydon assize in 1763, then again to Kingston assize in 1764 when a different tenant, John Baker, led the tenants' action and claimed £30 in damages. During this hearing the judgement from the earlier case in 1671 between Viscount Montague as lord of Pirbright Manor and Robert Woods, a tenant, was read out as evidence for the tenants.

Solomon's lack of employment might have caused him some financial hardship, because in January 1762 he was 'in the custody of the marshal of the Marshalsea', the debtors' prison in Southwark, although this was more likely related to a dispute over some specific debt rather than general insolvency, because Solomon had many valuable paintings and possessions which he retained until his death. This circumstance might explain the timing of the tenants' action, to coincide with his absence.

In 1764 Solomon proposed an agreement whereby he would have the sole right of cutting peat in the manor, but the tenants would automatically receive 20% of the value of the peat cut. His representative, James Phipps of Henley Park, communicated the terms to the tenants and said he 'hoped Mr Dayrolles would allow something more' and said he would try to persuade him to come to an agreement. In 1773, 34 years and some four court cases after the dispute started, formal articles of agreement were drawn up. In these, the lord and the tenants of the manor agreed that the tenants would receive 40% of the profits from the peat and 50% of the profits from the 'todds' (the turf covering the peat). A committee of managers had to be formed and their accounts were to be kept in a chest with two locks, one key being held by the tenants' manager and the other by the lord of the manor's. The number of loads to be cut in a year could not exceed 2,000 nor be less than 500. However, Henley Park Moor and Hodd's Moor were excluded and the peat there was acknowledged as Solomon's sole property. The tenants declared that their share of the profits was intended for the public benefit of the inhabitants of Pirbright, for support of the poor and repairing the church, and thus the dispute was finally over.

Unlike the next owners the Halseys who were deeply involved with Pirbright Church, Solomon seems to have taken little interest in the church or parish, and was simply one of the contributors when a petition was raised in 1783 for funds to rebuild the church, although only the nave and tower were actually rebuilt at this time. His children were baptised in London or abroad, and the family does not appear in any of the local parish registers.

Solomon may not have spent much time at Henley Park in the early years of his tenure while he pursued his diplomatic career abroad, but after he returned from Brussels he became more involved in local affairs in Surrey. Together with Lannoy Richard Coussmaker of neighbouring Westwood, Solomon attended a meeting held in October 1767 at the King's Head

Inn, Chertsey, to consider an application to Parliament for making a turnpike road from Chertsey to Guildford, Farnham and other towns. The road from Farnham to Chertsey would provide a more direct and convenient route to London from Winchester, Southampton and the West of England than the existing route via Staines, according to the proposal. The route of this branch would have run past Fox Corner and Bakers Gate in Pirbright and presumably along the route of today's Pirbright Road through Normandy towards Ash. This scheme did not go ahead, but if it had done the route could easily have developed into something like the A3 trunk road and Normandy, Pirbright and Ash would be very different places today.

When the Basingstoke canal was proposed there were various sections built into the Basingstoke Canal Bill 1776-78 to protect the interests of local property-holders and one of these stipulated that no water could be diverted from Solomon Dayrolle's ponds at Pirbright. These ponds fed the stream down to the mill pond in Pirbright and may have been essential to ensure a head of water to work the mill. Ironically, eighty years later when the railway was built no such protection was available and the railway embankment almost completely filled in one of the ponds. When the canal was built through Pirbright between 1788 and 1792 it passed across land in the manor owned by Solomon Dayrolle. As part of his compensation he received an annuity of £25 a year from the company and this annuity passed with the property to the Halseys, although Henry Halsey apparently regarded it as his own personal property to dispose of as he wished.

Solomon's London house was in Hanover Square and he apparently split his time between there and Henley Park during the 1760s and 1770s, but by 1781 Henley Park was let to tenants and he and his family seem to have lived exclusively at their London home. In 1781 Henley Park was occupied by Sir John Sheffield, Baronet and he paid £9 9s window tax as the property had 93 lights (windows). He was there until 1784 and paid £90 a year rent to his landlord, then it was briefly occupied by Sir Sunyan Stoneard at the same rent. It seems that the property may have been deteriorating during this period because soon after it was sold to the Halseys it was reported to be 'much improving'.

As a British Ambassador Solomon and his family were part of court society and their comings and goings were reported in the press. As well as his movements to and from his postings at The Hague and Brussels and activities relating to his duties there, their social activities are mentioned such as the family's arrivals in Bath in the summer and Mrs Dayrolle's presence at a 'Drawing Room' at Saint James', attended by the royal family and numerous nobility. Solomon played an active part in mid-18th century London Society and one of his acquaintances must have been the playwright, poet, merchant and politician Richard Glover, who lived at Albemarle Street, St James Westminster, and like Solomon was a student of antiquities. Their children were certainly acquainted because Glover's son Richard is said by Horace Walpole to have eloped in 1777 with one of Solomon's daughters and gone to stay with Lady Amelia, the daughter of Robert D'Arcy fourth Earl of Holdernesse (the Secretary of State to whom Solomon had reported during his Residencies). Lady Amelia's mother-in-law the Countess of Carmarthen clearly disapproved of the elopement and refused to speak to her daughter, causing Walpole much cruel satisfaction at this 'great breach' in the household.

Glover left his daughter Mary over £8,000, a significant sum in those days, as well as all his papers. Mary, an intelligent and well-educated person, was responsible for the posthumous publication of some of her father's work, including a play called 'Jason' which was deemed too elaborate to stage and a 30-volume epic about the wars between Athens and Persia. She was later to marry Henry Halsey whose family were to own Henley Park for a century and a half after he purchased it from Solomon Dayrolle.

Solomon and Christabella had four children, one son and three daughters. Their youngest daughter Mary was apparently the unwilling prototype of the voluble and vivacious character Miss Larolles in Fanny Burney's novel Cecilia - she was reported by a respondent to the Gentleman's Magazine to have been 'very indignant' about it.

Their son Thomas Philip Dayrolle was educated at Eton and went into the Army, becoming a lieutenant then captain in the 10th Dragoon Guards. By 1786 he had married a Mademoiselle Tomaset, the daughter of a 'respectable Swiss gentleman' and they apparently settled in Switzerland, where he died in Lausanne in the early 1800s. Thomas had one son, George, who was born in 1795 and became Superintendent of Forests to the Grand Duke of Hesse Darmstadt. George married but died in 1823 without issue and this male branch of the Dayrolle family died out. Solomon must have hoped that Thomas would inherit his Surrey properties because in May 1777 they undertook an 'exemplification of common recovery' legal action to establish Thomas' right to the property, but Thomas must have decided otherwise because in July 1784 father and son conveyed Henley Park and his other properties in Surrey to trustees to be sold, and in 1784[*] they were bought by Henry Halsey. The sale price was reported to be £19,000, something like £850,000 at today's values.

Solomon apparently did not want to be any trouble to anyone. In his will he expressed a desire to be buried in whichever parish he happened to die, and that his servants should not be put into mourning for him. As well as monetary bequests he willed a series of specific items to his wife and daughters including harpsichords, violins, music books, silver and gold watches, rings and silver plated candlesticks. To his son he left all his firearms, swords and all his books, manuscripts and portraits, as well as a gold watch and two diamond rings. He did have second thoughts, however. In a codicil to his will ten months later, he stipulated that if any of his daughters should profess the Roman Catholic religion or should marry a Catholic, or if they should reside outside Great Britain and Ireland, then all his provisions for them should be void. Perhaps he remembered his uncle's refugee status and persecution of his family in France at the hands of Catholics.

In 1786 Solomon was at his leasehold house on the south side of Hanover Square London, and when he died on the 16th of March he was buried at St George Hanover Square parish church. He was described as a man of great benevolence and exemplary piety and his manners were the most correct cast of the old school. In the months following his death a series of auctions was advertised by the executors of his will, to sell his collections of paintings (including works by Rubens, Jordeans, Brueghel and several other named artists), his library of books, musical instruments, elegant household plate, glassware, furniture and the lease of the house itself (see Figure 15). Solomon's widow Christabella died in 1791 at her house at number 11 George Street,

---

[*] It has not been possible to confirm the date. The sale of Henley Park was recorded in the Surrey Feet of Fines, Trinity term 25 George III, where it was apparently seen by historians in the early 20th century, but while the other Feet of Fines are now preserved at The National Archive, that particular one is missing. In his will of November 1784 Solomon mentions his estate at Henley Park, but in a codicil of November 1785 he confirms that all his estates in Surrey had been sold.

Hanover Square and the household furniture and lease of the house was advertised for sale by her son Thomas Philip.

The Dayrolle family's tenure of Henley Park only lasted for 45 years and during much of that time they were elsewhere, yet it provided the most tangible reminder of its long history that survives today - the mansion that still stands at the centre of Henley Park.

By Mr. CHRISTIE,
On the Premises, on SATURDAY May the 6th.
By Order of the EXECUTORS pursuant to the WILL,
A CAPITAL and VALUABLE COLLEC-
TION of ITALIAN, FRENCH, and DUTCH
PICTURES, being an assemblage of the UNDOUBTED
WORKS of the most esteemed and admired Masters, in the
highest State of Preservation, late the Property of
SOLOMAN DAYROLLES, Esq. deceased,
At his Late HOUSE on the SOUTH SIDE of HANOVER
SQUARE.
AND on the following Day will ALSO be SOLD the
SIDEBOARD of PLATE, fine OLD CHINA, and two
capital fine TONED VIOLINS.
To be viewed two days preceding the sale, when Catalogues
may be had on the Premises, at the Rainbow coffee-house,
Cornhill, and in Pall Mall.
AND ALSO in the FIRST DAY's SALE, will be
SOLD by AUCTION, the unexpired Term of 28 Years,
of the ELEGANT SPACIOUS House with extensive
OFFICES, NINE STALL STABLE, and DOUBLE
COACH HOUSE, &c. The Premises have been recently
put into the most elegant and complete repair, and fit for
the immediate possession of a genteel family.
To be viewed with Tickets preceding the sale, and printed
Particulars will be forthwith ready.

Figure 15. Advertisement in the Morning Post
for sale by auction of Solomon Dayrolle's effects.

69

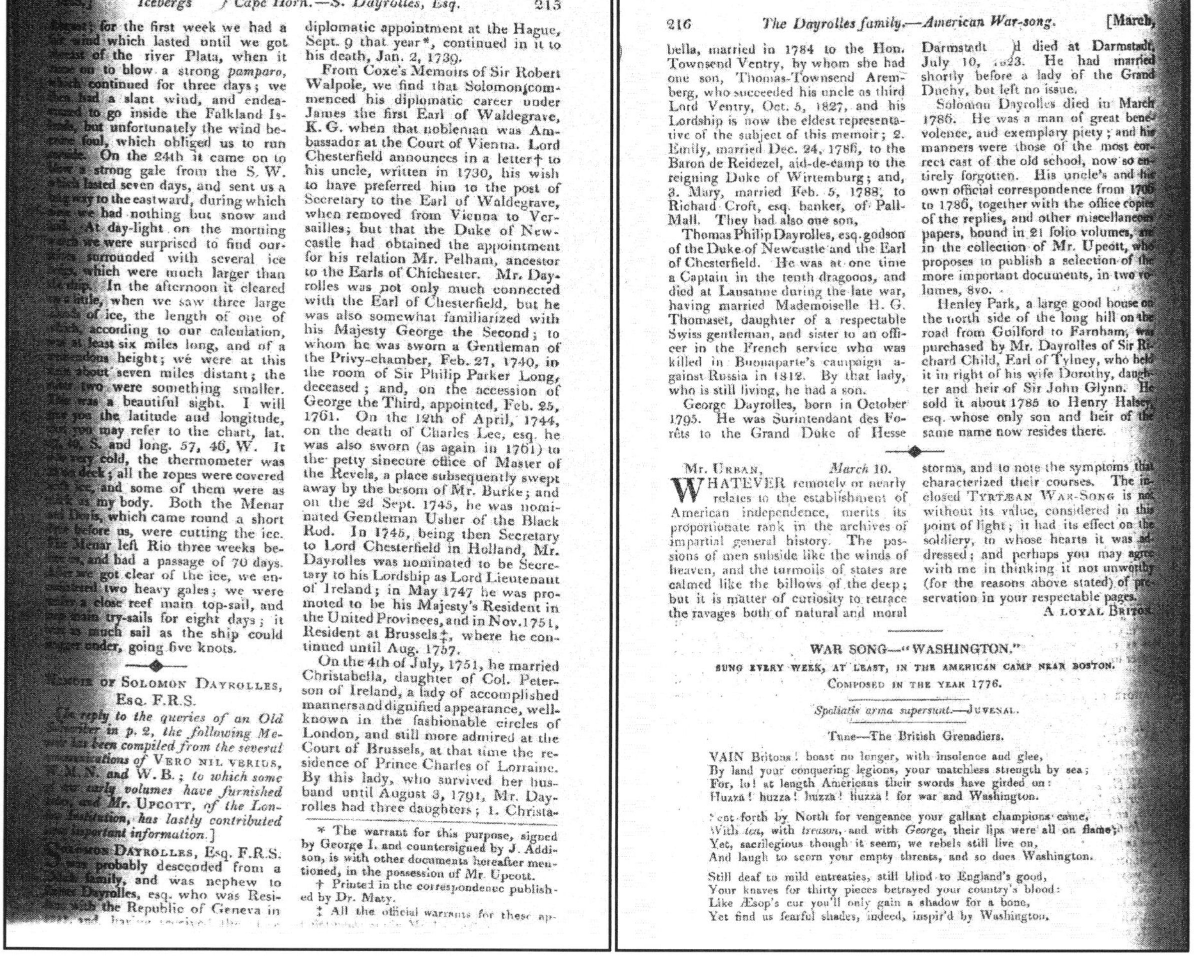

for the first week we had a ... which lasted until we got ... of the river Plata, when it ... to blow a strong *pamparo*, ... continued for three days; we ... had a slant wind, and endea... to go inside the Falkland Is... but unfortunately the wind be... foul, which obliged us to run ... On the 24th it came on to ... strong gale from the S. W. ... lasted seven days, and sent us a ... way to the eastward, during which ... had nothing but snow and ... At day-light on the morning ... we were surprised to find our... surrounded with several ice ... which were much larger than ... In the afternoon it cleared ... while, when we saw three large ... of ice, the length of one ... according to our calculation, ... least six miles long, and of a ... height; we were at this ... about seven miles distant; the ... two were something smaller. ... a beautiful sight. I will ... the latitude and longitude, ... may refer to the chart, lat. ... S. and long. 57, 46, W. It ... cold, the thermometer was ... all the ropes were covered ... and some of them were as ... my body. Both the Menar ... which came round a short ... us, were cutting the ice. ... Menar left Rio three weeks be... and had a passage of 70 days. ... got clear of the ice, we en... two heavy gales; we were ... close reef main top-sail, and ... try-sails for eight days; it ... much sail as the ship could ... under, going five knots.

—◆—

OF SOLOMON DAYROLLES, Esq. F.R.S.

[In reply to the queries of an Old ... in p. 2, the following Me... been compiled from the several ... tions of VERO NIL VERIUS, ... N. and W. B.; to which some ... early volumes have furnished ... Mr. UPCOTT, of the Lon... tion, has lastly contributed ... important information.]

SOLOMON DAYROLLES, Esq. F.R.S. ... probably descended from a ... family, and was nephew to ... Dayrolles, esq. who was Resi... the Republic of Geneva in ...

diplomatic appointment at the Hague, Sept. 9 that year*, continued in it to his death, Jan. 2, 1739.

From Coxe's Memoirs of Sir Robert Walpole, we find that Solomon commenced his diplomatic career under James the first Earl of Waldegrave, K. G. when that nobleman was Ambassador at the Court of Vienna. Lord Chesterfield announces in a letter† to his uncle, written in 1730, his wish to have preferred him to the post of Secretary to the Earl of Waldegrave, when removed from Vienna to Versailles; but that the Duke of Newcastle had obtained the appointment for his relation Mr. Pelham, ancestor to the Earls of Chichester. Mr. Dayrolles was not only much connected with the Earl of Chesterfield, but he was also somewhat familiarized with his Majesty George the Second; to whom he was sworn a Gentleman of the Privy-chamber, Feb. 27, 1740, in the room of Sir Philip Parker Long, deceased; and, on the accession of George the Third, appointed, Feb. 25, 1761. On the 12th of April, 1744, on the death of Charles Lee, esq. he was also sworn (as again in 1761) to the petty sinecure office of Master of the Revels, a place subsequently swept away by the besom of Mr. Burke; and on the 2d Sept. 1745, he was nominated Gentleman Usher of the Black Rod. In 1745, being then Secretary to Lord Chesterfield in Holland, Mr. Dayrolles was nominated to be Secretary to his Lordship as Lord Lieutenant of Ireland; in May 1747 he was promoted to be his Majesty's Resident in the United Provinces, and in Nov. 1751, Resident at Brussels‡, where he continued until Aug. 1757.

On the 4th of July, 1751, he married Christabella, daughter of Col. Peterson of Ireland, a lady of accomplished manners and dignified appearance, well-known in the fashionable circles of London, and still more admired at the Court of Brussels, at that time the residence of Prince Charles of Lorraine. By this lady, who survived her husband until August 3, 1791, Mr. Dayrolles had three daughters; 1. Christa-

* The warrant for this purpose, signed by George I. and countersigned by J. Addison, is with other documents hereafter mentioned, in the possession of Mr. Upcott.
† Printed in the correspondence published by Dr. Maty.
‡ All the official warrants for these ap...

bella, married in 1784 to the Hon. Townsend Ventry, by whom she had one son, Thomas-Townsend Aremberg, who succeeded his uncle as third Lord Ventry, Oct. 5, 1827, and his Lordship is now the eldest representative of the subject of this memoir; 2. Emily, married Dec. 24, 1786, to the Baron de Reidezel, aid-de-camp to the reigning Duke of Wirtemburg; and, 3. Mary, married Feb. 5, 1788, to Richard Croft, esq. banker, of Pall-Mall. They had also one son,

Thomas Philip Dayrolles, esq. godson of the Duke of Newcastle and the Earl of Chesterfield. He was at one time a Captain in the tenth dragoons, and died at Lausanne during the late war, having married Mademoiselle H. G. Thomaset, daughter of a respectable Swiss gentleman, and sister to an officer in the French service who was killed in Buonaparte's campaign against Russia in 1812. By that lady, who is still living, he had a son.

George Dayrolles, born in October 1795. He was Surintendant des Forêts to the Grand Duke of Hesse Darmstadt ... died at Darmstadt July 10, 18..3. He had married shortly before a lady of the Grand Duchy, but left no issue.

Solomon Dayrolles died in March 1786. He was a man of great benevolence, and exemplary piety; and his manners were those of the most correct cast of the old school, now so entirely forgotten. His uncle's and his own official correspondence from 1700 to 1786, together with the office copies of the replies, and other miscellaneous papers, bound in 21 folio volumes, are in the collection of Mr. Upcott, who proposes to publish a selection of the more important documents, in two volumes, 8vo.

Henley Park, a large good house on the north side of the long hill on the road from Guilford to Farnham, was purchased by Mr. Dayrolles of Sir Richard Child, Earl of Tylney, who held it in right of his wife Dorothy, daughter and heir of Sir John Glynn. He sold it about 1785 to Henry Halsey, esq. whose only son and heir of the same name now resides there.

MR. URBAN, March 10.

WHATEVER remotely or nearly relates to the establishment of American independence, merits its proportionate rank in the archives of impartial general history. The passions of men subside like the winds of heaven, and the turmoils of states are calmed like the billows of the deep; but it is matter of curiosity to note the ravages both of natural and moral storms, and to note the symptoms that characterized their courses. The inclosed TYRTÆAN WAR-SONG is not without its value, considered in this point of light; it had its effect on the soldiery, to whose hearts it was addressed; and perhaps you may agree with me in thinking it not unworthy (for the reasons above stated) of preservation in your respectable pages.

A LOYAL BRITON.

WAR SONG—"WASHINGTON."

SUNG EVERY WEEK, AT LEAST, IN THE AMERICAN CAMP NEAR BOSTON.

COMPOSED IN THE YEAR 1776.

Spoliatis arma supersunt.—JUVENAL.

Tune—The British Grenadiers.

VAIN Britons! boast no longer, with insolence and glee,
By land your conquering legions, your matchless strength by sea;
For, lo! at length Americans their swords have girded on:
Huzza! huzza! huzza! huzza! for war and Washington.

Sent forth by North for vengeance your gallant champions came;
With *tea*, with *treason*, and with *George*, their lips were all on flame:
Yet, sacrilegious though it seem, we rebels still live on,
And laugh to scorn your empty threats, and so does Washington.

Still deaf to mild entreaties, still blind to England's good,
Your knaves for thirty pieces betrayed your country's blood:
Like Æsop's cur you'll only gain a shadow for a bone,
Yet find us fearful shades, indeed, inspir'd by Washington.

Figure 16:
'Memoir of Solomon Dayrolles', in the Gentleman's Magazine 1828.

6. THE HALSEYS; RISE (1784-1850)

Many made their fortunes in India in the 18th century and Henry Halsey, by repute, was one of these, because when he bought Henley Park he was already very rich.

When the East India Company was founded in London in 1599, ten pounds of nutmeg which could be purchased in the remote spice islands for less than a penny, could be sold in London for more than £2 10s - a staggering markup of 60,000 per cent. The chances of success were slim, but a sackful successfully brought back to London could set a man up in luxury for life. By the 1700s the trade had largely switched to the Indian subcontinent itself, and to goods such as silks and saltpetre. Business had become more regularised and the risks had reduced somewhat but the profits were still huge and life in such a remote outpost lacked many of the refinements and conventions of English society.

Little is known about Henry Halsey's early background or how he came to be involved in the East India trade. He was born about 1744 or 1745 as he is recorded as being 62 years old when he died in 1807, and he was in Calcutta by about 1772 when his natural daughter Henrietta was born. More than half the baptisms in Bengal at this time were of 'natural' children of British fathers, so Henry's lifestyle was not unusual. In 1777 Henrietta was baptised in Calcutta and was sent aboard ship to England, where she apparently became part of Henry's family and in due course married at Ash Church. By 1781 he appears to have been a substantial merchant handling large sums of money, living in a 'garden house' in the wealthy Mirzapore district of Calcutta. A contemporary source described the luxurious lifestyle of the East India Company merchants of the time, with every action from being dressed in the morning, carried on his visits in a palanquin to having the tube of the hookah pipe placed in his hand performed by a bevy of salaaming servants, and concluded 'with no greater exertions than these do the Company's servants amass the most splendid fortunes'. Early in 1784 when Henry was preparing to leave Calcutta and return to England he was still being sued for the return of 200,000 rupees which had apparently been advanced to him for the provision of cloth from India to Europe, and he had to leave sufficient security behind which he lost when the decision went against him. Two envelopes from the East Indies in 1797 addressed to him at Henley Park which still survive, probably contained messages relating to these activities.

When he bought Solomon Dayrolle's estates later in 1784 Henry not only acquired Henley Park but also his other properties in Ash, Pirbright and Worplesdon, as well as the manor of Pirbright and an annuity of £25 from the Basingstoke Canal company. This was his first and largest property purchase, but having established his country seat it appears he was looking for ways to invest the rest of his fortune because he continued to buy considerable numbers of properties in Surrey, London and Somerset for the rest of his life.

The prominent city merchant and Member of Parliament Richard Glover strongly promoted the interests of overseas commerce with London as its hub, and this could have first brought him into contact with Henry Halsey. Halsey probably met Solomon Dayrolle through Glover and hence bought Henley Park, and in 1787 he married Glover's daughter Mary, by then a wealthy heiress who was 22 years younger than him, at Saint George Hanover Square in London. They made their home at Henley Park where they quickly assumed the role of country gentry. Although Henry and his family spent time in Bath for 'the season', their main residence was always Henley Park, which he never let to tenants and all their children were baptised at the church in Ash. Their first five children were daughters, born from 1788 to 1795. Then in 1797 they had a son, baptised Henry, but he died within a year. Finally on 23 November 1801 they had another son and possibly sensing that he might be their last child, they bestowed on him the resounding name of Henry William Richard Westgarth Halsey.

The Halsey family's ownership of Henley Park was to span the whole of the 19th century and the first two decades of the 20th century, a period which saw momentous economic, social, technological and political changes. The family's fortunes were eventually to suffer as a consequence of these changes but that was a long way off when Henry began to establish his family as one of the most important local landowners and to enhance his mansion at Henley Park to reflect his growing status in the community.

In the late 1700s several factors including a stiff brick tax to pay for the American war of independence caused brick to fall dramatically out of fashion, to be replaced by stone. Faced with a suddenly undesirable brick building, it may have been soon after he purchased the house that he had the whole exterior covered with stone-coloured wash, traces of which were still visible when the Historic Buildings Consultants produced their report in 1994. In addition Henry made some interior alterations of which the report found traces of a leaf cornice in the north-west room and part of the carriage of the simple timber back stairs. In 1789 it was reported in the press that Henley Park was 'much improving'. EW Brayley in his *History of Surrey* published in 1841 provides us with the earliest surviving description of the house which reads as follows:

> 'The house, which is approached by a double avenue of elms nearly half a mile in length, consists of a centre and two wings which project a short distance from the middle part of the building. The front entrance is by a handsome doorway, on each side of which are three large sash-windows. In the second storey is a range of seven windows. The attic is partly concealed by a parapet, which in the centre rises by curved lines into a gable-end, surmounted by a low pediment under which is a square window. Similar gables surmount the wings and the western wing is fronted by a colonnade. Though of some age, this house has a modern character from some late repairs, and the front has the appearance of stone.'

Brayley went on to describe the gardens and pleasure grounds which were beautifully laid out and remarked that Henley Park, being situated on an eminence, formed an 'oasis in the desert' looking more beautiful than the 'wild and blackened heath' around it.

Further alterations were made to the house but these might have been carried out by Halsey's son Henry William. Some but not all of the windows in the east front of the mansion were replaced with ones of a different design. It is interesting that the symmetry of the façade was not retained and the earlier windows had thicker oak frames with 15 panes whereas the replacement windows had 12 panes with thin mahogany frames (see Plate 101). The house was extended by adding a dining room in the middle of the western façade which led off the entrance hall, and some further rooms for domestic quarters which 'squared off' the mansion in the northwest corner. The inventory made when Baron de Worms leased Henley Park in 1891 provides a comprehensive list of the rooms in the house at that time. There were nine attics and a pump room on the top floor, seven bedrooms and a bathroom and two WCs on the first floor and on the ground floor a billiard room, boudoir, morning room, hall, gun room, drawing room, dining room, lobbies and a 'glazed smoking lounge'. Adjoining the main mansion were twelve servants' rooms, kitchens, larders and a boot room, and downstairs were a cellar, butler's pantry and a wine cellar. Also described in 1891, although they might have been different a hundred years earlier, were the outbuildings: a brew house, a 'wash-up house', a dairy, boiler house, gun room, apple room, game larder, an 'old soup kitchen', a granary on stone piers, stables with loose boxes and stalls and a coach house. In addition there was a farmyard with a range of cow stalls, barn, fowl house, bullock stall and pigsties.

With the estate that Henry acquired there were six tenanted farms; the Home Farm and Henley Park Farm in Ash parish, the ancient Manor Farm in Pirbright with its great field still communally worked in strips on the medieval pattern, Rails Farm in Pirbright, Cowshot Farm overlapping Pirbright, Bisley and Chobham parishes and Whipley Farm in Worplesdon, with a total annual rental value of over £400. If the acreages of these properties were similar to those shown in the tithe maps half a century later, this amounted to about 915 acres (452 in Normandy, 256 in Pirbright, 154 in Worplesdon and 53 in Bisley and Chobham). At this time the area to the north of the Pirbright Road was common land called Henley Heath, a large part of which was a

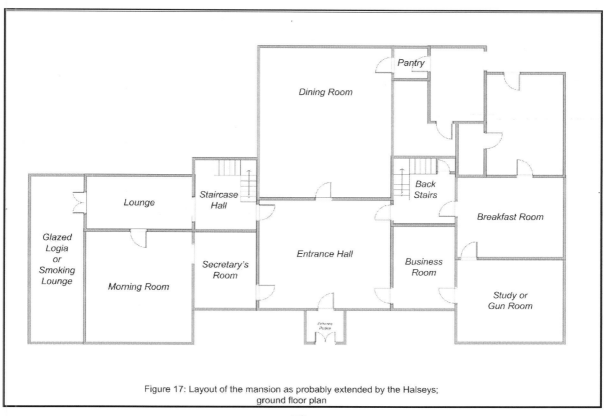

Figure 17: Layout of the mansion as probably extended by the Halseys; ground floor plan

peat moor, which was not yet enclosed according to Rocque's map of 1768.

Almost immediately Henry embarked upon an ambitious programme of expansion. Some of his earliest purchases were in Ash and Worplesdon close to Henley Park. These were 'Bakers Cottage' and a barn and 1 acre on Normandy Green, copyhold of the manor of Cleygate, which he purchased from John Taylor in 1786; Longerend Farm, about 60 acres freehold (with a tanyard) and Bailes Farm, about 76 acres freehold, from Thomas Cadell in 1788 for £2,800; a house and lands (now Longerend Cottage), copyhold of Cleygate Manor, and Marley Ground, 13 acres freehold in Normandy, from Henry Martin in 1791. Other than these he and his successors made no more substantial purchases in the parish of Ash for over 100 years. The reason may be that to the south there were already influential local landowners who owned the main farms - the Woodroffes of Poyle who were also lords of the manor of Cleygate, the Coussmakers of Westwood, the Onslows and Mangles of Wanborough and the Chitty family who owned several farms in Worplesdon.

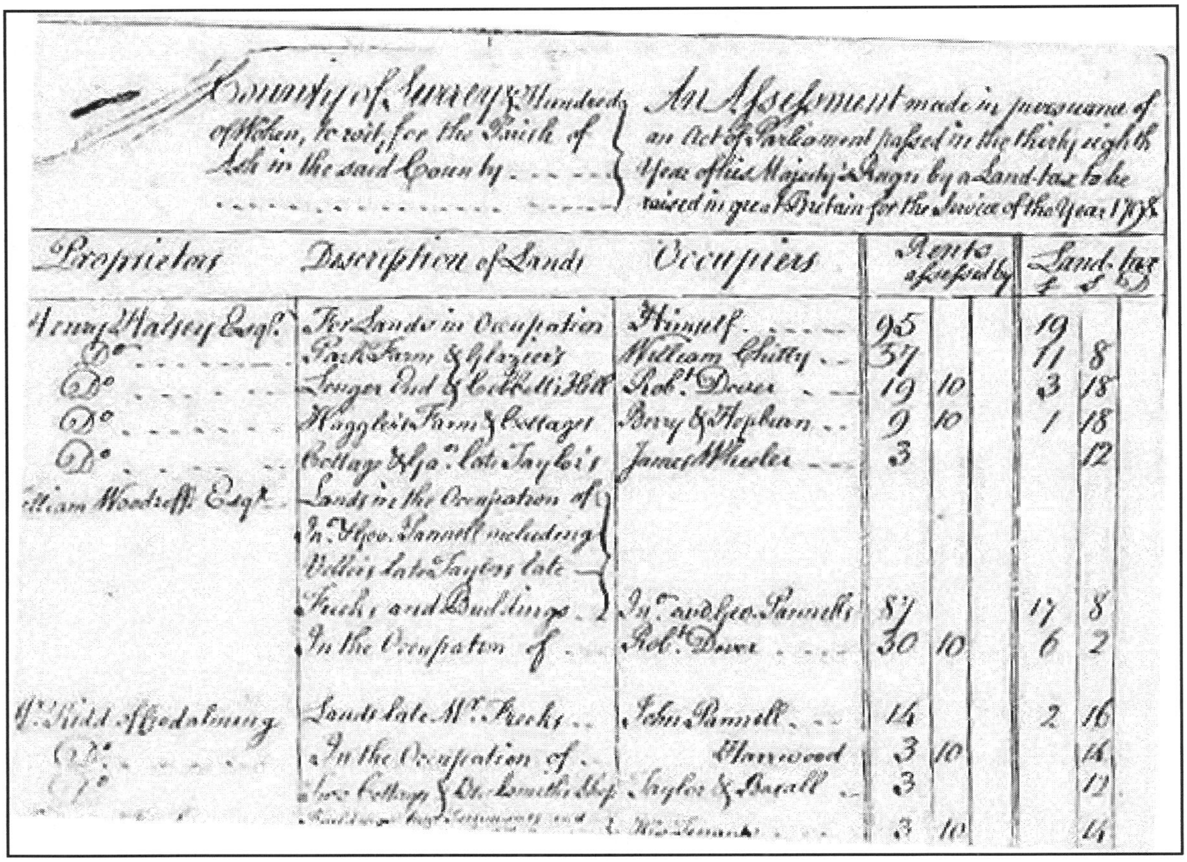

Figure 18: Page from the Ash land tax 1798
showing Henry Halsey's properties in Normandy.
Copyright of Surrey History Centre.

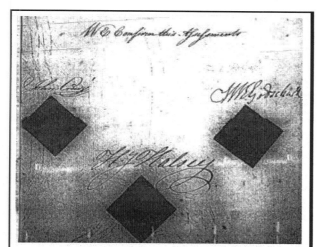

Figure 19: Henry Halsey's signature on the 1798 Pirbright land tax. Copyright of Surrey History Centre.

In the other direction at Pirbright there was by contrast a 'vacuum' with no large estates, and as lord of the manor Henry Halsey stepped into the role of major landowner. He started in 1789 when he made two purchases: Fell Moor, 40 acres copyhold, from George Linnard and Jordans, a house and 17 acres of land, from John Woods. Then in 1793 he purchased Hovers & Lushers, a tenement and 45 acres, from William Faggeter. In 1801 he purchased the properties in Pirbright owned by George Tate Esq and Robert Shuttleworth Esq. These included Wickham Farm, 23 acres, Burrow Hill Farm, 45 acres, and the glebe lands 12 acres, which were all incorporated into Wickham Farm, and Mount Byron, now The Lodge, with 6 acres, The Duchies, a house, barn and 11 acres and Castle House, 6 acres, which became part of Rails Farm. The glebe lands brought him the tithes of Pirbright parish, worth £66 10s a year. In 1803 he purchased Whites Farm, 40 acres, from Mary Stovold late Martin, and in 1805 a house and 8 acres of land from George Terry.

Further afield, he purchased, probably at auction, the manor and rectorial tithes of Farnham in 1789 and in 1805 he leased the Parsonage House of Farnham and Parsonage Mead, 3 acres, from the Archdeacon of Surrey. At about this time he purchased a piece of ground on East Street, Farnham as well, and erected 5 new hop kilns there.

His purchases outside Surrey seem quite random and it is hard to discern a pattern. In the 1790s he bought several properties amounting to over 900 acres in the Yeovil area of Somerset and the family retained these for over a hundred years. The three properties he bought in London are clustered in a fairly small area although they were in two different parishes and again Richard Glover could be the connection because this area was known for its theatrical associations and Glover, a friend of David Garrick, was also a playwright whose works were staged at nearby Drury Lane and Covent Garden theatres. In July 1787 Halsey purchased five plots in Newcastle Court for £1,575 which were probably part of a property development scheme by a group of noblemen including the Duke of Newcastle who apparently gave his name to the Court and nearby Newcastle Street at the bottom of Stanhope Street. Other parties to the sale were the Earl of Hertford a Knight of the Garter like the Duke of Newcastle, the Countess of Lincoln and Sir Henry Clinton a Knight of the Bath. On the same date and from the same vendors he bought a house on the west side of Stanhope Street for £475, which was probably part of the same property development. Unlike the Newcastle Court plots which soon became an area of slum tenements, the Stanhope Street house was respectable and well-built and was already let to Francis Bedwell as tenant. He then bought the Blue Boar Inn in High Holborn in January 1791 from the Tufnell family, father son and nephew, for £3,450. It was a long-established coaching inn with 40 bedrooms and stabling for 52 horses, as well as three dwelling houses on the north side of High Holborn 'abutting on the gateway' of the inn. The inn and one of the dwelling houses were let to Christopher Ibberson who presumably had to do the actual day-to-day work of running the Inn. The Tufnells also assigned to Halsey a piece of ground demised in trust for the relief of poor people of St Clement Danes. It was demised in June 1746 for 61 years, so this term ran out just days before Henry Halsey died, and this piece of ground is not mentioned again. Two of the London properties, the Blue Boar Inn and the tenements in Newcastle Court, were clearly investments and there is no record of him ever occupying the house in Stanhope Street, although he may have intended it to be his London home.

Back in Surrey, in 1798 he purchased some properties in Woking from the executors of the late Reverend Edward Emely, including Parsonage Farm and its strips in the common field, a total of 31 acres, and also Runtley Wood Farm, about 75 acres. About 1801 he purchased more land in Woking which was probably added to these farms and then in 1806 even more land, which was added to Runtley Wood Farm.

By the time of his death in 1807 Henry Halsey had purchased more than 560 acres in Surrey, completing a transaction every two years on average in his desire to establish himself as a major presence in the community. The estates now comprised about 1,480 acres (543 in Normandy, 525 in Pirbright, 38 in Bisley, 15 in Chobham, 250 in Worplesdon and 109 in Woking). His estates in Pirbright were so extensive that he commissioned a survey to record them, but although the surveyor William Newland produced a wonderfully detailed and decorative map of the parish (see Plate 16), Henry did not live to see it.

Henry probably also enjoyed the status and power that were part of manorial lordships, because he bought several of them even though it is unlikely that these were a very significant source of income by the late 18th century. He became the lord of the manor of Pirbright when he purchased Solomon Dayrolle's estates and titles and he may have been led to believe he was lord of the manor of Henley by the archaic wording of the deeds although it had been replaced by Cleygate centuries earlier. The manor of Pirbright was still very active and the manorial courts held every few years dealt with issues of property ownership and collected rents and heriots on behalf of the lord. Henry subsequently purchased the lordship of the manor of the Rectory of Woking from the Reverend Emely and the manor of Farnham with its tithes and courts from the Archdeacon of Surrey. Outside Surrey he owned the rectory and manor of Saint Peter the Great in the Cathedral Church of the Holy Trinity Chichester and two manors in Somersetshire. Even though the ancient manorial system was coming to an end when his son Henry William died in 1885, the value of the lordships was assessed for property tax then and found to be: Pirbright £57, Rectory of Woking £3 11s 2d and Henley - nil. His estate in turn was still liable for nearly £20 of heriots, payable to the lords of the manors of Cleygate, Worplesdon, Woking and Bisley for property he owned there.

The Halseys were Patrons and Lay Impropriators of Pirbright. The Patron holds the Advowson which is the right to nominate the curate or vicar of the parish, and Henry purchased the Advowson from William Moore of Heston Middlesex in 1804. The Lay Impropriator is the person entitled to receive the tithes of the parish out of which they pay the vicar's salary; it is not clear whether he acquired this with the Advowson or with the lordship of the manor or separately.

Like Solomon Dayrolle before him, Henry was aware of the value of the peat on Pirbright moor, and Henry had strong views about how to maximise its use. Unlike normal practice, which was to throw the surface of the trench into the bottom of the previous one, he preferred to burn the top surface, getting 'excellent ashes' which he sold for 12s a load of 60 bushels, the labour cost being a mere three or four shillings. He also believed that the growth of the peat was encouraged if the moor was flooded in the winter and left dry in summer. Surprisingly, unlike Solomon, there is no evidence that Henry alienated his tenants by taking the peat.

Henry Halsey was clearly a very ambitious and determined man and by 1794 his high-handed attitude to manorial procedure was drawing censure from the authorities in the adjacent manor of Cleygate. In the court of that year it was noted that he had encroached on the common land of the manor in several places; enclosing a pond and piece of ground into his farmyard at Longerend Hill, putting up an old turf house on another piece of common nearby, enclosing land into the yard of the house he bought from Henry Martin and putting another turf house on it, encroaching at Henley Park Gate (by what is now Pirbright Road) by building a 'necessary house' on the wasteland there and finally enclosing a large piece of land at Standing Hill north of the Pirbright Road and making a plantation of trees. It had been found that the Scots Pine would flourish on the poor soils of the Surrey heaths and in the 18th and 19th centuries many commercial plantations were established, so Henry Halsey was clearly quick to grasp this new opportunity. In 1797 the court grumbled that he had further encroached on the common at his lodge at Cobbett Hill Lane, added 4 or 5 rods of land at the farmhouse formerly occupied by John Chitty and enclosed another small piece into the hop garden occupied by James Berry, which was probably somewhere near Longerend Cottage. The court ordered that all these encroachments must be thrown open within one month, but a year later nothing had changed and the order was repeated. Henry continued to ignore the orders of his neighbour's manorial court because in 1802 and 1803 his encroachments remained in place and he enclosed a further piece of ground at Cobbett Hill, adjacent to 'his old Furze Field'. After that the court records are quiet on the subject. Possibly he was more sympathetic towards the manorial procedure at Pirbright for which he was the lord of the manor.

The story of 'Halsey's highway' or the Squire's new road as recounted by RJ Palmer in his *Pirbright Papers*, illustrates the lengths Henry was prepared to go to in order to get his own way. To further enhance his country seat, he decided to enlarge the lake which he had acquired with the land he had enclosed north of the Pirbright Road. Unfortunately this brought him into conflict with the authorities who in 1801 made a presentment to the Justices at the quarter sessions claiming that his enlarged lake had 'drowned' the old road to Frimley. Henry made a representation to the effect that he had not obstructed an ancient route but nevertheless, in order to dispose of the opposition to his plans, he agreed to build a new road across the common which would be a more direct route than the old one. Whether this meant that he intended to build a new road from Cobbett Hill Lane or just a diversion at the north end of the lake is not clear. Work was started on the new route but in autumn 1803 another presentment was made to the quarter sessions claiming that the part of the 'ancient' road which had been diverted was still not capable of taking traffic. This presented the Justices with a problem as they were unwilling to prosecute a fellow landowner and one of their peers. They commissioned an enquiry, applied for the case to be tried in another county and threatened Henry with indictment, but it was another three years before the matter was finally settled and the new section of the road completed to everyone's satisfaction.

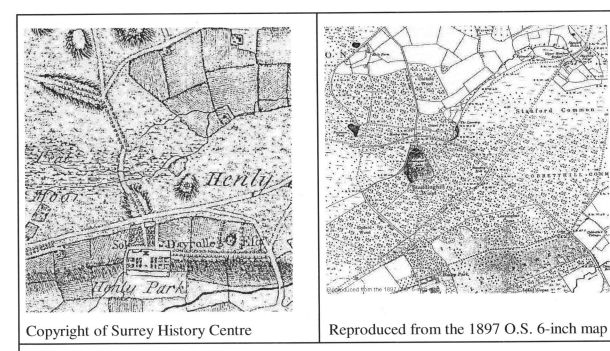

Reproduced from the 1897 O.S. 6-inch map

Figure 20: 'The Squire's new road'.
Plans of the route of the Guildford to Frimley road,
as it existed in the 18th century and
as diverted in the 19th century to avoid the enlarged Henley Park lake.

Whatever Henry's intentions, the whole episode shows his determination and he did not lose out, because not only did he enlarge his lake but he was allowed to formalise his ownership of the common land he had enclosed.

Henry Halsey's will which runs to 13 pages and was drawn up in 1807 two months before his death, provides further insights into his character. Since his only son Henry William was a minor, he not only laid down very detailed and precise instructions as to how his estates should be managed during his son's minority but he also set out to extend his authority over future generations of his family, which was to have profound consequences for the fate of Henley Park.

He began by instructing the sale of specific assets. These included his estates and manors in Farnham and Chichester with their respective glebe lands and tithes. Perhaps he considered that these were now rather peripheral to the estates he had built up in Ash, Pirbright and neighbouring parishes although he still retained the assets in Somerset. More significantly he directed that his properties in London should be sold as well, probably an acknowledgement that, as he could now be considered a member of the landowning classes and his son was being brought up as a gentleman of independent means, there would no longer be any need to keep them and the money they would fetch could be put to better use. All three properties were sold by the trustees in the last few days of December 1807, less than five months after the will was proved and less than 20 years after they were purchased. Interestingly, the tenements in Newcastle Court were sold to Christopher Ibberson, a stable keeper of High Holborn, who appears to have been the tenant of the Blue Boar Inn when Halsey bought it. All four tenements, numbered 2, 3, 4 and 5, were let to Alexander Brodie by the Halsey trustees in July 1807, just a couple of weeks after Henry

Halsey's death, possibly regularising an existing verbal arrangement. The house in Stanhope Street was sold to Richard Pack of Thames Street London, an oil merchant and the Blue Boar Inn and adjacent houses were sold to Thomas Dodd of Sloan Square, Knightsbridge. As an astute business man Halsey must have had a very shrewd idea as to how much these sales would realise but the sale prices are not mentioned in the deeds. Elsewhere in his will and despite the entail he set up, he made allowances for further sales or mortgages of property (with the exception of Henley Park itself) should it become necessary to raise funds to meet any future financial obligations as they arose, but it appears that very few further sales took place for some time.

He appointed his wife Mary and his friends Westgarth Snaith of London, Caleb Woodyer of Guildford and John Antrobus of Cheam as executors of his will and guardians of his children, and as trustees to hold the estates during his son's minority, and thereafter they and their successors to be trustees for the entail of 200 years which he set up for Henley Park and all his other real estate in Ash, Pirbright, Woking and Somerset. The entail directed that all his estates, except where they were already subject to certain conditions, should always pass in trust to his male heirs successively, i.e. to every elder son, and if the male line should die out, then to his or their female heirs, also in a strict order which he laid down, but only to them as tenants in common, that is to share between them equally the rents and incomes of the estates during their lives. 'Estates tail' were still the favoured means of family settlements at this time and in this respect there was nothing unusual in the entail that Henry set up. Indeed Henley Park and its estates had been entailed before in the time of the Tylneys and Dayrolles and even for 'a thousand years' by Henry's marriage settlement in 1797, but the very detailed terms of his will give it the appearance of being not only that of a very able man but an extraordinarily autocratic and dictatorial one, and this is heightened by the repetitious, obfuscating, tortuous and labyrinthine legal style in which it is written. He clearly believed that he knew what was best for his descendants and by endeavouring to leave nothing to chance he was attempting to ensure the continued existence of his family as a landowning dynasty and to prevent the estates he had built up from, in the words of his will, 'being defeated and destroyed'. The entail he set up was to prevail for 80 years but even he, with his thoroughness and regard for every eventuality, could not envisage agricultural depression and the effects that declining rents would have on the landowning classes and the fortunes of his family.

He directed that if any of his daughters should marry before the age of 26 without the consent of her guardians (the trustees) she would lose all rights to her inheritance, and any other provision made for her under his will would cease as if she 'were actually dead', and this stern clause was applied to daughters of future generations as well.

His wife Mary was given the choice of Henley Park mansion, Pirbright Lodge or the house he had recently acquired in The Circus at Bath to have as her home, but not the house in Stanhope Street, London. During her lifetime the house she chose was not subject to the terms of the entail but was to revert to the main estate and be incorporated into the entail on her death. The will also dealt with other provisions for his wife and for their children including arrangements for setting up and paying Mary the annuity due to her under her marriage settlement, and the amount to be paid to her as a guardian of their son while a minor for his maintenance and education (although, should she remarry, she was to cease to be a trustee and guardian). He specified the exact sum of money to be invested for the benefit of his daughters, the annual proceeds of which were to be spent on their maintenance and education and the capital to provide a lump sum for each of them to be paid when they reached the age of 26 or the day of their marriage. He not only gave instructions as to what should be done if the investment did not yield sufficient income but even what should be done if none of his daughters survived to inherit. When he came to the amount that sons could charge on the estate for marriage settlements, he sought not only to limit the amount his own son could grant to his wife when he married, and grant to his children as their 'portions', but he also placed the same limitations on any future son who held the estate in trust. Under no circumstances was a charge permitted on the mansion of Henley Park. Another example of his attempts to exert his authority over any future descendant was in the provision for letting any part of the estate, which he decreed could not exceed a term of seven years and should be for 'the best rent that could reasonably be obtained'.

Should any of the trustees be in any doubt as to the powers they held during his son's minority, those were specified in detail. A proportion of the income from the estate was to be put towards the upkeep and repair of the mansion and other houses, buildings, gardens and plantations. They were empowered to cut down trees for repairs but with due regard being taken 'not to cut down or spoil ornamental trees and plantations' and any timber not needed for repairs should be sold and the money to be added to the residue of the estate. They were directed to finance and finish the work he had started on the house in The Circus at Bath, to his plan and within the budget he stipulated. In addition they were to erect a chancel to the church at Pirbright (see Plate 18) and a family mausoleum or burying place within it 'according to such plan as I shall have adopted in my lifetime', or in the case of his not having adopted any such plan, then according to such plan as the trustees should approve so that the total expense did not exceed £1,500. Any surplus rents or other monies if not added to the residue of the estate and held in trust for the use and benefit of his son, were to be invested in the purchase of more lands and tenements and made subject to the same provisoes as the rest of his estate.

Various other clauses were taken up with personal bequests to his wife and a sum of money to be distributed amongst the poor families in the neighbourhood of Henley Park and to such of his labourers as his wife should in her discretion direct. Rather surprisingly because he was so precise where other sums of money were concerned, he left it to her discretion as to the actual amounts which should be distributed and to whom. Another clause dealt with the arrangements for his funeral which, with the same meticulous care and regard to cost of his other plans and actions, he decreed should be 'as plain as my rank in life and decency will permit, and without pomp and unnecessary expense'. He should be carried to his grave by his tenants at Pirbright and such of his friends as his executors should select.

He made provisions for the payment of other expenses including those of his trustees and laid down the precise procedure to be taken to replace them on death or retirement. Many who were to succeed the original trustees were also friends and professionals and several were members of the family. In 1810, two years after Henry's death Caleb Woodyer, a trustee, married Henry's daughter Mary Anne Eleanor whose birth he is said to have attended in his capacity as the family doctor 22 years previously. The Reverend Lawrence Eliot was another future son-in-law to act as a trustee. Later his son Henry William's brother-in-law Alfred Whitmore became a trustee as did Henry William's father-in-law Edward Whitmore, while in the next generation his grandson Edward Joseph Halsey and his grandson-in-law Samuel Bircham a solicitor, were also appointed trustees (see Figures 22 and 23).

Although Henley Park was the family's main home during Henry's lifetime, they also spent time at their houses in Bath. Bath was a pleasant resort and spa where fashionable society gathered for the 'season' in the winter months and the Halseys spent time there from at least 1797 when they were at number 8 Queen Square while Mrs Halsey was recovering from an illness. It appears that they originally took short lets for the season as their name does not appear in the rate books, but by 1806 Henry had acquired number 13 (subsequently renumbered 11) The Circus, one of the largest houses in what is considered to be a great architectural masterpiece. Henry set about some major improvements which may have included erecting a cottage and coach house to the rear of the premises but as his will shows these were not completed at the time of his death. He made his will at Bath in April and died at his house at The Circus on 19 June 1807, and was buried in the family mortuary chapel in Pirbright Church which was built between 1807-12 in accordance with his will.

It is not known for sure which house his widow Mary chose for her home but as she died before their son Henry William attained his majority, it is unlikely that she maintained a household separate from that of her son. The ratebooks show Halseys as ratepayers at The Circus until 1809, then the property was let until Halseys appear again in 1813-14. After that the property was apparently let although they retained ownership until they sold it in 1886. Mary was residing in Bath in 1816 and Guildford in 1818 but when she died in July 1819 at the age of 52, she was described in the burial register of Pirbright as being 'of Brighton'. She clearly felt that her husband's will had leaned too heavily towards their son, and in her own will she redressed the balance by leaving the great majority of the £15,000 under her control to her daughters. Her remains were placed in the family mausoleum with those of her husband and their first son who had died in infancy, and with those of their daughter Elizabeth Caroline Nangle and her infant son, both of whom had died in 1817, and of another grandson, the son of their daughter Mathilda Elizabeth Eliot, who had died in 1818 at the age of four (see figure 22).

Andrew and Anna Stirling probably became the tenants of Henley Park in 1815. The Stirlings came from Glasgow and had a bleaching and calico business based in Scotland and London. In 1822 when Henry Halsey's son Henry William took up residence after probably being away on the Grand Tour they moved to Pirbright Lodge. On 2 November 1822 Henry William married their daughter Mary Noel Stirling at Pirbright. The two families were very close and when Andrew and Anna Stirling died in 1823 and 1830 respectively, they were laid to rest in the Halsey mausoleum. It would appear that their son James, later Admiral Sir James Stirling, continued to live at Henley Park and used it as his base when he was not away at sea. In March 1827 he explored the Swan River in south western Australia and named an area on the upper reaches of the river 'Henley Park' (see Plate 20). A nearby stream is still called Henley Brook. He proposed the idea of a new colony and in 1829 he sailed on the ship 'Parmelia' as the first Lieutenant Governor of the colony of Swan River, Western Australia, accompanied by his wife Ellen a daughter of the Mangles family of Woodbridge, Guildford, and their small son Andrew. Also on board were George Eliot who was Henry William Halsey's nephew, George Mangles and a Mr P Brown and his family, described as 'Colonial Secretary'. The ship was a ready-made floating colony, with a surveyor, storekeeper, horticulturalist, surgeon, cooper, bricklayer and boatbuilder on board. They carried a pre-fabricated wooden house with them and erected it 20 miles up Swan River at a place they named 'Woodbridge' after the Mangles' mansion in Stoke next Guildford.

Henry William and Mary Noel Halsey had two sons and five daughters but Mary died in 1834 aged only 36 years, and in 1835 Henry William married Caroline Whitmore at Epsom in Surrey. Henry and Caroline had two sons and two daughters and their youngest daughter Caroline Elizabeth born in March 1842 was probably the last baby to be born at Henley Park mansion until modern times.

Henry William was still a minor when the expansion of the estates started up again in pursuance of the terms of his father's will. About 1815 his trustees purchased West Hall Farm, 73 acres in Pirbright, from Richard Vincent. Then about 1820 they bought several small properties in Pirbright: a house and four acres of land from George Watts, which was subsequently added to Stanford Farm; and about 1821 Henley Park Laundry and Smallborne Cottage with 3 acres, from James Davey. Once he had come of age, Henry William Halsey continued adding to the estates. In 1823 he purchased part of Mansland, a copyhold house, orchard and garden with 4 acres in the common field of Pirbright, from the heirs of William Russell Sherett for £200. In 1825 he purchased Stanford Farm, 13 acres in Pirbright, from John Linnard for £650.

In 1825 he made the Halseys' main purchase in Worplesdon, acquiring Littlefield Farm and Pusseys Farm, 208 acres, as well as Barlands, a 12-acre meadow in Normandy, from the Right Honourable Fletcher Lord Grantley. Then in 1826 he purchased Rickford Malt House with 28 acres of land spread across the parishes of Woking, Worplesdon and Pirbright and also the tithes of 'Crastock' or Bridley, worth £23 a year, all from William Evershed. In 1840 he bought a house and garden of half an acre in Old Woking Street.

Returning to Pirbright, in 1828 he purchased one part of Goldmoor Farm, 10 acres, from John Wakeford for £500 and in 1833 he purchased the other part, 12 acres, from the executors of Henry Pope Nye for £450. In 1839 he purchased Waldens Field, 3 acres, from James Honer's trustees for £100. At some time he also purchased West Heath Cottage, apparently from Stephen Saunders, and a tenement called Little Cut.

By the time of the tithing surveys in the 1840s, Henry William and his trustees had purchased over 500 acres and the total size of the Halsey estates in Surrey had now more than doubled to an impressive 2,027 acres, with an annual rental income of £1,225 10s. The most dramatic increase in land was in Pirbright parish where they now had almost 800 acres (more than half of the cultivated land in the parish), while they had 555 acres in Normandy, 462 in Worplesdon, 160 in Woking and still 53 in Bisley & Chobham.

Henry William apparently joined in the sporting activities of the day, and when he was a young man he kept a pack of harriers for hare-hunting. Stream House was two cottages at the time and one part housed the kennels while the other was occupied by the Henley Park laundry staff (presumably making use of the stream rather than the limited water supply from Henley Park's well).

Like his father, Henry William was active in the affairs of Pirbright and was a great benefactor of the parish church. In 1822, when he married Mary Stirling there, he presented a new peal of five bells to the church and the old peal was removed to Henley Park and installed in the stable turret where it is said they chimed regularly "with a pleasant gentle chime" up to the 1960s. The Halseys' first major works at Pirbright were the addition of the mortuary chapel on the north side of the chancel and a matching vestry room on the other side, built as directed in Henry's will. In niches in each of these was an inscribed marble tablet in the form of a sarcophagus, with inscriptions commemorating Henry and his will. Henry William funded some further extensive changes in 1848 when the chancel was remodelled from Classical to Gothic style, possibly executed by his nephew Henry Woodyer the architect. All this time as owners of Henley Park the Halseys were entitled to the use of the two front-row pews on one side in the parish church at Ash, but it seems likely that they actually worshipped at Pirbright so the pews may have remained empty.

Henry William added an annexe to the Stock House (subsequently the Old School House) in Pirbright to house the Free School, and then donated land in 1870 to build a new school when the Education Act came into force. Although most of his attention was directed to Pirbright, he was one of the principal subscribers, together with Lannoy Arthur Coussmaker of Westwood, who contributed to the cost of building the new church of St Mark at Wyke in 1847, the architect of which was again his nephew Henry Woodyer of Guildford.

Henry William Halsey also had strong links with the County - he was a JP and Deputy Lieutenant for Surrey. He might have thought that Henley Park was the centre of a settled and unchanging way of life that would continue to pass through the generations according to his father's wishes, but there were problems ahead. Both the actions of his family and unforeseeable shifts in the economic situation were to have significant consequences for Henley Park.

Figure 21: The Halseys' Surrey Properties 1784-1926.

In the parish of Ash		
Property	Date Purchased	Date Sold
Henley Park, mansion and grounds and 'the manor of Henley'	1784 from Solomon Dayrolle	1925 to E Ramsay Moodie *[but the manor was not specified]*
Henley Park Farm, 120 acres	1784 from Solomon Dayrolle	1925 to E Ramsay Moodie
'Bakers' Cottage, with a barn and 1 acre on Normandy Green	1786 from John Taylor. Added to Longerend Farm	*See Longerend Farm*
Barlands, 12 acres of meadow	1825 from Lord Grantley	Between 1844-95, owned by Mr Deedman in 1895
Longerend Cottage	1791 from Henry Martin. Added to Longerend Farm	*See Longerend Farm*
Longerend Farm, c 60 acres	1788 from Thomas Cadell for £2,800 (with Bailes Farm)	1922 auction to Mr EH North for £2,000
Marley Ground, 13 acres	1791 from Henry Martin. Part added to Longerend Farm	Part *see Longerend Farm*, Other part 1922 auction to Mr Ramez for £330
Marlins, 13-acre smallholding with cottage [now Halsey Cottage]	1784 from Solomon Dayrolle. Land added to Longerend Farm	Land *see Longerend Farm*, Cottage 1922 auction to Mr EH North for £340
Purse's Copse, 11 acres [later Glaziers otherwise Barretts then Pussey's Copse]	1784 from Solomon Dayrolle	1922 auction to Mr Ramez for £440
A piece of land at Standing Hill, made into a plantation	1794 enclosed from the waste of Cleygate Manor	1925 to E Ramsay Moodie
Woodland, 34 acres between Henley Park and Pirbright Road and more on the north side of the road including the lake	1887 from the War Department	1925 to E Ramsay Moodie
A smallholding, 3 acres [now Normandy Hill Farm and Quinta Cottage]	1895 Normandy Manor Estate sale	1922 auction to Humphrey Quin for £500
Four fields, 24 acres between Longerend & Henley Park Farms	1895 Normandy Manor Estate sale. Added to Henley Park Farm	*See Henley Park Farm*

Figure 21: The Halseys' Surrey Properties Continued.

In the parish of Pirbright (1)		
Property	Date Purchased	Date Sold
Binners Meadow, 4 acres	1874 from Morris Ashby	Apparently by 1922
Burrow Hill Farm, 45 acres	1801 from George Tate. Added to Wickham Farm	*See Wickham Farm*
Castle House, 6 acres	1801 from Robert Shuttleworth. Added to Rails Farm	*See Rails Farm*
Court Farm, c 120 acres, also known as Manor Farm, including the Manor House and Manor Mill; and the manor of Pirbright	1784 from Solomon Dayrolle	Manor Mill 1919 auction to LJ Harding for £1,200. Manor Farm 1922 auction to Mr Ramez for £2,500. Manor House 1896 to the Armstrongs, ground rents 1922 auction to Mr Ramez for £660.
Cove Cottage	Apparently between 1841-81	1919 auction to Miss AM Goddard for £520
Cowshot Farm, 103 acres, including some land in the parishes of Bisley and Chobham	1784 from Solomon Dayrolle	1889 to the National Rifle Association for firing ranges
The Duchies, house [later two cottages], barn and 11 acres	1801 from Robert Shuttleworth. Land added to Stanford Farm	Land *see Stanford Farm*, Cottages did not reach their reserve of £450 in 1922 auction
Fell Moor, 40 acres copyhold	1789 from George Linnard. Added to Rails Farm	*See Rails Farm*
Goldmoor Farm and Appletree Cottage (part of), 10 acres	1828 from John Wakeford for £500 Probably added to West Hall Farm	*See West Hall Farm*
Goldmoor Farm (the other part), 12 acres	1833 from the executors of Henry Pope Nye for £450. Probably added to West Hall Farm	*See West Hall Farm*
Grove Farm, 20 acres	1900 from the trustees of Samuel Greenfield for £1,000	1919 auction to Henry Layton for £850
Henley Park Laundry, 3 acres [adjacent to Smallborne Cottage]	1821/22 from James Davey	1922 auction to Mr Charnock for £710
Hodds Field, 9 acres	Between 1841-77. Added to Goldmoor Farm	*See Goldmoor Farm*

Hovers and Lushers, tenement & 45 acres	1793 from William Faggetter. Part added to Court Farm	Part *see Court Farm*, Other part probably sold 1919 to Messrs Skelton & Kirby for £1,000
The Humble, messuage and lands at Hog Sty Lane	By 1807	Probably sold at auction in 1919
Jordans, messuage and 17 acres	1789 from John Woods	Apparently between 1841-1922
Little Cut, 'the poors tenements', 1 acre	Between 1807-41 from the parish of Pirbright	Apparently before 1922
Manor Farm, Manor House and Manor Mill - *see* Court Farm		
Mansland (part of); copyhold messuage, orchard & garden, and 4 acres in Pirbright common field	1823 from the heirs of William Russell Sherett for £200. Mansland added to The Lodge, Land in common field added to Court Farm	*See Mount Byron/The Lodge and Court Farm*
Mount Byron, subsequently The Lodge, 6 acres	1801 from Robert Shuttleworth	1919 by private treaty to Mr Q de Quincy for £3,500
New Mead (location unidentified)	1856 from Henry Faggotter's trustees for £240	Not known
Newmans, once a beerhouse called The Swallow, 3 acres	1874 from Morris Ashby for £630	Apparently by 1922
The Nursery, 9 acres	1907 from Lady Pirbright	1919 auction
The Old School House, formerly The Stock House, now The Old House	By 1807	Conveyed to Edwina Countess de Kerdrell in trust in 1934 then freehold in 1954
Rails Farm, c 86 acres	1784 from Solomon Dayrolle	Apparently between 1922-45, possibly to Major Armstrong-Jones
Rails Meadow, 6 acres copyhold	Between 1807-41. Added to Stanford Farm	*See Stanford Farm*
Rapley's Fields, 8 acres	Between 1841-1922. Added to Court Farm	*See Court Farm*
Smallborne Cottage	1821/22 from James Davey	1922 auction to Humphrey Quin for £200

House [now Stanford Cottage] and 4 acres	1819/20 from George Watts. Land added to Stanford Farm	Land *see Stanford Farm*, Stanford Cottage 1922 auction to Mr Avenell for £210
Stanford Farm (part of?), 13 acres	1825 from John Linnard for £650	1922 auction to Mr HB Baverstock for £1,200
Stanford Farm, another part of	1909 from John Cherryman. Combined with rest of Stanford Farm	*See Stanford Farm*
Stream House Farm, 5 acres	1909 from Lady Pirbright for £460	1922 auction to Mr EB Faggetter for £670
Terry's Cottage or Box Cottage (now The Old School House) and 8 acres	1805 from George Terry	Terry's Cottage 1919 auction to Henry Faggotter for £300, the land sold between 1841-1922
Throat Moor Meadow, 2 acres	1874 from Morris Ashby. Added to Court Farm	*See Court Farm*
Inner & Outer Throat Moor, 5 acres	1907 from Lady Pirbright for £145. Added to Stanford Farm	*See Stanford Farm*
Till Moor (part of), 10 acres	Between 1841-1922. Added to Stanford Farm	*See Stanford Farm*
Waldens Field, 3 acres	1839 from James Honer's trustees for £100. Added to Stanford Farm	*See Stanford Farm*
West Hall Farm, 73 acres	1815/16 from Richard Vincent	1919 auction to Albert Thompson for £1,900
West Heath Cottage	Between 1807-41, apparently from Stephen Saunders	Apparently between 1910-19
West Heath - 5 other cottages	Built around 1880	1919 auction to Percival Kirby, James Keen and ED Faggotter, for £1,630 in total
Whites Farm, 40 acres	1803 from Mary Stovold late Martin	1919 auction to John Cherryman for £2,200
Wickham Farm, 23 acres	1801 from George Tate	1919 auction to William Thompson for £1,600

The glebe lands, 12 acres	1801 from George Tate. Added to Wickham Farm	*See Wickham Farm*
Unidentified land	1804/05 possibly from Widow Chitty	*Not known*
Unidentified land	1815/16 from Webb	*Not known*
Two pieces of land (unidentified)	*Not known*	1869/70 to the London & South Western Railway Company
Four strips in Pirbright common field, 6 acres	1870 at the Fords Farm Estate sale. Added to Court Farm	*See Court Farm*
The 'wastes' of Pirbright Manor, 3,072 acres	1784 from Solomon Dayrolle, with the manor of Pirbright	1877 to the War Department

In the parish of Worplesdon		
Property	Date Purchased	Date Sold
Bailes Farm, 76 acres	1788 from Thomas Cadell for £2,800 (with Longerend Farm)	1922 auction to Mr EM Tenant for £2,800
Dairymead, 2 acres	1784 from Solomon Dayrolle. Added to Henley Park Farm	*See Henley Park Farm, Ash Parish*
Littlefield Farm and Pusseys Farm, 208 acres	1825 from Lord Grantley	Apparently between 1838 and 1882 to Charles Peto Shrubb
Whipley Farm, 152 acres	1784 from Solomon Dayrolle	1925 to E Ramsay Moodie

Figure 21: The Halseys' Surrey Properties Continued.

In the parish of Woking		
Property	Date Purchased	Date Sold
Cowshot, 18 acres on Hook Heath	Between 1849-53	1853 to Mrs Smith
House and garden, ½ acre in Old Woking Street	1840	1906 to Miss Mary Ross for £600
Ostend, a house adjacent to land near Rickford Malt House	Possibly c. 1827	1853 to James Honer Snr
Parsonage Farm, 31 acres including strips of land in the common field. Also the manor of the Rectory of Woking, and the tithe	1797 or 1798 from Rev Mr Emely	1886, 37 acres in Old Woking to Edward Ryde for £3,225 *The manor was apparently never sold*
Rickford Malt House and 21 acres of land in Woking, with 4 acres of meadow in Worplesdon and 3 acres in Pirbright	1826 from William Evershed	1853
Land near Rickford Malt House, 18 acres	Possibly c. 1827	1853 to Robertson
Runtley Wood Farm, c. 75 acres	1797 or 1798 from Rev Mr Emely	Between 1885-91
A piece of land (near Runtley Wood Farm)	1806. Added to Runtley Wood Farm	*See Runtley Wood Farm*
15 unidentified acres in Old Woking	Between 1839-78	*Not known*

In the parish of Farnham		
Property	Date Purchased	Date Sold
East Street: a piece of ground with hop kilns	*Not known*	Between 1846 and 1885
The manor of Farnham and rectorial tithes	1789 at auction	Between 1846 and 1885
The Parsonage House and Parsonage Mead, 3 acres	1805 as a 'lease for lives' from the Archdeacon of Surrey	Between 1846 and 1885

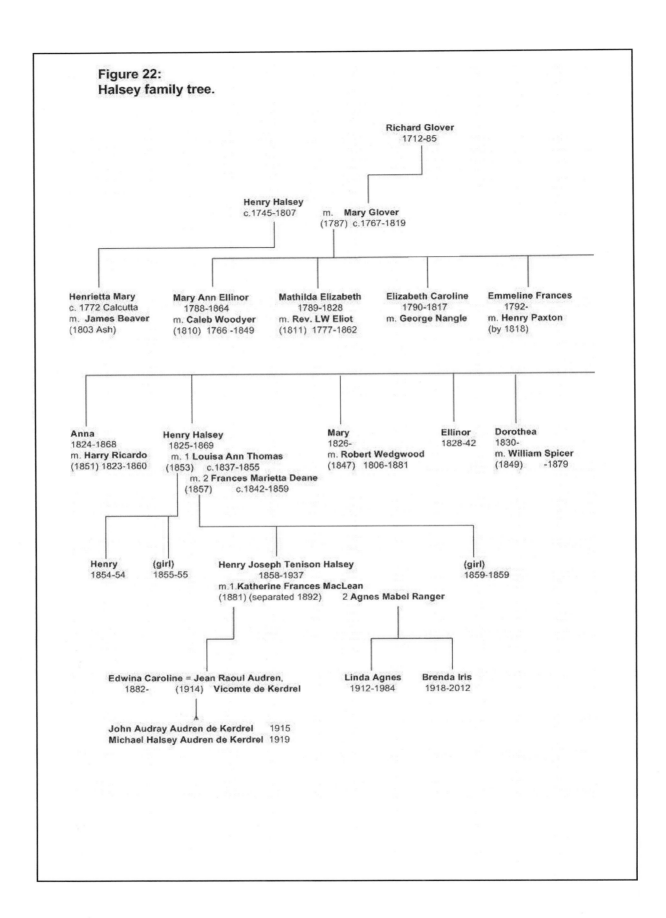

Figure 22:
Halsey family tree.

Richard Glover
1712-85

Henry Halsey
c.1745-1807
m. Mary Glover
(1787) c.1767-1819

Henrietta Mary
c. 1772 Calcutta
m. James Beaver
(1803 Ash)

Mary Ann Ellinor
1788-1864
m. Caleb Woodyer
(1810) 1766 -1849

Mathilda Elizabeth
1789-1828
m. Rev. LW Eliot
(1811) 1777-1862

Elizabeth Caroline
1790-1817
m. George Nangle

Emmeline Frances
1792-
m. Henry Paxton
(by 1818)

Anna
1824-1868
m. Harry Ricardo
(1851) 1823-1860

Henry Halsey
1825-1869
m. 1 Louisa Ann Thomas
(1853)   c.1837-1855
m. 2 Frances Marietta Deane
(1857)   c.1842-1859

Mary
1826-
m. Robert Wedgwood
(1847) 1806-1881

Ellinor
1828-42

Dorothea
1830-
m. William Spicer
(1849)   -1879

Henry
1854-54

(girl)
1855-55

Henry Joseph Tenison Halsey
1858-1937
m.1.Katherine Frances MacLean
(1881) (separated 1892)   2 Agnes Mabel Ranger

(girl)
1859-1859

Edwina Caroline = Jean Raoul Audren,
1882-   (1914)   Vicomte de Kerdrel

Linda Agnes
1912-1984

Brenda Iris
1918-2012

John Audray Audren de Kerdrel   1915
Michael Halsey Audren de Kerdrel 1919

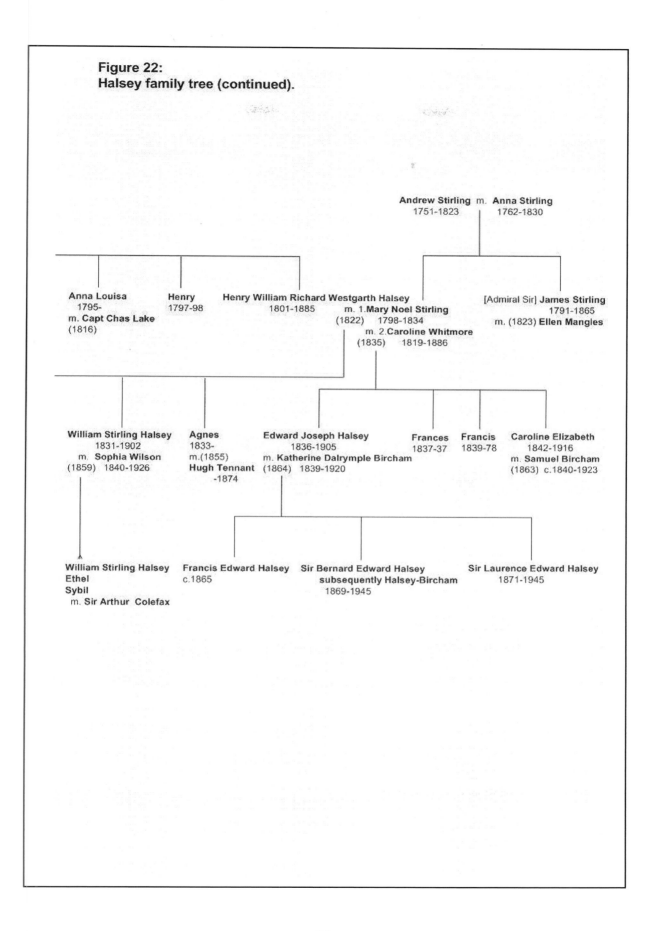

Figure 22:
Halsey family tree (continued).

Andrew Stirling m. Anna Stirling
1751-1823   1762-1830

Anna Louisa
1795-
m. Capt Chas Lake
(1816)

Henry
1797-98

Henry William Richard Westgarth Halsey
1801-1885
m. 1.Mary Noel Stirling
(1822)   1798-1834
m. 2.Caroline Whitmore
(1835)   1819-1886

[Admiral Sir] James Stirling
1791-1865
m. (1823) Ellen Mangles

William Stirling Halsey
1831-1902
m. Sophia Wilson
(1859) 1840-1926

Agnes
1833-
m.(1855)
Hugh Tennant
-1874

Edward Joseph Halsey
1836-1905
m. Katherine Dalrymple Bircham
(1864) 1839-1920

Frances
1837-37

Francis
1839-78

Caroline Elizabeth
1842-1916
m. Samuel Bircham
(1863) c.1840-1923

William Stirling Halsey
Ethel
Sybil
  m. Sir Arthur Colefax

Francis Edward Halsey
c.1865

Sir Bernard Edward Halsey
subsequently Halsey-Bircham
1869-1945

Sir Laurence Edward Halsey
1871-1945

Figure 23: The Halseys' Trustees 1787-1930, as named in various documents.

Appointed	Details	Relinquished
Trustees of Henry Halsey's marriage settlement		
1787	Alexander Higginson of Harley Street	
1787	John Harrowes of Hanover Street	
1787	John Antrobus, tea dealer of the Strand	(see below)
	(also a trustee of Richard Glover's will)	
1787	John Bellamy of Covent Garden	
1787	Richard Treward of Norfolk Street	
Trustees of Henry Halsey's will		
1807 by will	Wife Mary Halsey	Died 1819
1807 by will	Westgarth Snaith of London	Deceased by 1846
1807 by will	Caleb Woodyer of Guildford	[still in 1846]
1807 by will	John Antrobus of Cheam	Deceased by 1816
1816 settlement	Rev Laurence William Eliot of Peper Harrow	Still in 1874, deceased by 1880
	appointed in place of John Antrobus deceased	
1816 settlement	Thomas Wilkinson	1831 desires to be discharged from execution of the trusts
1816 settlement	Broome Philips Witts	[still in 1830s]
by 1830s	John Hopton Forbes	
by 1846	Edward Whitmore	Died 1856
by 1846	Frederick Mellersh of Godalming	Still in 1888, deceased by 1894
1870	Edward Joseph Halsey of Pirbright appointed	Died 1905
	in place of Edward Whitmore, deceased	
[1880	William James Farrer, owner in trust of	ref: Indenture/Title
	all the estates]	
Trustees of Henry William Richard Westgarth Halsey's will		
1862 by will	Alfred Whitmore & Robert Edmund Mellersh	(no further reference)
Still in 1888	Frederick Mellersh	Deceased by 1894
Still in 1888	Edward Joseph Halsey	Died 1905
By 1894	Samuel Bircham appointed in place of Frederick Mellersh, deceased	
1905	Francis Edward Halsey of Chelsea appointed in place of Edward J Halsey, deceased	Still in 1930
By 1908	Bernard Edward Halsey Bircham	
1922 by indenture 15/2	James Robert Nicolson Macphail of Edinburgh	Still in 1930
Mortgagees of Henry Joseph Tenison Halsey		
1886-98	John Moxon Claborn, Robert John Porcher Broughton & Frederick Peake	
1893	Samuel Bircham, Harrington CJ Groves & Edward Arthur Bonnor Maurice	
Trustees of Henry Joseph Tenison Halsey's will		
1926 by will	Sir Bernard Edward Halsey Bircham	

92

7. THE HALSEYS; DECLINE (1850-1922)

It all seemed to be going so well. By 1850 Henry William Richard Westgarth Halsey was a significant landowner in Surrey with estates of over 2,000 acres (see Plate 31) and he was the lord of the manors of Pirbright and the Rectory of Woking. He was living at his country seat at Henley Park with a retinue of 12 servants, including a butler, page, cook, housemaids, kitchenmaids and a groom. In the lodges and cottages within the park were gardeners, a coachman and a dairymaid. Henley Park was described as 'an agreeable oasis' in the 'bleak and weary desert' of Surrey Heath. He had a large family all born at Henley Park, including four sons to carry on the family name and traditions. Two of his sons were to become upstanding, respectable pillars of society but the fatal flaw in the plan was his eldest son, Henry Halsey.

Locked in the stranglehold of the entail set up by his father's will, Henry William had to pass on the estates to his eldest son, but Henry, although undoubtedly dependent on his father for his income, had interests elsewhere. As the first step in implementing the terms of the will, an indenture of settlement was drawn up when Henry junior reached 21 years of age in 1846 which granted him powers over Henley Park, but these powers were never exercised. Instead Henry appears to have preferred the hedonistic attractions of London and after returning from the Grand Tour to Germany, Switzerland, Italy and France he lived at Cox's Hotel, Jermyn Street St James' as well as other addresses in London, Romsey in Hampshire and Dorking rather than returning to live at Henley Park. His lifestyle clearly exceeded whatever allowance his father was giving him because in July 1850 he was sued in the Court for Relief of Insolvent Debtors. There must have been a serious breach between father and son for it to have got that far and clearly Henry senior was not ready to bail his son out. Then in 1853 Henry junior married Louisa Ann Thomas, the 16-year old daughter of John Alfred Thomas, a hatter of Rupert Street. She gave birth to a son eight weeks later but this son died the same year and for some unknown reason Henry gave a false name on the baby's death certificate. In 1855 Louisa died giving birth to a daughter who also died a few days later.

No longer encumbered by a family, Henry departed for New York, where in April 1857 he married the 15-year old Frances Marietta Deane. Both parties to this wedding gave false details; Henry called himself Harry Percy Howard Halsey of Bath, England, and reduced his age by six years to 26, while Frances increased her age by six years to 21 and gave her place of residence as La Prarie, Canada. They married again five months later at a different church, this time giving more accurate details of themselves. By the time of their second wedding Frances was pregnant and on 1 March 1858 she gave birth at 136 West 20th Street, New York to a son whom they named Henry Joseph Tenison Halsey. His baptism on the 21st of July was certified by the British Consulate in New York.

But Henry Halsey was still not destined for a normal family life. In April 1859 Frances gave birth to a girl, but then disappeared on the 1st of June. Her body was found eight days later floating in New York Bay opposite Bay Ridge above Brooklyn. The inquest returned a verdict of accidental drowning. After the death of his wife, Henry asked a certain William D Tenison to take charge of his children, and nothing more is known of him until 10 years later when he died of kidney disease in New York on 5 April 1869 at the age of 43. Unlike his brothers, he has no mention in the family memorials in Pirbright Church.

- - - - -

Possibly disillusioned with country activities and probably saddened by his eldest son's dissolute way of life, Henry William spent more time in London. His father's 'town house' had been in Bath and there is no record that the elder Henry lived in London but as Bath's social attractiveness declined Henry William appears to have started to use London as his town base instead. By 1854 he had purchased 132 Westbourne Terrace, north of Kensington Gardens, then about 1860 a development of new town houses was built at nearby Norfolk Square, Hyde Park, and he acquired Number 34 where he lived until about 1870, apparently spending less and less time at Henley Park. But Henry William was afflicted with a physical disability as well, because by 1871 he was registered as blind, and for the rest of his life he and his wife lived with their youngest daughter Caroline and her husband Samuel Bircham, a solicitor, first at Lancaster Gate then at Elvaston Place in Kensington.

During the last 35 years of Henry William Halsey's life the pace of change slowed and the size of his estates did not alter dramatically. In 1870 he purchased the last four separate strips in Pirbright Common Field at the Fords Farm estate sale and added them into Manor Farm, thus finally removing all trace of the medieval strip-farming system which had survived in the form of sections of the great common field, which in 1800 had still belonged to nine separate farms within Pirbright. He made a series of other small purchases, mostly in Pirbright, to enhance his existing properties, but he also made several major sales. In 1853 he disposed of Rickford Malt House and its adjacent land, and he sold Littlefield and Pussey's Farms in Worplesdon to Charles Peto Shrubb of Merrist Wood House, probably in the 1860s. In 1870 Edward Ryde, a surveyor of Woking, offered him £2,380 for 'the farm in Woking common field' occupied by Mr Bayley, but the sale apparently did not go through because Ryde eventually bought it in 1886 for a considerably higher price. In April 1877 Henry William sold the greater part of the wastes of Pirbright Manor and 'divers old enclosures' including Stony Castle and Small Shot, amounting to 3,072 acres, to Her Majesty's Principal Secretary of State for War for £48,314. By the time of his death in 1885 Henry William's estates in Surrey had reduced to 1,770 acres but despite the agricultural depression, caused by the sudden availability of food arriving in quantity from overseas in refrigerated transport, the annual rental had risen to about £2,000.

The Halseys continued their close association with Pirbright Church and Henry William presented a new stone font for the church in 1873 and donated more land for a new churchyard in 1874. In 1877 he donated glebe land for a parsonage house and his son Edward Joseph Halsey gave funds for the building, gardens and outhouse. Continuing the tradition, in 1908 Edward's wife Katherine and their three sons put up the new lychgate.

By the 1870s alternative arrangements had to be made for burials because there was probably no more room in the family's mortuary chapel and it was not fashionable or acceptable to have a private mausoleum monopolising space in the church. At the instigation of Edward Joseph Halsey it was closed and the coffins were probably re-interred under the chancel floor. In the 1890s the mortuary chapel was converted into the vestry. Henry William purchased a piece of ground within the churchyard in 1879 from the Bishop of Winchester at a cost of £7 11s 6d for a family burial place. It was 440 square feet in area and was marked out by granite stones with the letter 'H' at the four corners (see Plate 27). It was allocated to the Halseys 'as long as the family shall continue parishioners of the parish'.

Henry William RW Halsey died on 7 October 1885 at the age of 84 and was buried in the family plot in Pirbright churchyard on the 13th of October. The funeral was simple and unostentatious; no carriages followed the hearse. The mourners walked from the Old School on Pirbright Green where they had assembled (see Plate 23). The weather was bitterly cold. The epitaph on his gravestone seems to echo the sadness and disappointment of his later life - it reads 'Whom the Lord loveth, He chastiseth'.

A century later residents still recalled that when Henry William lived at the park the farms were well kept up, employment was found for all and he is reported to have given away one way or another £200 at Christmas. He made many improvements and changes to his properties and acquired a reputation as a great one for 'building up and pulling down'. He was referred to as 'the old squire' and regarded with great respect by the local people, long after he had stopped living at Henley Park. At a sale at Henley Park in 1853 Mr Leftwich, the miller at Pirbright, bought a huge wooden tub as a memento, it having been the 'squire's tub'! He put it on the mill pond and local children would paddle themselves about in it until it became worn out.

Even in the 1880s when Edward Joseph Halsey and his wife Katherine lived in Pirbright they found that there was still an old-fashioned friendliness and courtesy locally and a respect for the 'squire' and his family. Katherine Halsey noted in her notebook that local people used to tap the larches in Rails Lane, leading to Henley Park pond, for 'May beer'. There was plenty of game in Henley Park woods and she thought that hares and rabbits must often have been poached, to judge by the children's caps of rabbit skins.

- - - - -

Francis, Henry William's fourth son had also predeceased him. He was born in 1839 and died in 1878. Little else is known of him apart from his memorial in the chancel of Pirbright Church which states that he died in Venice and was buried at Pirbright on what would have been his 39th birthday.

Of Henry William's other two sons, his second son William Stirling, born in 1831, joined the Indian Civil Service and spent most of his life in India where he was Inspector General of Registration and Commissioner of Excise and Stamps. He was still in the Punjab in 1886 but by 1893 was living in South Kensington, London. He died in 1902 and is also buried in the family plot at Pirbright. It was however Henry William's third son Edward Joseph, born in 1836, who made his home in Pirbright and carried on the Halsey tradition of involvement in local affairs (see Plate 28).

Edward Joseph was educated at Durham and Charterhouse and apparently made the Grand Tour in his youth, having spent 'many years after leaving school in other parts of the world'. In 1864 he married Katherine Dalrymple Bircham at St George Hanover Square, London. By 1870 he had been appointed a trustee of the Halsey Surrey estates in place of another trustee who had died. Edward and Katherine leased the Manor House in Pirbright in 1872 and stayed there during the next three summers while retaining a London residence in Belgrave Road. Then in 1876 they moved into The Cottage, now called Langley House, opposite the White Hart and Pirbright green.

In the same year Edward Joseph was elected the parish of Pirbright's representative on the Guildford Board of Guardians and worked tirelessly to implement important reforms in the administration of the Poor Law, serving as chairman from 1880 to 84. In 1880 he qualified as a county magistrate like his father had been and in 1889 he was elected to Surrey County Council where he served as chairman from 1893 to 1903 and his portrait still hangs in the Ashcombe Suite at County Hall. He took an active interest in many of Pirbright's social activities as well. In 1877 he is recorded as going to Woking to watch 'his' Pirbright cricket XI play the local team and in 1880 he gave a reading and Mrs Halsey played the pianoforte at the Musical Society. He clearly felt an affinity with the locality, but in 1885, the year of his father's death, he and his family moved back to London. In recognition of his good works in the parish he was presented with a massive silver tankard by the people of Pirbright (see Plate 29).

Edward Joseph died in Kensington 20 years later and was buried in the family plot at Pirbright. Although he did not live in Pirbright for the latter part of his life, two of his three sons subsequently settled in the area. His second son Bernard Edward Halsey who changed his name by deed poll to BE Halsey Bircham and was later knighted, became the senior partner in Bircham and Co solicitors. He became private solicitor to King George V, served as a JP for Surrey and was elected to Surrey County Council where he became chairman. In 1904 or 1905 he built the house called Admiral's Walk in Pirbright and divided his time between here and his house in London, and in 1911 he was chairman of Pirbright's Coronation Festivities Committee.

Edward's third son Laurence Edward Halsey, knighted in 1919, lived at Goose Rye Farm in Worplesdon, described in 1915 as a 'charming brick and tile residence converted from a farmhouse' with 24 acres worth £4,760. In 1936 he purchased Worplesdon Place for £10,000 although he apparently continued to live at Goose Rye Farm. He is remembered as being a great benefactor of Worplesdon over the years, having anonymously built the Memorial Hall in 1922 and providing a cottage for a surgery to the village's first resident doctor.

Edward's eldest son Francis Edward and second son Bernard Edward also became trustees of the Henley Park estate after their father died, and it was probably due to their local knowledge that the last local land purchases for the estate were made. Edward and his sons could have been fitting 'squires' of Henley Park but instead, on the death of Henry William, it passed to a virtual stranger.

- - - - -

When Henry William Halsey left Henley Park for London the mansion was let once more and although the Halsey family were to own Henley Park for another 70 years, they never returned to live there. A gentleman by the name of George Reid is recorded as being in residence in 1855, followed by General Sir George Scovell GCB until his death there in January 1861 age 86. In the 1861 census the house was unoccupied and one gets the impression of a sad and deserted place at this time, with the 'old squire' gone and no-one to care for it. From 1862 to 1867 Edward Brettle Esq and James Startin Esq were tenants.

Charles Douglas Burnett became the next tenant in 1869. He was a member of the family distilling company founded by his grandfather Sir Robert Burnett which raised the standard of production during London's 'gin craze' in the 18th century. Sir Robert, who became Lord Mayor of London and lived at Morden Hall now owned by the National Trust, first established the Vauxhall Distillery south of the Thames in Vauxhall High Street. During the 19th century the company was run by his four grandsons Charles Douglas, Fassett Charles, John Robert and George Richard who moved the distillery to the nearby Albert Embankment, Lambeth. Charles Douglas Burnett originally lived at Park Crescent, Regent's Park, but during his thirties he and his family lived at a series of houses in Surrey and Hampshire - Birtley near Guildford, Hawley Hill House in Farnborough and Hartley Grange in Winchfield - all within easy commuting distance of the distillery at Vauxhall. Then in 1869 at the age of 42, he and his family took up residence at Henley Park and it is possible that this choice was influenced by the close proximity of Brookwood station, which had been opened five years earlier. Their youngest daughter Ruby, who had been born in Putney, was baptised at Wyke in December. In 1873 Burnett leased Henley Park with its land and sporting rights from Henry William Halsey and his trustees for 14 years at

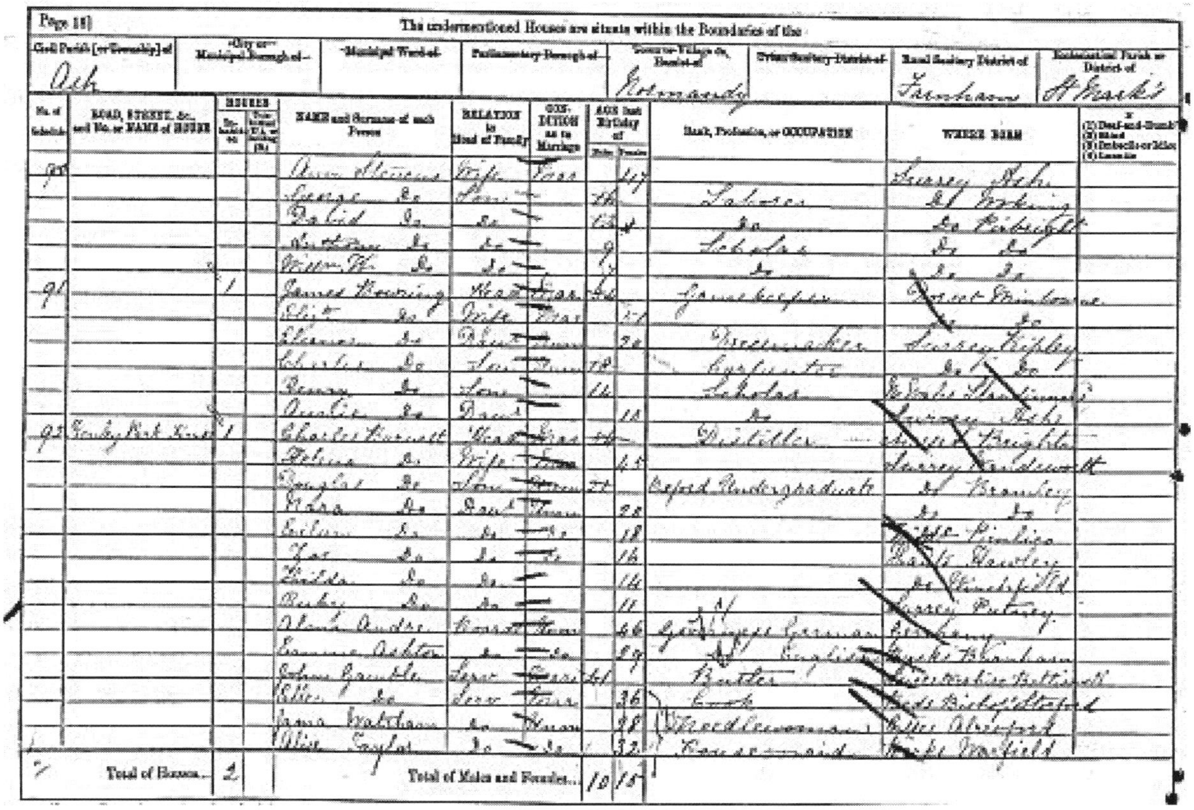

Figure 24: The 1881 Census page showing the Burnett family at Henley Park.

an annual rent of £500, although in 1877 the rent was reduced to £425 because some of the land had been sold to the War Office. The 1881 census lists a full complement of staff and Burnett was in residence with his wife, son, five daughters, a German governess, an English governess and 11 indoor servants; butler, cook, needlewoman, housemaids, kitchenmaid, scullerymaid, footman and hallboy.

Charles Douglas Burnett lived at Henley Park for 20 years, longer than subsequent tenants Lord and Lady Pirbright or Sir Owen and Lady Roberts but, unlike them and 'the old squire' Henry William Halsey, he is not remembered in local folklore. He might well have wished to stay on even longer when his lease expired in 1887, but by this time his landlord had changed. In 1885 Henry Joseph Tenison Halsey had inherited Henley Park and its vast estate on the death of his grandfather and now some serious financial negotiations were about to take place.

- - - - -

The daughter born in New York to Henry and Frances Halsey in 1859 had died a few months later, but their son Henry Joseph survived. Despite his father's request to William Tenison to take charge of the children, it appears that he was brought up by his uncle Henry A Deane, a dentist of New York. In 1880 having reached the age of 21, he came to England and the family papers contain a flurry of sworn affidavits and indentures of settlement as he established his claim. He was assigned powers over the Henley Park estate by his grandfather in an act of settlement on 2 December 1880, under the trusteeship of his uncle Edward Joseph Halsey and the family solicitor, Frederick Mellersh of Godalming. The settlement gave him powers to raise mortgages on the estate up to £7,000 and within two weeks he did exactly that, taking a loan up to the limit allowed. It would appear that he had no further immediate interest in the estate because in 1881 he was back in New York where he married Katherine Frances MacLean. Their only child was a daughter Edwina Caroline born in 1882. The marriage does not appear to have been a success as they were to negotiate a contract of separation in October 1892. Despite Henry Joseph's disapproval, the contract stipulated that their daughter Edwina was to be brought up in the Roman Catholic faith.

There is no record that Henry Joseph visited England again during his grandfather's lifetime, but he returned in March 1886 following Henry William's death and visited Henley Park for a day with Mr Mellersh. After his visit Henry Joseph said that he preferred his house in New York, but if he could not let Henley Park he would spend the three summer months there and shut it up for the rest of the time. In fact the house continued to be let and such was the reputation and standing of the subsequent tenants - Lord and Lady Pirbright and Sir Owen and Lady Roberts - that many people forgot that it was the Halseys who owned the mansion.

During his visit the Burnetts, who were still in residence, showed him round the house and told him they would stay on if he would further reduce the rent when the lease expired the following year. Their request indicates that the mansion might have become rather run down, and indeed an inventory taken five years later lists several signs of decay. Henry Joseph's response is not recorded, but not long afterwards the Burnetts moved to Fernhill, a mansion north of Farnborough, and on 25 December 1889 Baron Henry de Worms leased Henley Park for 28 years at an annual rent of £378, significantly lower than the rent which the Burnetts had been paying.

As well as letting the house, Henry Joseph almost immediately started to raise money on Henley Park by other means. Six months after his grandfather died he extinguished the 'two-hundred-year' entail that Henry Halsey set up 80 years earlier, in an indenture signed by twelve parties including all his grandfather's surviving children. He now had much more freedom to dispose of the estate and within three months he started raising a series of additional mortgages on Henley Park itself, until by 1897 the total sum borrowed was £21,400. By 1904 this had risen to £22,000.

In addition he boosted his income by selling the timber on the estates. From 1885 to 1891 this raised less than £10 a year, but then it started to increase - £40 in 1892, £171 in 1895, £277 in 1896, £264 in 1898, £71 in 1899 and £388 10s in 1900. After the cost of sale, this brought him over £1,000 in the five years to 1900. It may be that the price of timber had increased or perhaps Henry Joseph had realised that here was another useful source of revenue and felled more trees.

At first the properties that he sold were in outlying parts of the estate. In 1886 he sold Parsonage Farm in Old Woking to Edward Ryde for £3,225 and in July 1889 he sold Cowshot Farm to the Trustees of the National Rifle Association. At about the same time he sold Runtley Wood Farm in Woking. In 1906 he sold his last property in Woking, a house and garden in Old Woking Street which had been occupied by the Ross family for 65 years, to Miss Mary Ross for £600. The few purchases during this period were probably due to the local knowledge of the trustees who saw the opportunity to consolidate the estate closer to Henley Park. When the Normandy Manor estate was put up for sale in 1895 they acquired the 3-acre smallholding on Normandy Green which is now Normandy Hill Farm and Quinta Cottage. They also acquired the Woodroffe's four fields between Longerend and Henley Park Farms which they added to Henley Park Farm, so extending its boundary outside the former royal park. In 1907 and 1909 they bought The Nursery and Stream House Farm from Lady Pirbright.

In 1910 Henry Joseph's Surrey estates still totalled 1,657 acres and the National Valuation Survey calculated their gross freehold value in 1913 at £77,647, split roughly into £40,000 in the parish of Ash, £30,000 in Pirbright and the rest in Worplesdon. The market value of the mansion and its grounds was originally assessed in April 1913 at £22,273, being 40 years' annual rent of £575, less £427 for the tithe rent charge and £300 for the footpaths that ran through the estate. The survey was conducted for taxation purposes so most people were trying to talk down the value of their properties but in December 1913 it was agreed with Mr Mellersh that the value of the mansion and grounds should be assessed at £29,273 (a gross value of £30,000 less the tithe and footpaths). It could be that Mr Mellersh was trying to 'talk up' the value on behalf of Henry Joseph, with the mortgage value or an eventual sale in mind.

Henry Joseph might have run out of options for raising loans against the property because by the First World War he started selling major parts of his estates. In 1916 he sold his estates in Somerset. Then in 1919 he turned to Pirbright and by July of that year he had sold Pirbright Lodge to Mr Q de Quincy for £3,500 and on the 6th of September he auctioned the Manor Mill, two smallholdings, 10 cottages and five farms - Whites Farm, Wickham Farm, West Hall Farm, Grove Farm and The Nursery, about 290 acres in total. The Pirbright sales raised £15,460, enabling him to pay off the rest of his mortgages.

Henry Joseph always seems to have found it difficult to settle. From 1886 to 1892 he lived in Edinburgh (when he sometimes referred to himself as 'of Henley Park' even though it was let to tenants) and from 1896 to 1898 he lived in Willesden Green, London. In 1898 he put all his goods in storage as if he were going abroad, but by 1911 he was back in England and lived near Leicester Square in London. He leased a shop and premises in Wolverhampton, but what became of this venture is not recorded. He was never divorced from his first wife because she was a Catholic, but in 1910 or 11 he met Agnes Mabel Ranger and they had two daughters, Linda Agnes born in 1912 in Edgbaston, Birmingham, and Brenda Iris born in 1918 in Windsor. In 1915 he granted a strip of his land to the north of Pirbright Church to the parish for an extension of the churchyard and in return he received an extension of the plot reserved for the Halsey family, so it is probable that he intended to be buried there.

As Henry Joseph was an absentee landlord, it would be easy to believe that he had no interest in the affairs of his estate and used it solely as a source of income, leaving all the decisions during his 40 years of ownership to his trustees. Indeed family members say that in his later years when he was living in Monte Carlo he was a playboy, having affairs and playing the Casino, until his partner Agnes Mabel left and returned to England with one of their daughters. On the other hand both he and his trustees might have attempted to keep the estate together as long as they could in the difficult circumstances caused by the depression in farming and declining rents.

A series of Property Acts from 1882 to 1922 significantly reduced the power of entails, releasing any remaining restrictions imposed by Henry Halsey's will of 1807, so that Henry Joseph was free to sell. By 1922 the Halsey holdings in Woking, Bisley and Chobham had disappeared completely and those in Pirbright had fallen to 463 acres and in Worplesdon to 256 acres. On the other hand he had acquired the additional properties and land in Normandy which had increased his holdings there to 615 acres. In 1922 he and his trustees finally took the momentous decision to sell the whole estate including Henley Park and the mansion, following the trend set over the last 30 years by the sale of other estates in the area such as Normandy Manor Farm and Wanborough.

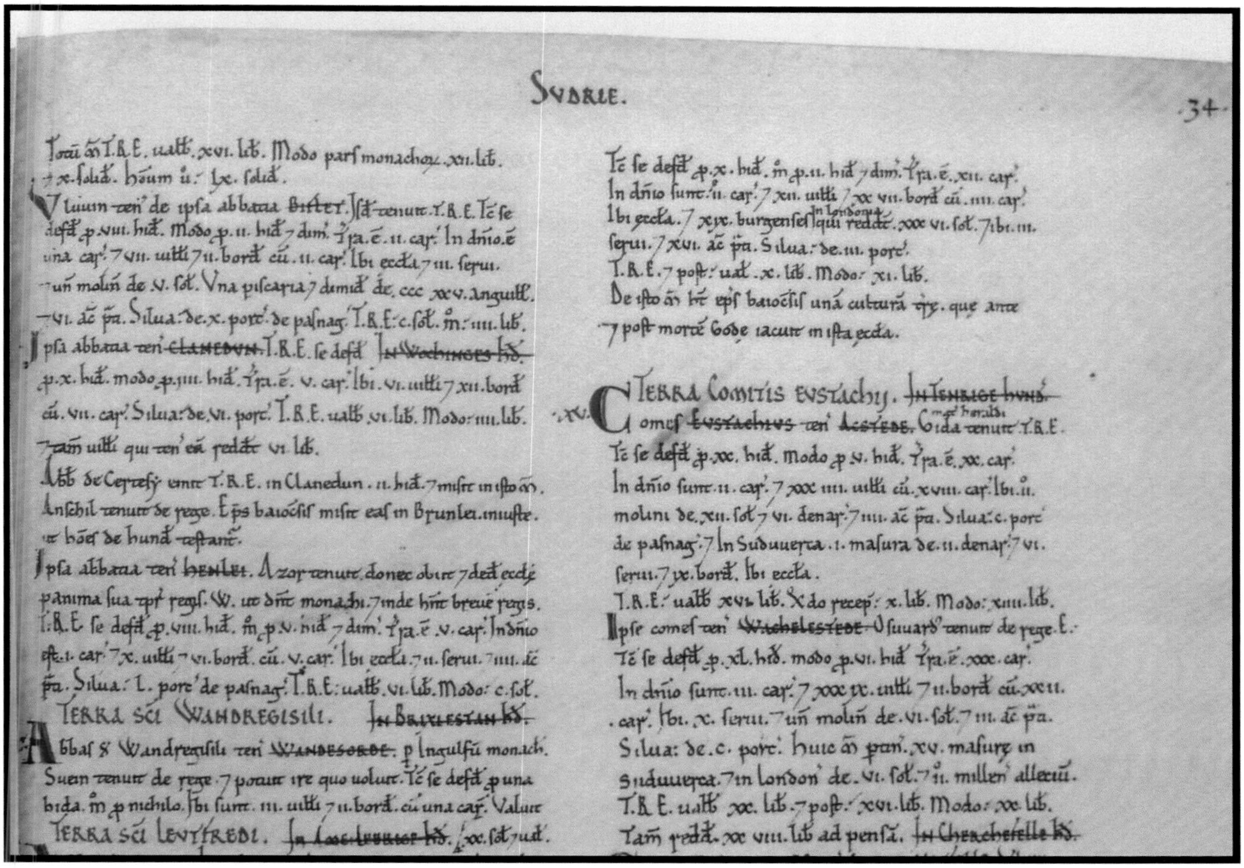

Plate 1.

The Domesday Book. Entries in the left column are for Byfleet, Clandon, Henley and Wandsworth.
Henley's entry translates as:
The same abbey [*Chertsey*] holds HENLEI. Azor held it until he died, and gave it to the church for his soul in the time of King William, as the monks say, and they have the king's writ therefor. In the time of King Edward it was assessed for eight hides; now for five hides and a half. There is land for five ploughs. In demesne there is one plough; and [*there are*] ten villanes and six bordars with five ploughs. There is a church; and two serfs; and four acres of meadow. Wood for pannage of fifty hogs. In the time of King Edward it was worth six pounds; now a hundred shillings.

Plate 2.
The first royal owners of Henley Park;
19th Century representations of King Edward II (left) and King Edward III.

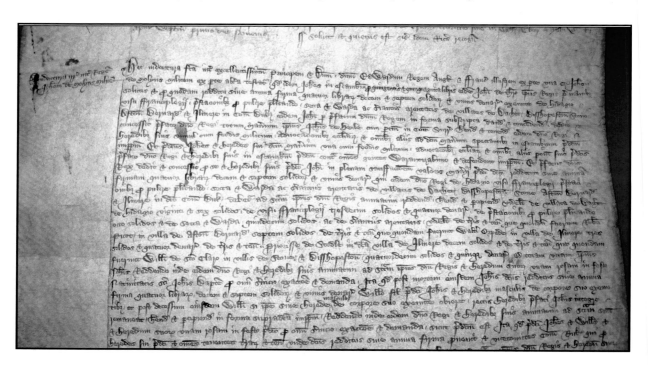

Plate 3.
Royal purchase; John de Molyns knight to King Edward III for £550.
Part of Close Roll 26 June 1351. The first seven lines translate as:
This indenture made between the most excellent prince and lord the lord Edward illustrious King of England and France of the one part and John de Molyns Knight of the other part bears witness that the same John in exchange for £550 paid to him in hand from the treasury of the same king and for a certain rent or annual farm of £4 17s 1d issuing from the hidage view of frankpledge prests for beaupleader suit and ward and rented serjeanties of the vills of Datchet Bishopston Stone Aston Bernard and Ilmer in the county of Buckingham to be given and granted to the same John by the aforesaid lord king in the form underwritten has given and granted to the aforesaid lord king all that the same John's manor of Henley with the appurtenances in the county of Surrey to have and to hold to the same lord king and to his heirs together with the knights' fees advowsons of churches and all other things belonging to the said manor in exchange aforesaid forever.

Plate 4.
Fragment of a highly-decorated 14th century floor tile
believed to be from the medieval manor house, discovered in fields near Henley Park.
Drawing alongside shows the pattern of the full tile (50 pence coin for scale).

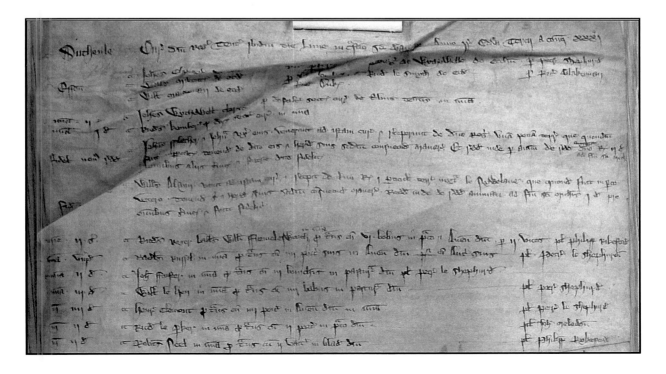

Plate 5.
Extract from the only known court roll of the manor of Henley, 12 June 1357.
Begins: Suthhenle   court of the lord king held there on Monday on the morrow of St Barnabas
in the year of the reign of King Edward III after the conquest the 31st.

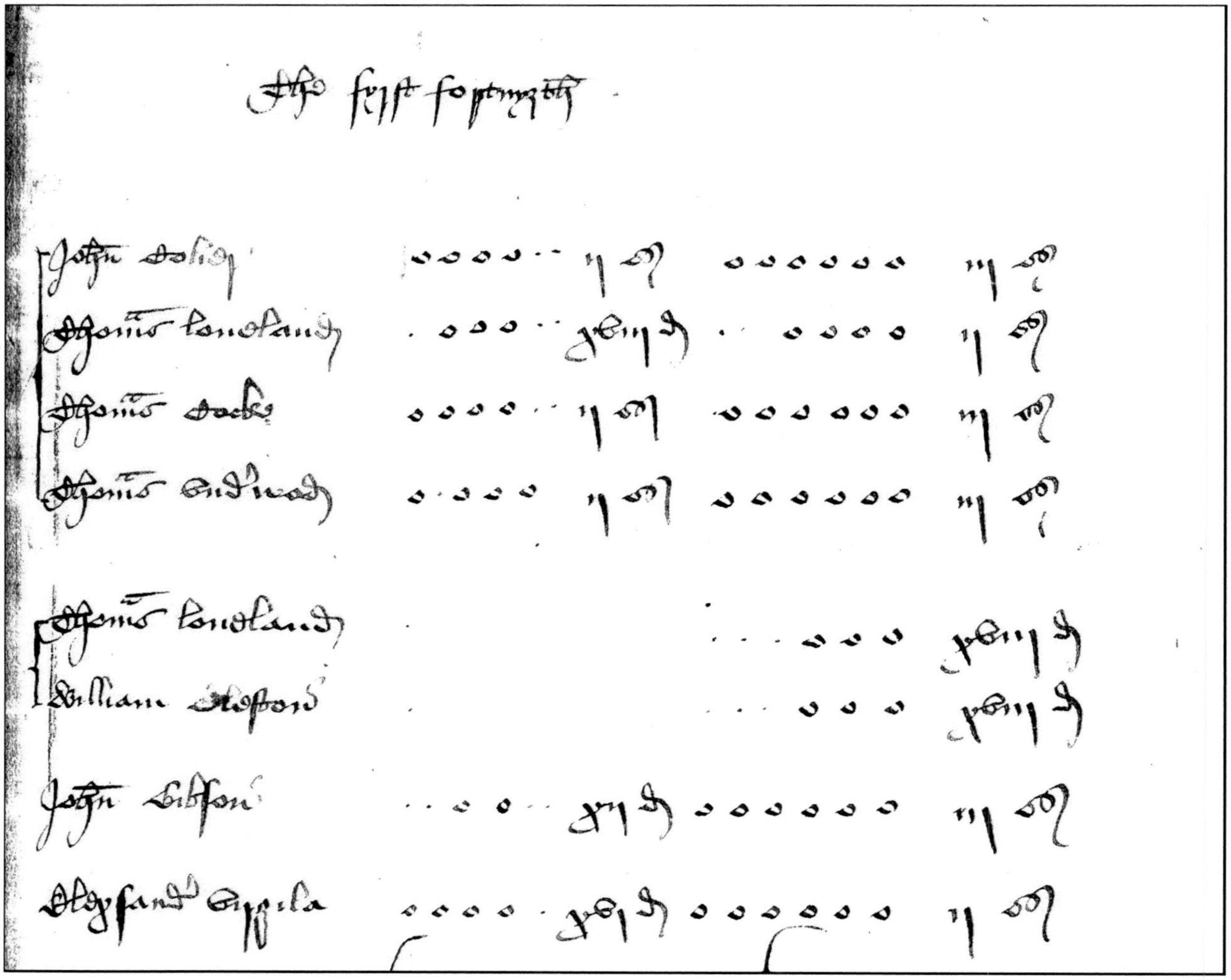

Plate 6.

Excerpt from accounts for repairs to the lodge and great barn at Henley Park;

the fyrst fortnyght (20th Aug to 1st Sept 1515)

John Colier (a carpenter)	oooo..	ii^s (4 days, 2 shillings)	oooooo	iii^s (6 days 3 shillings)
Thomas Loveland (carpenter)	.ooo..	xviii^d	..oooo	ii^s
Thomas Cock (carpenter)	oooo..	ii^s	oooooo	iii^s
Thomas Undrwod (carpenter)	o.ooo	ii^s	oooooo	iii^s
Thomas Loveland (sawyer)			...ooo	xviii^d
William Clefton [*Clifton*] (sawyer)			...ooo	xviii^d
John Gibson (tyler)	..oo..	xii^d	oooooo	iii^s
Alexsandr Virgila? (labourer)	oooo..	xvi^d	oooooo	ii^s

Plate 7.
William Fitzwilliam, Earl of Southampton,
close friend of King Henry VIII and
keeper of Henley and Guildford royal parks
from 1516 to 1542,
by Hans Holbein the Younger.

Plate 8.
Sir Anthony Browne, 'dissolution profiteer' and friend of Henry VIII,
keeper of Henley and Guildford royal parks 1543 to 1548.

Plate 9.

Sir Anthony Browne,
first Viscount Montague,
a staunch Catholic but was
rewarded for his loyalty to
Queen Elizabeth. Keeper
of Henley and Guildford
royal parks from 1553 to
1592.

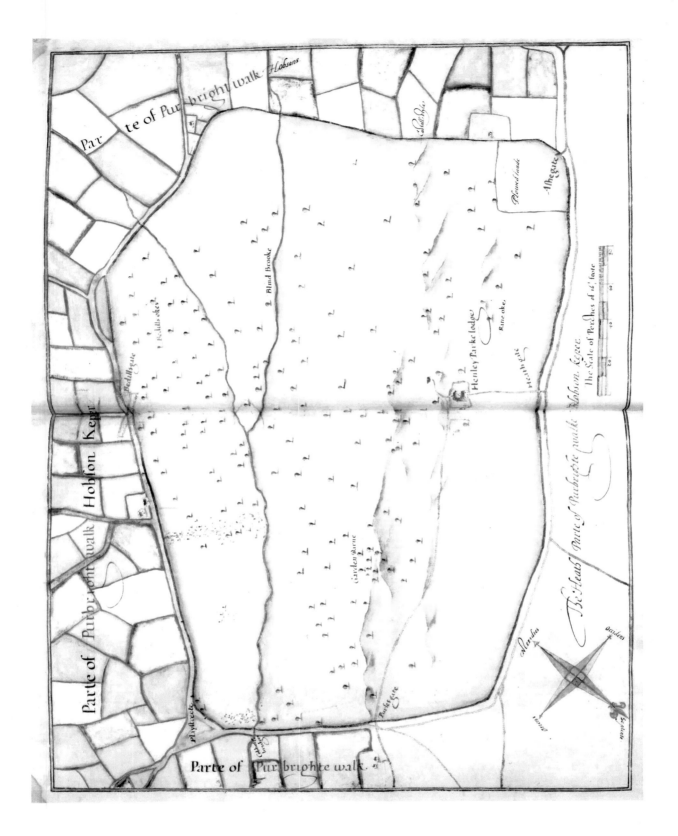

Plate 10.
John Norden's 1607 map of Henley Park drawn from the north-west,
beautifully hand-drawn and coloured, measuring 15¾ by 21 inches
from the volume dedicated to King James.

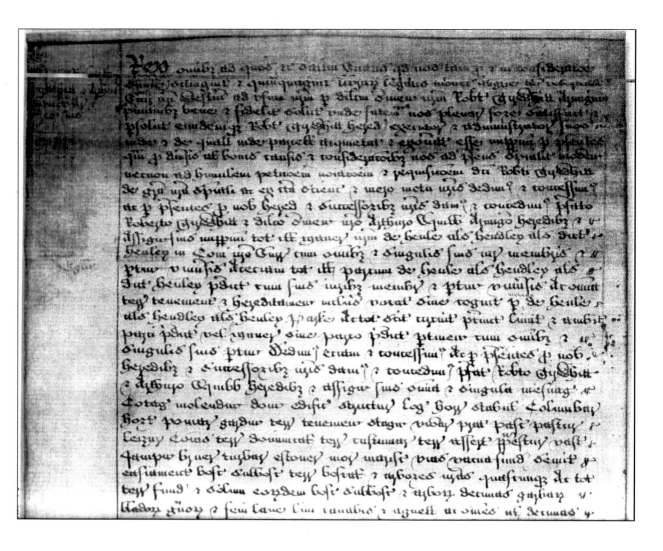

Plate 11.

Royal sale: King Charles I to Robert Tyrwhitt for £850.
Part of Patent Roll 13 July 1632. The first few lines of convoluted legalese translate as:
The King to all whom these presents shall come. Whereas that We for and in consideration of the sum of eight hundred and fifty pounds of legal money of England do grant unto the use of Robert Tyrwhitt Esq and by trust in him to faithfully acknowledge to release unto him the said Robert Tyrwhitt, his heirs, executors and administration unto the property to forbear and discharge in perpetuity with good cause and consideration and he hath humbly craved to take over by grace and also out of merit moving of the Lord and to grant unto his present and known heirs and successors and for him the said Robert Tyrwhitt to declare and grant unto Arthur Squibb Esq, his heirs and assigns half of the whole to share with the whole in such manner to be agreed of Henle otherwise Hendley otherwise called Henley in the County of Surrey with all and singular part and parcel of the whole in the Park of Henle otherwise Hendley otherwise called Henley aforesaid with their parts and parcels of the lands, tenements and knight's hereditaments called or known by the name of Henle otherwise Hendley otherwise Henley Parke.

Plate 12.

The east façade of the Jacobean-style mansion and outbuildings at Henley Park.
The main mansion was probably built by Arthur Squibb in the 1630s.
On the extreme left is the earlier lodge house shown on Norden's survey.

Plate 13.
Portrait of Sir John Glynne in the robes of Chief Justice of the Upper Bench,
with his second wife Ann Manning and their two children Mary and John. John, the child on the left,
is attired in a dress which was the custom for boys before they were 'breeched'.

Plate 14.
The Tylney family in the splendour of their home at Wanstead, by Old Nollekens.
Richard Earl Tylney is in black seated on the right, his wife Dorothy in front of him at the card table.
Reproduced by courtesy of York Civic Trust, Fairfax House, York.

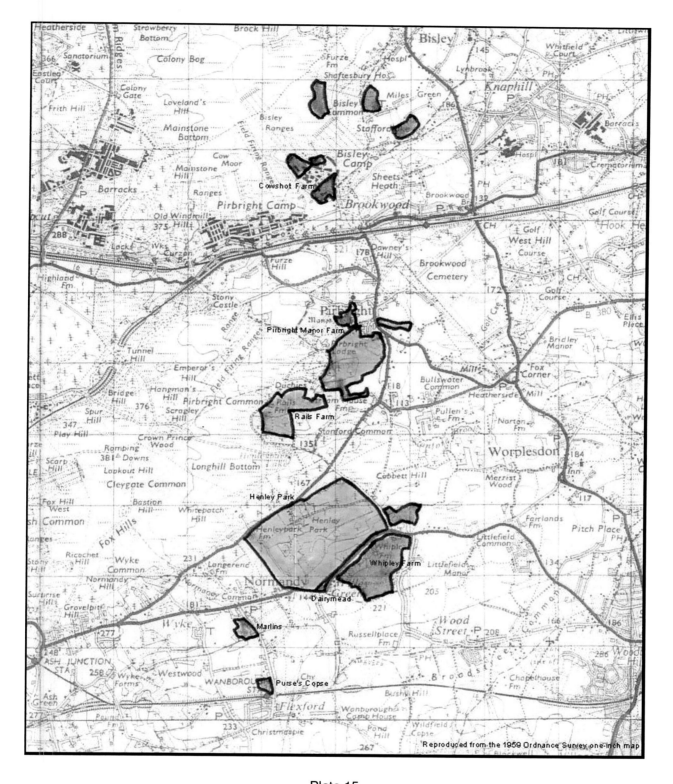

Plate 15.
The lands purchased by Solomon Dayrolle.
Henley Park, Pirbright Manor Farm, Rails Farm, 'Marlins' smallholding and Purse's Copse
(shown in green) were included in his original purchase in 1739.
He added Cowshot Farm in 1750, Whipley Farm in 1775 and Dairymead in the 1740s
(shown in blue) during his ownership of the estate.

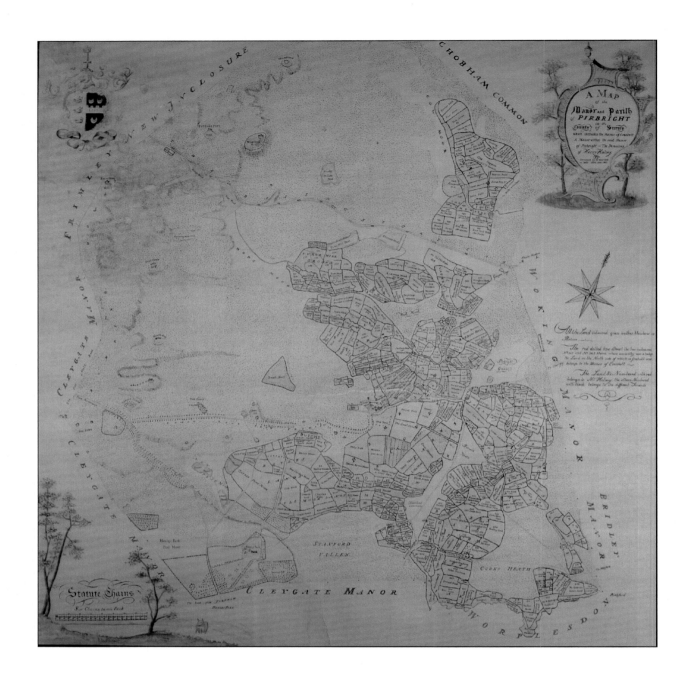

Plate 16.

Henry Halsey's estates in Pirbright were so extensive that in 1805 he commissioned a survey to record them, and for three years the surveyor William Newland mapped out all the cultivated land and residences in the parish. The result was a wonderfully detailed and decorative map, a copy of which now hangs on the wall of Lord Pirbright's Hall, and an accompanying schedule held at the Surrey History Centre in Woking which shows that Henry Halsey owned 525 acres in Pirbright, more than a third of the cultivated land in the parish. By the time William Newland finished his work he had run up a bill for £92 9s 5d, but Henry Halsey did not live to see it. Newland presented his bill to the estate and it was paid by Caleb Woodyer, one of the executors.

Plate 17.
Drawing of Pirbright Church in 1808 by William Petrie FSA,
before the east end was rebuilt for the Halseys' mortuary chapel.

Plate 18.
Pirbright Church in 1823 from *Surrey Churches* by CT Cracklow,
showing the Halseys' mortuary chapel, built according to the terms of Henry Halsey's will.

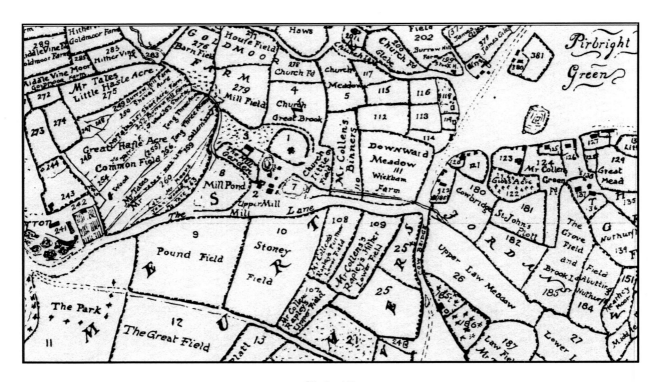

Plate 19.
Detail of Newland's map showing the centre of Pirbright village in 1807.

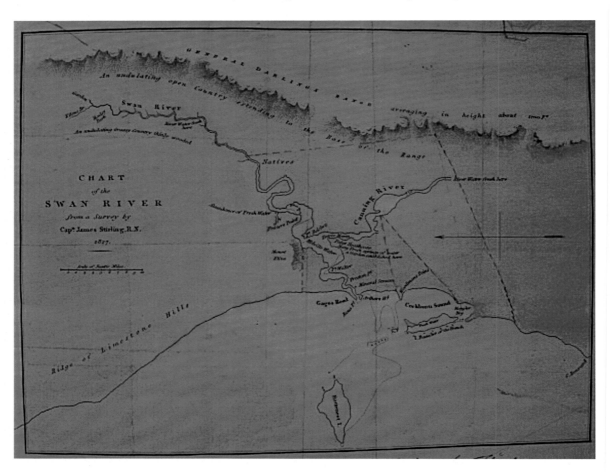

Plate 20.
Survey of Swan River, Western Australia, by Captain James Stirling in 1827.
Note 'Henley Park' in the upper left near the source of the river
and 'Mangles Bay' on the coast at the mid-right.

Plate 21.

Henry William Richard Westgarth
Halsey c.1834.
Portrait presented to the
Union Club, London, of which
he became a member in 1853
by his grandson
Sir Bernard Edward Halsey Bircham.

Plate 22.

Henry William Richard Westgarth
Halsey in his later years.
Copyright of Surrey History Centre.

Plate 23.
The Old School House, Pirbright, the only property retained by the Halseys after the estate sales.
Henry WRW Halsey's funeral cortege set out from here to the church in 1885.

Plate 24.
Edward Ryde's diary for 13th October 1885,
when he attended Henry WRW Halsey's funeral.
'No carriages follow the hearse
but all the friends walk from the Old Schools
at Pirbright where they had assembled.'
Copyright of Surrey History Centre.

Plate 25.
The Chancel of Pirbright Church,
showing the Halsey memorials
on the north and south walls
next to the chapel doors.

Plate 26a. Halsey memorials on the north wall of the Chancel in Pirbright Church:
(Left) Sacred to the memory of H W R W Halsey ~~ And of Caroline his wife ~~
Both are buried in Pirbright churchyard "her children arise up and call her blessed"
(centre) To the memory of Henry Halsey and Mary his wife ~~ And of their children ~~ Also of Andrew
Stirling ~~ and Anna his wife ~~ Their mortal remains were laid in a Mortuary Chapel built on the North
side of the Chancel of this Church ~~ and subsequently in the year 1877 were lowered into a grave
beneath and the Mortuary Chapel closed for Interments
(Right) Francis Halsey youngest son of H W R W Halsey born at Henley Park xvi August 1839. Died at
Venice vii August 1878. Buried in the churchyard on his 39th birthday

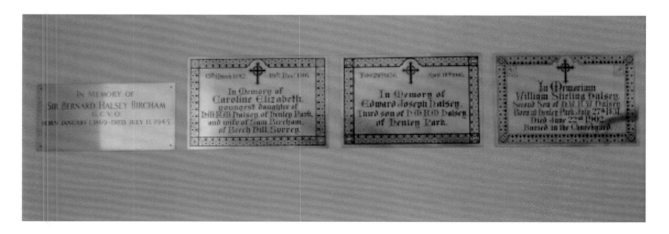

Plate 26b. Halsey memorials on the south wall of the Chancel in Pirbright Church.

Plate 27. Halsey gravestones in Pirbright churchyard. Left to right:

William Stirling Halsey, Born July 27 1831 Died June 22 1902, and of his wife Sophie Victoria Halsey,
Born May 7 1840 died Jan 26 1926, Fifth daughter of the Rt Hon James Wilson MP
"Truly the light is sweet and a pleasant thing it is for the eyes to behold the sun if a man live many years
and rejoiceth in them all"

Caroline, wife of HWRW Halsey, Born May 10 1816 Died September 26 1886
"Blessed are the pure in heart for they shall see God"

Henry WRW Halsey, Died October 7th 1885 in his 84th year
"Whom the Lord loveth He chastiseth"

In remembrance of Edward Joseph Halsey, Third son of HWRW Halsey of Henley Park
Born February 28th 1836 Died April 18th 1905
He was chairman for 13 years of the Surrey County Council and for 25 years was untiring in educational
and philanthropic work for his much loved county
"It is good to be zealously affected always in a good thing"
And of his wife Katherine Dalrymple Halsey

Francis Halsey, Born August 16 1839, Died August 7 1878
"Underneath are the everlasting arms"

Francis Powys Halsey Bircham, Died 13th March 1907 aged 5½ months
Without spot to God

And to the right beyond the edge of the picture -
Bernard Halsey Bircham GCVO, Died 1945; Ivy Cecilia Halsey Bircham widow of
Sir Bernard Edward Halsey Bircham GCVO & daughter of Arthur Powys Vaughan died 15 Apr 1951

Plate 28. Edward Joseph Halsey,
Chairman of Surrey County Council, 1893-1905.
Copyright of Surrey History Centre.

Plate 29.
Edward J Halsey's presentation tankard
from the people of Pirbright, 1885.

Plate 30. The Manor House, Pirbright.
Edward J Halsey and his family lived here 1875-1877.

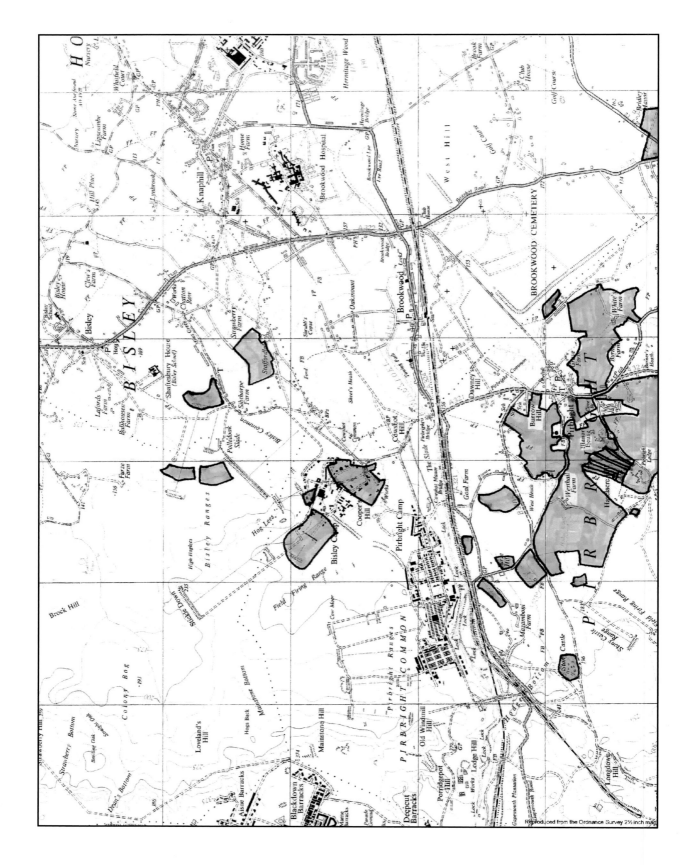

Plate 31a.
The Henley Park estates at their greatest extent around 1850 (shown in green),
northern section. The properties shown in blue were purchased later by the Halseys
after some of the larger farms had already been sold.

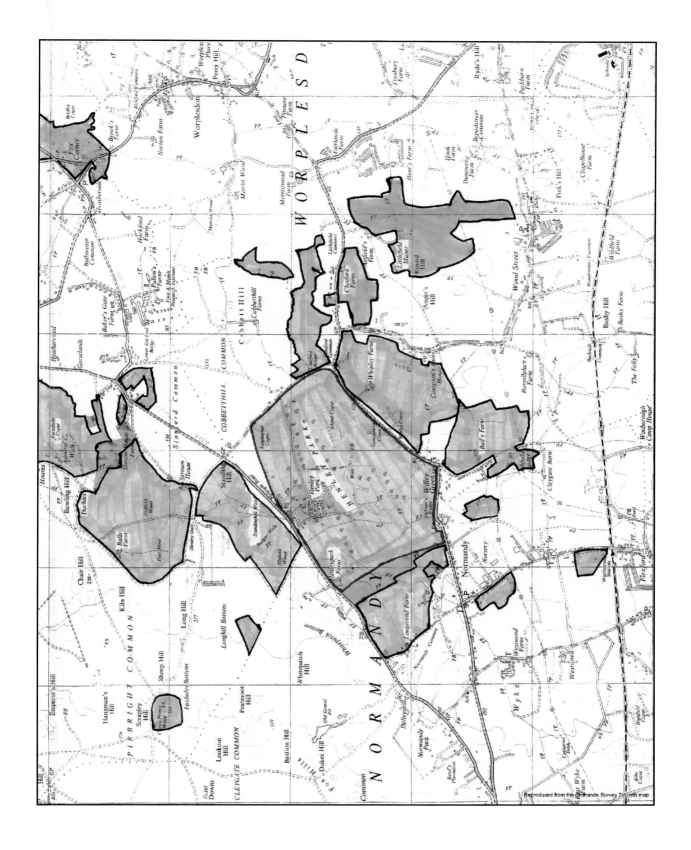

Plate 31b.
The Henley Park estates at their greatest extent, southern section.
The former royal park is outlined in blue.

Plate 32.

Henry Joseph Tenison Halsey,
the last member of the family
to own Henley Park.

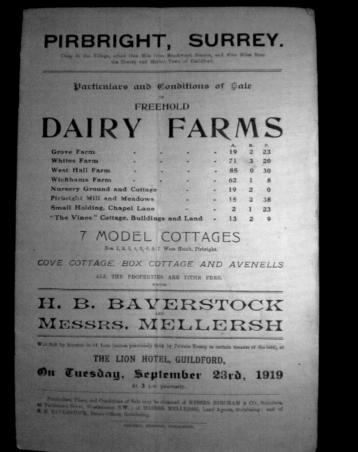

Plate 33.

The first estate sale:
Sale catalogue for sale by auction
of the Pirbright farms in 1919.

Plate 34.

Henry Baron de Worms (later Lord Pirbright)
as a younger man,
a contemporary portrait
by Sandor Liezen-Mayer.

Plate 35.

Meet of the Ripley and Knaphill Harriers outside the east front of Henley Park in 1895.
Lord and Lady Pirbright are standing to the right of the doorway.

Plate 36.
The Queen's Jubilee celebrations on Pirbright village green in 1897.
Lord and Lady Pirbright are in the centre, in front of the new drinking fountain
that Lord Pirbright donated to the village.

Plate 37.
Lord Pirbright's Hall in about 1905 showing the elaborate stained glass window in the south wall, which had Lord Pirbright's full armorial bearings and motto, 'vinctus non victus' - to restrain but not to conquer.
The window had to be removed when the hall was extended in about 1950 and subsequently disappeared without trace.

Plates 38 and 39.

Portraits of
Lord and Lady Pirbright
hanging in Lord Pirbright's Hall.

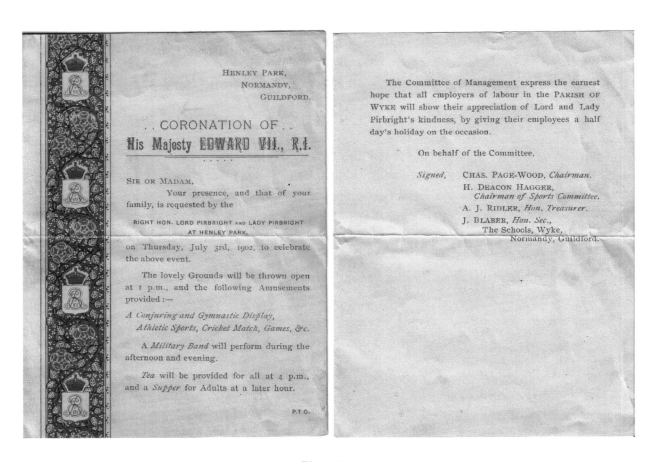

HENLEY PARK,
NORMANDY,
GUILDFORD.

.. CORONATION OF ..
His Majesty EDWARD VII., R.I.
. . . . .

SIR OR MADAM,
Your presence, and that of your
family, is requested by the

RIGHT HON. LORD PIRBRIGHT AND LADY PIRBRIGHT
AT HENLEY PARK,

on Thursday, July 3rd, 1902, to celebrate
the above event.

The lovely Grounds will be thrown open
at 1 p.m., and the following Amusements
provided:—

A Conjuring and Gymnastic Display,
Athletic Sports, Cricket Match, Games, &c.

A *Military Band* will perform during the
afternoon and evening.

Tea will be provided for all at 4 p.m.,
and a *Supper* for Adults at a later hour.

P.T.O.

The Committee of Management express the earnest
hope that all employers of labour in the PARISH OF
WYKE will show their appreciation of Lord and Lady
Pirbright's kindness, by giving their employees a half
day's holiday on the occasion.

On behalf of the Committee.

Signed,   CHAS. PAGE-WOOD, *Chairman.*
H. DEACON HAGGER,
Chairman of Sports Committee.
A. J. RIDLER, *Hon. Treasurer.*
J. BLABER, *Hon. Sec.,*
The Schools, Wyke,
Normandy, Guildford.

Plate 40.
Invitation to an event at Henley Park
to celebrate the coronation of King Edward VII in 1902.

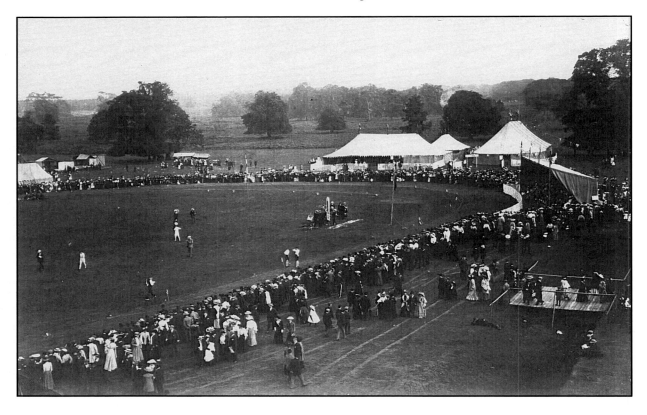

Plate 41. 'Normandy Show'.
A picture postcard believed to be the coronation celebrations
in the fields at Henley Park in 1902.

Plate 42.
'Lord Pirbright's cottages' at numbers 1 to 3 Pirbright Road, Normandy
showing the familiar 'crowned P' motif and the date 1896.

Plate 43.
The gatepost outside one of the villas at Dawney's Hill built by Lord Pirbright.

Plate 44.
The summerhouse at Tumbling Bay as rebuilt by the Moodies.
Lord Pirbright spent many a quiet hour here watching the fish.

Plate 45.
Lord Pirbright's elaborate Grade II-listed tomb in Wyke churchyard.

Plate 46.

Portrait of Sir Owen Roberts
by Herkomer, commissioned
by the Clothworkers' Company.
Now hanging at Plâs Dinas,
the former family home
in north Wales.

Plate 47.

Portrait of Lady Roberts
painted in 1904
by Nora Butson.

Henley Park, East Front.

HENLEY PARK, FROM THE TERRACE.

Plates 48 and 49.
Henley Park before the First World War, on postcards produced by local shopkeeper J Horne:
Top: The front (east face) of the mansion on a summer's day;
the Virginia Creeper appears to be in need of a trim.
Bottom: The back (west face) of the mansion, showing greenhouses on the left
and Lord Pirbright's grand extension on the right.

Plates 50 and 51.
Henley Park before the First World War, on postcards produced by local shopkeeper J Horne:
Top: The south face, Lord Pirbright's extension on the left, Solomon Dayrolle's mansion on the right.
Bottom: 'On the river', on the man-made lake south of the pleasure gardens.

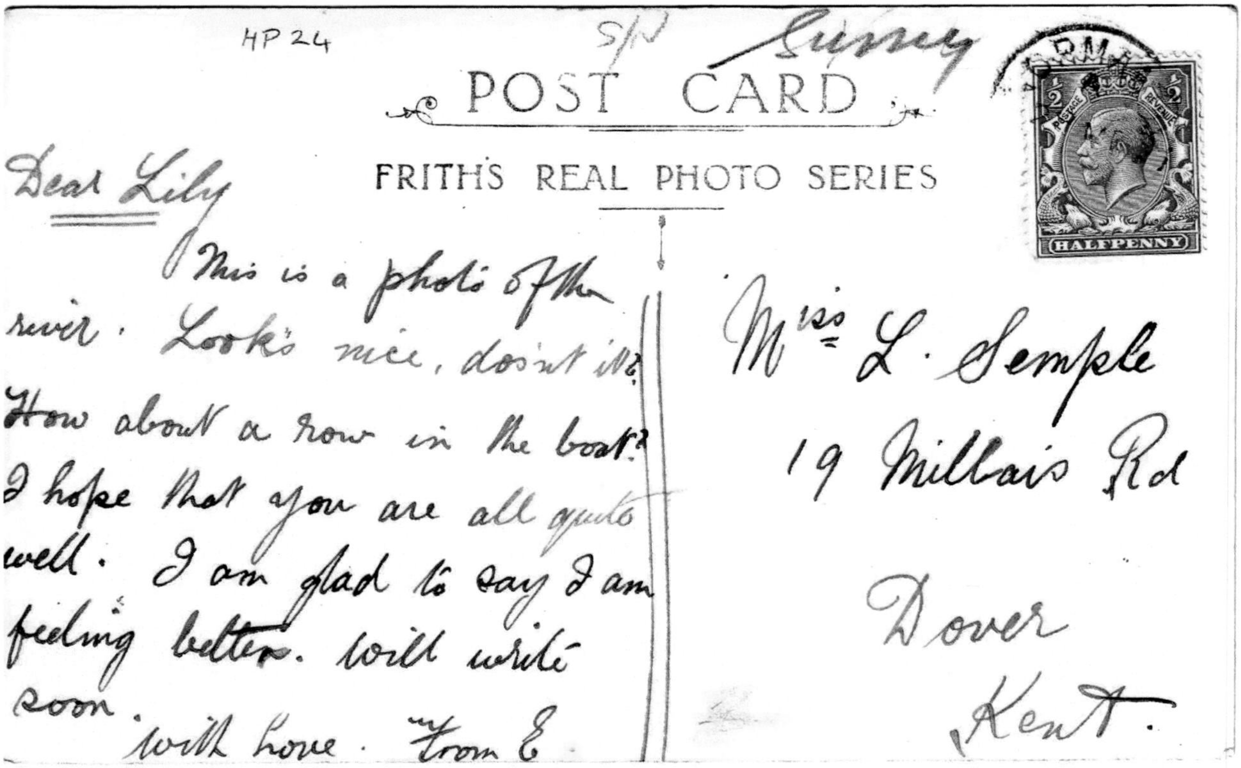

HP 24   S/N   *Surrey*

POST CARD
FRITH'S REAL PHOTO SERIES

Dear Lily

This is a photo of the
river. Looks nice, doesn't it?
How about a row in the boat?
I hope that you are all quite
well. I am glad to say I am
feeling better. Will write
soon. With love. From E

Miss L. Semple
19 Millais Rd
Dover
Kent.

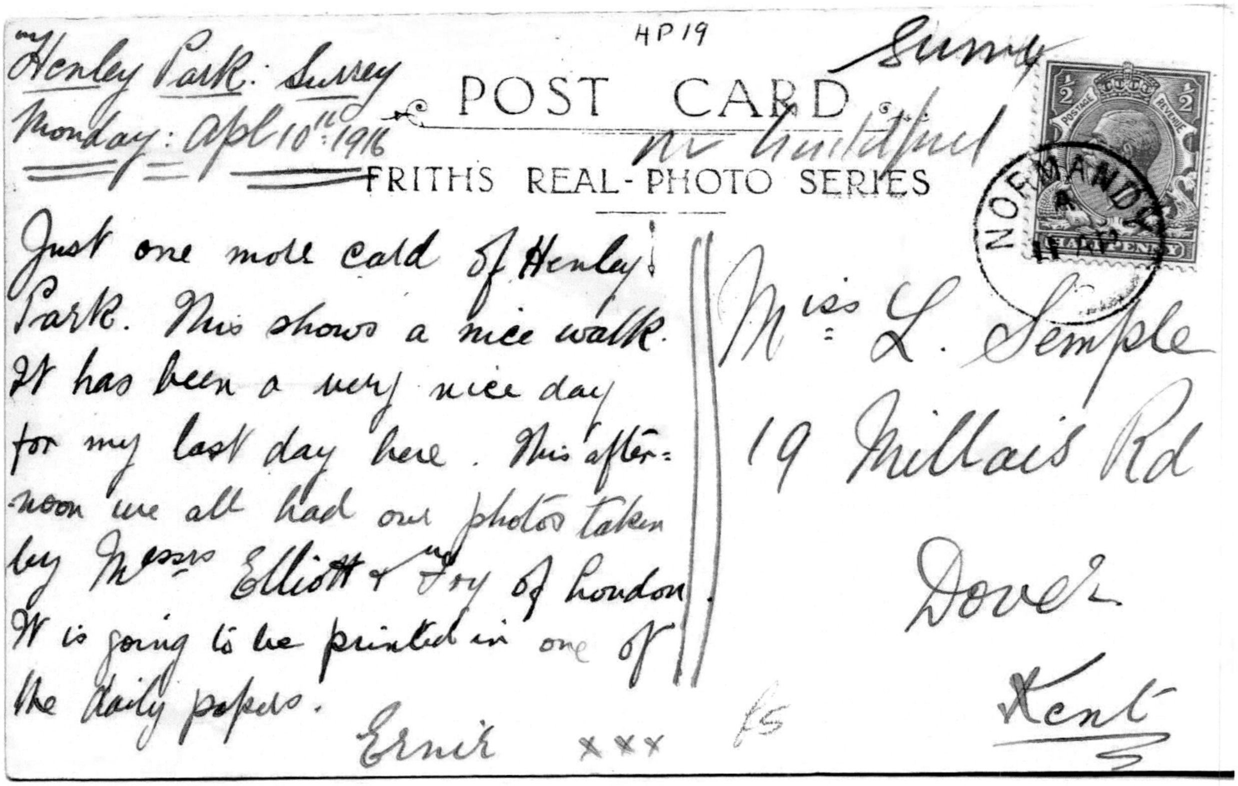

Henley Park: Surrey   HP 19   *Surrey*
Monday: Apl 10th 1916

POST CARD   nr Guildford
FRITH'S REAL-PHOTO SERIES

Just one more card of Henley
Park. This shows a nice walk.
It has been a very nice day
for my last day here. This afternoon we all had our photos taken
by Messrs Elliott & Fry of London.
It is going to be printed in one of
the daily papers.
    Ernie   x x x

Miss L. Semple
19 Millais Rd
Dover
Kent

Plate 52. The soldier's messages.
Postcards from Henley Park Auxiliary Hospital during the First World War.
The first is on the back of 'On the River' (Plate 51)
and the second on the back of 'Henley Park Green Walk' (Plate 72).

Plate 53.
Titled 'Five servant girls in service at Henley Park during the First World War'
in fact this may be a photograph of nurses at the wartime auxiliary hospital.

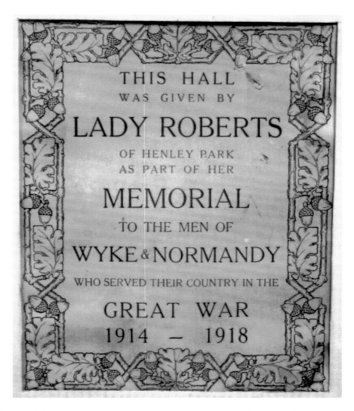

THIS HALL
WAS GIVEN BY
LADY ROBERTS
OF HENLEY PARK
AS PART OF HER
MEMORIAL
TO THE MEN OF
WYKE & NORMANDY
WHO SERVED THEIR COUNTRY IN THE
GREAT WAR
1914 — 1918

Plate 54. Memorial commemorating Lady Roberts' gift of a village hall to Normandy
with the compensation money she received for Henley Park's use as a hospital during the war.

Plates 55 and 56. Inside Henley Park in Lady Roberts' time,
pictures from the estate sale catalogue, 1922:
Top: The Entrance Hall, in the middle of the east front;
the main entrance is off the picture to the right, the door on the left leads through to the dining room.
Bottom: The Finely-proportioned Dining Room, with the bow window in the west façade.

Plates 57 and 58. Pictures from the Henley Park estate sale catalogue, 1922:
Top: The Noble Drawing Room or Saloon; formerly the ballroom in Lord Pirbright's extension.
Bottom: The Handsome Billiard Room; on the first floor over the dining room.

Plate 59 (facing page).

The kitchen gardens and pleasure gardens in a postcard of about 1909.
From left to right: the head gardener's cottage at the bottom of the hill
and the chauffeur's cottage at the top of the hill with smoke issuing from their chimneys,
the palm house, vineries and peach and nectarine houses
and the stable block and coach houses with their bell tower in the centre,
and below them the walled fruit and kitchen garden with its 2-acre orchard
with more greenhouses, a stoke hole, packing and potting shed, mushroom house
and fruit and onion rooms,
and beyond the wall on the right the pleasure gardens with their specimen trees,
behind which rises the mansion itself.

Plate 59a.

A detail of the palm house and the bell tower on the stable block.

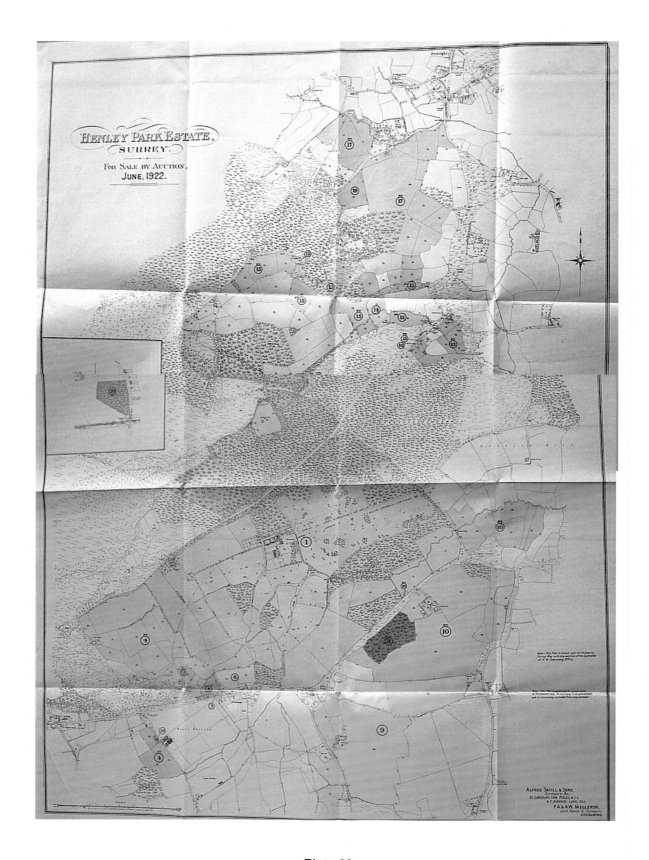

Plate 60.

Map of the lots in the 1922 estate sale
from the sale catalogue.

Plate 61.

Edwin Ramsay Moodie,
the country gentleman.

Plate 62.

Ramsay Moodie and his grandchildren Robin and Serena
outside the front porch at Henley Park in about 1937.

Inside the mansion in the Moodies' time:
Plate 63. The Entrance Hall (compare with plate 55 from the 1922 sale catalogue).

Plate 64.
The Moodies' Library, probably one of the rooms off the Entrance Hall.

Plate 65.
The Morning Room, located in the south-east corner of the mansion, with east and south aspects.

Plate 66.
The Morning Room,
showing the oil painting
in the centre of the ceiling
and the full-length mirror
by the window.

Plate 67.
The Dining Room in the Moodies' time (compare with plate 56 from the 1922 sale catalogue).

Plate 68.
The Saloon, complete with sprung ballroom floor (compare with plate 57).

Plate 69.
Interior hallway, running lengthways through the mansion and linking the two stairways;
looking towards the north with the main stairway just visible on the left.

Plate 70. Deb in the Lily Garden.
Ramsay Moodie added this garden to the grounds of Henley Park
by incorporating a piece of the adjoining field into the pleasure gardens.

Plate 71.
An aerial view of the mansion from the east, looking west.
The façade of the stable block to the right is almost as imposing as the mansion itself in the centre.

Normandy, Henley Park Green Walk

Plate 72.
Henley Park Green Walk;
the three pathways from the
gate on Pirbright Road
leading to the mansion
and the stable block.

Plate 73.
Annotated 'The start for Burley', the family are about to set off on a trip in a selection of vehicles
with their two chauffeurs standing by.

Plate 74.
Henley Park, the family home;
Mike Day and Robin Moodie sailing boats in the swimming pool.

Plate 75.
Henley Park Farm in 1938;
Mr Clark, the Moodies' gamekeeper -
one of his duties was to keep down the moles
and he had killed 95 of them on the estate
in one month.

Plate 76.
Henley Park Farm in 1938; Mr Mullard ploughing with his Suffolk Punches -
he had worked at Henley Park Farm all his life except for the 1914-18 war.

Plate 77.

Mr Cecil Gordon Vokes
in his office at Henley Park,
his desk covered with
papers and 'gadgets'.

Plate 78.

Mr Vokes and Miss Collen
in the 'gun gallery' on the
first-floor landing at Henley Park,
with his collection of
antique firearms.

Plate 79.
Inside the wartime '9X' factory building in the grounds of Henley Park.

Plate 80.
The south lawn in front of
the mansion, ploughed up
for wartime cultivation.

Plate 81.
Vokes Home Guard.

(above) The platoon in front of Henley Park mansion,
with their officer in charge, Lieutenant CG Vokes (centre).

(Below) The plaque on the framed photograph of the Home Guard platoon.

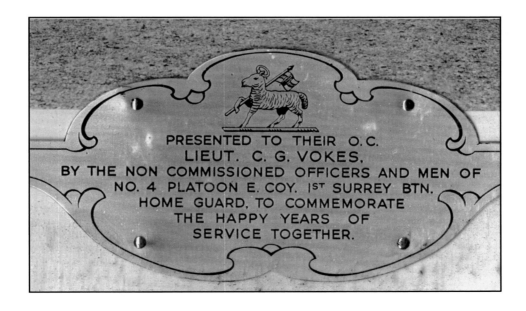

PRESENTED TO THEIR O.C.
LIEUT. C. G. VOKES.
BY THE NON COMMISSIONED OFFICERS AND MEN OF
NO. 4 PLATOON E. COY. 1ST SURREY BTN.
HOME GUARD, TO COMMEMORATE
THE HAPPY YEARS OF
SERVICE TOGETHER.

SUNDAY PICTORIAL

The Happiness of a Thousand Workers Is in the Balance

GET OUT!

Say the Gentry

MORRIS LINDEN REPORTS

Sir Philip Henriques was one of the gentry who found very odd reasons for wanting a factory moved.

YOU have probably never heard of Cecil Gordon Vokes. He is an engineer—secret saviour of our tanks in the desert, rescuer of thousands of RAF lives from the hell of tuberculosis — and now he is himself having the fight of his life.

For years he fought Government departments to accept his inventions—and won. Now he is fighting for himself and for 1,000 workers in an effort to maintain his model factory hidden in the woods of Henley Park, Surrey.

He is fighting men who can best be described as landed gentry. The "county," as these people describe themselves, are against him: the people are for him.

The Ministry of Aircraft Production say that he must be allowed to continue his experiments: the export trade say the same about his products. But

As Sir Philip Henriques, a former chairman of the Surrey County Council (club: Carlton), told me, "Mr. Vokes is paying fantastically high wages. You know, you can't get gardeners, and, if these workpeople stay here, my plum trees will be in danger."

It may seem incredible that views like this can be allowed to hinder an enterprise that was built up out of disaster during the war. But as the facts show that is the exact position today —unless the Government intervenes on behalf of the people

★

AFTER a lifetime of struggle against prejudice the Vokes concern, then a small business specialising in filtering plant, found itself recognised at the beginning of the war as one of the few firms in the whole

Vokes, the key brain of the concern.

And the firm of Vokes, harassed and quite bomb-happy, got out of London.

They found a mansion house at Henley Park, near Guildford. There were barns—and some big copses. It was ideal —and the owner of the estate agreed to sell out, in view, as he said, of the national emergency.

Fair enough. Cecil Vokes, scientist, antiquarian, and a lover of art, began to build low buildings in the heart of the copses. Long an advocate of the model factory, he was determined to build one for himself at last

. . . or series of small

the interested Government and County authorities and that it was recommended that the firm should leave Henley Park within five years.

A gentle murmur of satisfaction went around the council room.

I thought that perhaps the man who lives next door to Henley Park might be prepared to say a good word for this model factory, who lives in a mansion in Normandy Park.

"No, I haven't seen the place since Mr. Vokes took over, and I have no intention of doing so.

"And you know, it is not right that his workers should have lodgings with my cottagers. I've

Plate 82.

There was a lot of opposition to Vokes remaining at Henley Park after the war,
as reported in this *Sunday Pictorial* article. Sir Philip Henriques of nearby Normandy Park stated
that it was impossible to get gardeners because Mr Vokes was paying fantastically high wages
and his plum trees would be in danger!

Plate 83.
Vokes overcame the opposition and their 'new factory' was built at Henley Park by 1954.

Plate 84.

An aerial view of the factory about 1980, showing the newly-built research block between the main factory and the mansion (mid-left) and the remodelled front entrance (centre).

Plates 85 and 86.
Vokes at work and play at Henley Park:
(top) Lord Pirbright's former ballroom in use as the drawing office in 1954...
(bottom) ... and as the works dining room for Christmas lunch in the 1960s or 70s.

Plate 87.

Delivery vans lined up outside
the front of the mansion.
Note the two flagpoles,
one on the roof of the mansion
and a taller one on the lawn.

Plate 88.

The helicopter test.
Tony Vokes (2nd from
left) and Mr CG Vokes
(4th from left) with
ministers and officials at
Westland's.
Tony Vokes'
innovative silencer is
visible attached to the
helicopter.

The test in progress.
Would a civilian helicopter be allowed to fly
so close to the Houses of Parliament today?

Plate 89.
Vokes works outing - a boat trip on the river Thames about 1951/52.
The boy in the foreground is Derek George Crooke, does anyone know who the other people are?

Plate 90.
Vokes had their own ex-Aldershot and District bus, which was used to transport workers
between the factories at Alton and Henley Park.

Plate 91.

The 'House in the Wall'
(former gardener's cottage)
seen in the 1960s
across the staff allotments
(former kitchen garden)
from the gate to
Azalea Walk.

Plate 92.

Fire practice:
Vokes' own fire brigade
practising at Henley Park
in the 1960s.

The mansion in the 1980s, empty and unloved:
Plate 93. The south façade in 1984.

Plate 94. The north-west wing and brick archway.
The archway was the subject of a preservation order
and was re-erected behind the mansion after redevelopment.

Plate 95.

An atmospheric picture of the unused kitchen gardens and empty gardener's cottage in 1986. It is winter and the sun is low in the south-west behind a menacing cloud over Normandy village. The wall below the gardener's cottage is still intact and there is a gateway in it opposite the gate that still exists in the wall on the opposite side of the garden. The formerly cultivated land is a wilderness of scrub and grass.

Plate 96.

Greenhouses and the roof of the south-west wing of the mansion, from inside the derelict gardener's cottage in 1984.

Plates 97 and 98. Aerial views of the mansion in 1986;
from the east (above) showing the factory, and from the west (below).

Signs of decay
inside the mansion
in 1986:

Plate 99.
Damp marks in the ceiling are visible
at the top of one of the staircases.

Plate 100.
Although the plasterwork decoration
remains,
the painting has gone from the
ceiling of the Morning Room
(compare with plate 66).

Rapid decline: Plate 101. In 1986 the mansion was still mostly intact.
The different window styles (18th century 15 panes and 19th century 12 panes) can clearly be seen.

Plate 102. In 1987 the mansion was still intact but many of the windows were boarded up.

Plate 103. But by 1988 the windows, porch and internal fittings had gone.

Plates 104a and b.
The 'glass box' development proposal, approved by the planning committee in 1984. This model created by Manser Associates gives a good impression of how the development would have looked.

The mansion in ruins:
Plate 105. The east façade about 1996.

Plate 106.
The west façade in 1994, showing the effect of the various demolitions -
the dining room and billiard room in the centre, the ballroom to the right
and the old north-west wing to the left.

Plate 107a and b.
The mansion in ruins in 1994; an empty shell supported by scaffolding.
The fireplace in the Entrance Hall (left) and looking up from the Morning Room (right).

Plate 108. The cellars below the former north-west wing.
These were separate from the cellars under the main mansion and did not interconnect.

Plate 109. The remains of one of the fountains in the Lily Garden in 1998
(compare with plate 70 in the garden's heyday).

Plate 110. The broken bridge at Tumbling Bay, at the bottom of the pleasure gardens, in 1994.

HENLEY PARK

A superb development in a wonderful parkland setting

featuring the conversion of an historic mansion building

together with six detached family houses, three mews houses

and two attached cottages.

Plate 111.
At last, in 1998, redevelopment of the mansion got under way and the structure was saved from collapse. This is an excerpt from the glossy sale brochure produced by Browns estate agents.

Plate 112.
The mansion was largely rebuilt, with much of the brickwork being renewed or repointed and a whole
new roof structure except for a single roof truss 'retained as record of the historical structure'.

Plate 113.
The unusual shape
of the window of the
former Breakfast Room
in the north end
of the mansion
was retained.

The beautifully restored
interior of the mansion:

Plate 114.
The former Breakfast Room.

Plate 115.
The entrance hall to Robert Cecil Place.

Plates 116 (above) and 117 (below).

Residents and guests gather at Henley Park
to celebrate the Queen's Diamond Jubilee
in June 2012.

Plate 118.

Modern-day residents of Henley Park
pose for a group photograph
in front of the entrance to the mansion.

Plate 119.
The key to the mansion.
Front door key from the 1970s when the mansion was last occupied prior to redevelopment.

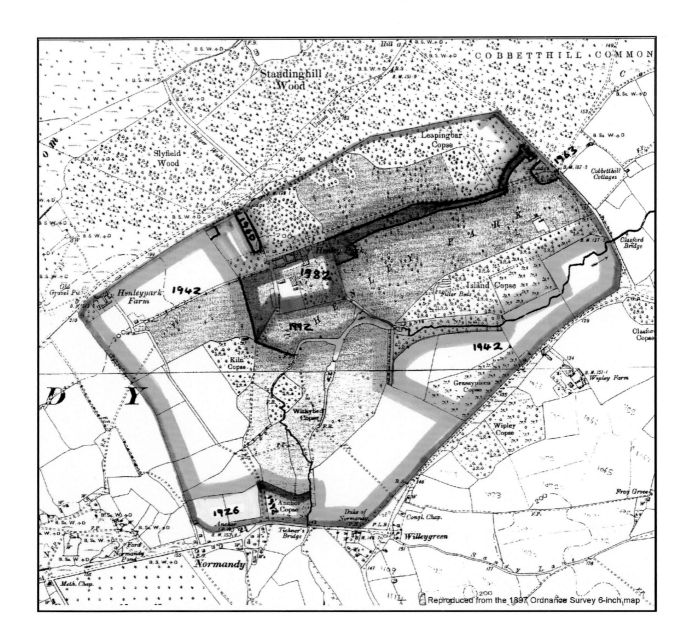

Plate 120.

Final break-up of the royal hunting park enclosed in 1355.
The park remained intact in single ownership until 1926
when the southwest corner was sold to A Wiltshire.
Then over the next 75 years the park was subdivided
into nearly 50 separate freehold properties
(see figure 46).

The boundary of the royal park today:
Plate 121 (above). Looking south from 'Costoll stile' on the west side of the park;
the slight ridge running up to the tree marks the position of the former embankment.
Plate 122 (below). The boundary embankment on the southern edge of the park
between Tickner's bridge and Willey Green.

Plate 123.

A modern photograph of Henley Park from the west
illustrating the ground rising to the 'high clearing'
on the upland ridge.

Figure 25: Inland Revenue; succession duty on real property estate of HWRW Halsey died 7 Oct 1885.

HJT Halsey of Saint Margarets Mansions Westminster Esq (the successor)

		Gross annual value
Estates mentioned in schedule A:	Surrey	£1942 10/-
	Somerset	£1163 1/-
Copse or woodland: 288a 0r 25p in occ. of the successor at Pirbright		£32
and at Yeovil 11a 1r 27p		£2

24 cottages at Pirbright, Ash and Normandy and cottages and land 2a 3r 12p near Henley Park let by lease of 14 Feb 1879 to CD Burnett at £13 per year £134

Cottage & land at Chilthorne Somerset £4

Rent charges in lieu of tithes:	Woking	299 14/6	
	Pirbright	217 3/3	
	Yeovil	373 11/3	
	Ilchester	7 10/6	
		897 19/6	
	average for three years of tithe received		£846 3/2

House No. 11 The Circus Bath sold to Mr Morris for £2,000. The purchase money was received by the trustees on 19 May 1886 £80

Interest of the successor as lord of the manors of

Pirbright, Surrey, assessed to property tax at	£57
Rectory of Woking, Surrey	£3 11/2
Henley, Surrey	—
(Two manors in Somerset)	—
The successor's right of donation to the curacy of Pirbright	£344 15/-
Total:	£4609 -/4

<u>Schedule A.</u> Dutiable properties

(22 properties in Surrey and several in Somersetshire listed).

<u>Schedule B.</u> Deductions against duty

Jointure rent charge of £200 p/a created by deed of 11 March 1835 in favour of Caroline Halsey [added: died Oct 1886] commencing 7 Oct 1885 payable during her life, charged on the estates devised by will dated 17 Apr 1807 of Henry Halsey who died 26 June 1807 (excepting Henley Park mansion and lands, right of donation to curacy of Pirbright, Manor of the Rectory of Woking and the Somersetshire estates and tithes) £200

Earl Sandwich's fee farm rent payable to the manor of Henley in respect of Henley Park Surrey £10 and acquitance 1s 4d, less land tax £1 £9 1/4

Figure 25: Inland Revenue; succession duty (continued).

Quit rent payable in respect of property held of Worplesdon Manor	£1 5/-	
Earl Onslow quit rent in respect of property held of Bisley Manor	3/10	
Earl Onslow quit rent in respect of property held of Woking Manor	£17 5/8	
Quit rent in respect of property held of Cleygate Manor	18/1	
Duchy of Cornwall rent payable in Stoke under Hambden, Somerset	£7 7/-	
Sir J Barthursts fee farm rent in respect of Chilton Vagg, Somersetshire	£2 10/-	
	Total	£238 10/11

Schedule C. Land Tax

Pirbright	(12 properties listed)	£28 10/9	
Bisley	James Mitchell	£1 9/3	
Chobham	James Mitchell	15/-	
Ash	Shadrack Mayhew	4/6	
Pirbright	RL Mangles	£6 12/5	
Woking		£3 3/2	
	Total	£40 17/1	

Schedule D.   Rates

Ash	Poor rate	£7 3/4	
	Tithe		
Worplesdon	Poor rate	16/6	
Woking	Poor rate	£31 -/8	
Pirbright		£36 6/6	
	Total	£75 4/-	
Yeovil, Chilthorne, Ilchester & Longport, Somerset		£48 17/10	
		£124 1/10	

Schedule E. Capital

3% Consols		£526 4/7	
Enfranchisement of copyholds, Pirbright (2)		£134 18/2	
Tithe redemption	Woking	£3 1/1	
	Yeovil (4)	£36 18/-	
	Total	£701 1/10	
More 3% Consols		£10,790 12/5	
	Total	£11,491 14/3	Income - £344 15/-

Back page:

Total gross annual value	£4609 -/4	
Deductions	£701 19/9	
Net annual value	£3907 -/7	

Signed by HJT Halsey.

8. LORD AND LADY PIRBRIGHT (1889-1914)

The next tenant of Henley Park after Charles Burnett was Henry de Worms, Baron of the Austrian Empire, Member of Parliament, Deputy Lieutenant for Middlesex, Undersecretary of State for the Colonies and Barrister (not practising), as he styled himself in the 1891 census. Better known to posterity as Lord Pirbright, the title he chose on being ennobled in 1895, he had a clear view of his own self importance and although he lived at Henley Park for only 12 years from 1890 until his death in 1903, he made a great impact on both the fabric of the house and on the local community.

Background and family

Baron de Worms was descended from Benedict Moses Worms, his grandfather having married a daughter of the Rothschilds, a family that rose from obscurity to become the richest in modern Europe. When Benedict married Jeanette, the daughter of Mayer Amschel von Rothschild in 1795, Mayer had already risen from running a second-hand shop with his brothers in an alley in the Jewish ghetto of Frankfurt, in one of the many princedoms that comprised what is now Germany, to become the unofficial financier of the head of state and most importantly, to have raised five sons who would come to control much of the finance of Europe and wield more power than the kings and emperors who entrusted them with their money. Without anybody noticing, by 1800 the energy and mobility of the Rothschild boys made them indispensable as bankers to the courts of Europe, even though they were still chained into the ghetto at night. The Battle of Waterloo established England as the foremost European power and it also established the Rothschilds as the foremost world financiers. By dint of their superb communications network they knew the outcome of the battle hours before anyone else in England - and a few hours was all it took to manipulate the stock market to make an unimaginable fortune. Throughout the next hundred years the Rothschilds confined the key positions in their empire to their sons and rigidly excluded the female line, so Benedict Worms and his family had to succeed in their own right. His sons came to England from Frankfurt and became coffee-traders, owning an extensive plantation in Ceylon. The third son, Solomon, was head of the family's City-based firm of bankers and colonial merchants, and was created an hereditary baron of the Austrian Empire. In 1874 Queen Victoria granted permission for him to use the title in England, in recognition of the family's services in developing the industry of Ceylon.

Solomon's third son Henry was born in London on 20 October 1840 and trained in the Law. He was both physically fit, being a proficient boxer, and intellectually active, writing book reviews for 'Punch' magazine and filing patents, for example for 'improvements in apparatus for elevating guns'. Baron de Worms entered politics and was elected at the third attempt, as the Conservative member for Greenwich. In due course he was appointed as Parliamentary Secretary to the Board of Trade and then Under-Secretary for the Colonies, and about the same time he became the first Jew to be appointed to Her Majesty's Privy Council. He had considerable talent as an orator and charmed everyone he met, although it was reported that the commitments he made were not always fulfilled. On reflection many felt that his abilities were brilliant rather than solid, and he was never seen as a great statesman. A pattern emerges of bitter disputes with those close to him, including his election agent in Greenwich and his first wife, Fanny von Todesco of Vienna, from whom he lived apart for many years and was divorced in 1887; and eventually the entire Jewish community, as we shall see later.

Unlike most of his predecessors at Henley Park, when he was embarking upon a second marriage Baron de Worms did not marry a younger woman who could continue to give him heirs. Perhaps he chose instead for status or wealth, marrying in 1887 Sarah, the daughter of Sir Benjamin Samuel Phillips a magistrate and former Lord Mayor of London, who was a widow and two years his senior, and they had no children.

A demanding tenant

It appears that Henry Joseph Halsey did not reduce the rent for Henley Park when Charles Burnett asked him to in 1886 because within a few years the Burnetts had left, so he had to find another tenant. In the end he agreed a price that was significantly lower than the rent the Burnetts had been paying, and on 25 December 1889 Lord Pirbright leased the estate for 28 years at an annual rent of £378.

He was clearly a demanding tenant. He apparently took up residence at the beginning of 1890 but before he would agree to complete the lease he insisted that his landlord had to lay on mains water to the mansion, and in January 1890 Halsey contracted with the Woking Water and Gas Company to establish an extension of the water main up to the Pirbright parish boundary nearest to Henley Park mansion, at a cost of £500. The remaining 1,000 yards up to the mansion was estimated to cost £175 and a considerable amount of work was required inside the mansion itself, estimated at another £175. Thus the total estimate was £850, but of course by the time the works were completed in March 1891 the total cost had risen to £917 16s 2d. Some things never change!

The mains water supply superseded use of the well located within the walled garden to the north-east of the mansion. The well, which was 4 or 5 feet in diameter, survived until around 1950 when Vokes filled it in for safety reasons.

Possibly in connection with these works, some new filter beds (a sewage works) had been constructed by 1895 down the hill to the south-east of the mansion. Soon afterwards a group of ditches or 'moats' were constructed just below the filter beds and linked to them by run-off channels. These ditches in the Island Copse site, forming two islands plus an extended western channel, have been suggested as the location of the medieval manor complex but they have been generally ruled out as being too small to accommodate the extensive buildings described in the records, and are of comparatively recent origin based on the evidence of Ordnance Survey maps.

As well as running water Lord Pirbright may also have insisted on the latest up-to-date electric lighting. In the 1870s Henley Park was probably lit by producer gas and there was a gas works in the grounds just to the west of the stable block. By 1891 this had been replaced by a 13 horse-power steam engine driving a generator charging a battery of 54 cells in the outbuildings, operated by James Marshall, an 'electric light engine driver' who lived at Dolley's

Hill. Despite the power of these modern contrivances, if a light was accidentally left on all night there would be no electricity in the morning because the batteries were flat.

Lord Pirbright finally signed the lease for Henley Park on 7 December 1891. Attached to the lease is a very comprehensive inventory of the fixtures and fittings in the property, from which it emerges that everything in the mansion was not in best condition - in the Billiard Room the iron stove was in a sculpted white marble mantel piece and surround which was 'cracked and chipped', in one of the bedrooms was a 4 foot 9 inch by 1 ft 9 in mirror with 'defective silvering' and in one of the attic rooms was a 'defective' 17 inch Oxford stove. Perhaps this is why he got Henley Park at such a favourable rent. It appears that his lease included many of the farms on the Halsey estates, including Rails Farm in Pirbright which he sub-let to J Tucker in 1893 for £75 per annum.

Although he was only a tenant, he certainly acted as if he owned the place. Indeed some local residents thought he did, and referred to him as the 'lord of the manor', which he probably did nothing to discourage. One of his older brothers lived at Thorpe Park and was lord of the manor there, and Lord Pirbright possibly yearned to have the same status, but he never achieved it.

Some major enhancements were carried out at Henley Park in the first few years of his tenure, which he apparently paid for himself because there is no record of the expenditure in the Halsey papers. In 1893 he received a large inheritance from his maternal uncle Mr George Samuel, and it may have been these funds that enabled him to perform such extensive works. By 1895 he had built the two-storey 'Victorian' extension, extending west on the southern side, turning the mansion into an 'L'-shape and giving it an imposing new southern façade overlooking the gardens sloping down towards Normandy village. On its ground floor was a fine ballroom nearly 50 feet long by 26 feet wide with a fully sprung floor, which was used as the state salon for royal visits. It was designed by Lady Pirbright and was hung with some splendid old tapestries. Above it was the suite of two bedrooms, a boudoir and a bathroom that was occupied by the Prince of Wales on his visits. Lord Pirbright also radically enlarged the dining room by adding a semicircular front in the middle of the western façade and raising the ceiling to add height to the room. He obviously wanted to create the right sort of setting for his fabulous collection of art treasures - the house was described in one magazine as a regular museum of beautiful and valuable things.

By 1913 the rental value of the property was assessed at £575 per year, an increase of more than half the price that Lord Pirbright was paying, probably because of his extensive enhancements to the property. These additional wings were demolished in the 1980s during one of the abortive attempts at redevelopment.

The pleasure gardens below the mansion were also considerably extended by 1895 and laid out with rockeries, a rose garden and ornamental walks. Many believe that Lord Pirbright created the boating lake by damming the little stream that flows through the fields below the mansion, but in fact he probably resurrected a feature created earlier by the Halseys. There was a boat house beside it and a summerhouse on the island in the lake. He may well have restored the boat house and created some new features downstream of the boating lake, which appeared between 1871 and 1895 according to the Ordnance Survey. The stream goes on to flow over 'Tumbling Bay', an ornamental waterfall made of Cumberland stone, and under another bridge. Between 1895 and 1912 the path was further extended around and beyond Tumbling Bay and another footbridge was

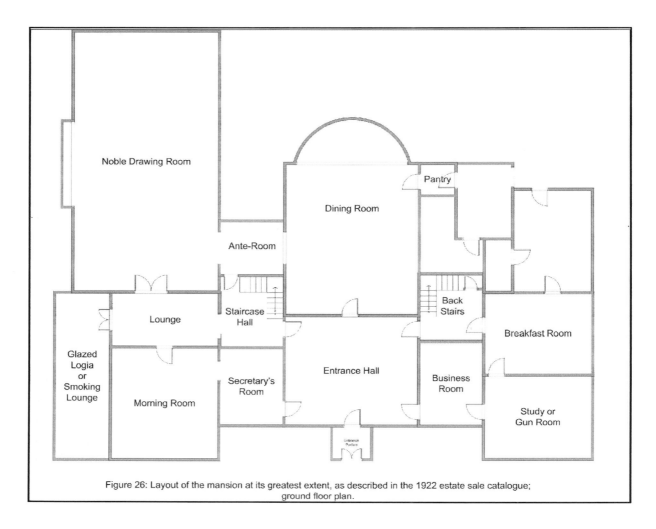

Figure 26: Layout of the mansion at its greatest extent, as described in the 1922 estate sale catalogue; ground floor plan.

Within the image, the following labels appear:

Noble Drawing Room

Pantry

Dining Room

Ante-Room

Lounge

Staircase Hall

Back Stairs

Breakfast Room

Glazed Logia or Smoking Lounge

Secretary's Room

Entrance Hall

Business Room

Morning Room

Study or Gun Room

Entrance Porch

created. The paths were all paved with York stone and there was another wooden summerhouse on the south side of the waterfall (see Plate 44). The pool was always well stocked with goldfish and Lord Pirbright was seen spending many a quiet hour watching them swim among the water ferns and lily pads. Sarah, Lady Pirbright, appears to have been very keen on horticulture and there were a number of greenhouses in the grounds, including some fine orchid houses. During royal visits the house was lavishly decorated with floral displays including numerous orchids.

There is a story that Lord Pirbright created the island in the top lake north of Pirbright Road. In the particularly severe winter of 1898 the lake froze over and Lord Pirbright had his labourers dig soil and take it onto the lake and pile it up, where it formed the island when the ice melted. They worked on it for several weeks, and there is still a big dip in the ground on the east side of the lake where they are said to have dug out the soil.

Lord and Lady Pirbright may have created one of the best-known features of Henley Park's grounds, the Chinese Bridge in the fields below the mansion towards Normandy. The origin of the name of this bridge is unclear, but a resident of Normandy remembers it being known as 'Cheyney's Bridge' just after the First World War, and there was a bricklayer and builder called Charles Cheyney working in south and west London at this time, so a less romantic interpretation is simply that Cheyney's Bridge became corrupted to its present form as the memory of Mr Cheyney faded.

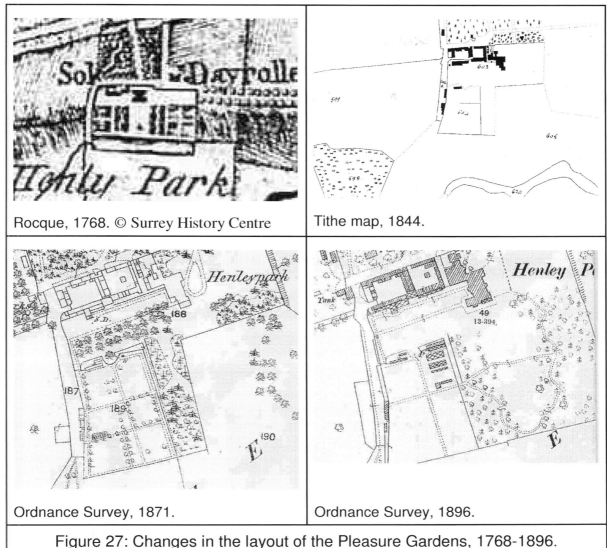

Rocque, 1768. © Surrey History Centre	Tithe map, 1844.
Ordnance Survey, 1871.	Ordnance Survey, 1896.

Figure 27: Changes in the layout of the Pleasure Gardens, 1768-1896.

There used to be four bee-boles (artificial bee-hives) in the wall bounding the west gardens of the mansion, 20 yards up from the gateway into the walled garden. In 1896 William Albert Woods established his building and apiary firm at The Firs on Pirbright Road and it is interesting to speculate whether the bee-boles were built by him during Lord Pirbright's improvements to the property. One was still there, well hidden in the ivy, in the 1980s but sadly it appears to have been destroyed during the recent renovations.

Lived like a lord

Lord Pirbright certainly lived like a lord and went to great lengths to impress his visitors and friends. He liked to move in exalted circles, he entertained royally and he entertained royalty. He managed to get himself mentioned in the newspapers several times, with reports of 'lavish hospitality' at Henley Park. Even when he was not entertaining he had a full complement of servants in the house - a butler, a cook, two housemaids, a kitchenmaid, a scullerymaid, two footmen and a lady's maid. The stillroom maid was responsible for bread, cakes and biscuits.

There were nine indoor servants resident, and this may have been limited more by the fact that there were nine servants' bedrooms on the top floor rather than Lord Pirbright's capacity to find work for them. There were also a gamekeeper and two gardeners resident in the grounds, and there were estate carpenters and bricklayers to look after the fabric of the property, as well as grooms to attend the six black horses that pulled Lord Pirbright's four carriages.

In the 19th century Henley Park typically had 10 to 12 indoor servants (an aristocrat's household might have up to 24). The essence of the whole country house system was hierarchy, it was built into the fabric of the servants' work situation. Footmen worked up to 16 hours a day and their job was infinitely varied, combining elements of display and drudgery, from accompanying the master's carriage wearing distinctive livery to cleaning and carrying. There was a huge amount of walking, often up and down stairs, and one footman recorded walking a distance of 18 miles in a day during the London season. Housemaids had a daily timetable of tasks, mainly cleaning and sewing and mending. Extra help was brought in for spring cleaning which lasted about a fortnight in May when no more fires would be needed. Washmaids did the heavy washing and laundrymaids were personal body servants who washed, starched and ironed small items. Infrequent washing was a status symbol showing that you were rich enough to accumulate large reserves of linen. Many country houses were unwilling to 'contract out' to commercial laundries because of the ever-present threat of disease being spread by damp laundered clothes.

Lord Pirbright entertained many distinguished visitors at Henley Park, especially during the shooting season. He occupied 173 acres altogether, with the mansion, home farm, orchard and garden occupying 130 acres plus 43 acres of shooting at Standing Hill. But this was not enough for him, because in 1892 and 1893 he leased the rights to shoot game, rabbits and wildfowl on Littlefield, Clasford, Rickford, Broad Street and other commons in Worplesdon from the Earl of Onslow.

During his tenancy the estate was visited on several occasions by royalty. Three of Queen Victoria's children were his guests: Edward Prince of Wales, Arthur Duke of Connaught and Helena, Princess Christian of Schleswig-Holstein, as well as Prince George, Duke of Cambridge. Two large trees in the gardens used to bear plaques commemorating their planting by royalty, a Wellingtonia and a Cedar planted by HRH the Duke of Connaught. A fir tree to the right of the entrance to the mansion forecourt was planted in 1900 by HRH the Prince of Wales, later King Edward VII, who attended the shooting parties at Henley Park several times. Lord and Lady Pirbright were described as being 'fond of sport of every kind' and entered fully into the country sporting life. In December 1895 the Duke of Connaught and the Infanta of Spain were their guests and the shooting was described as excellent. In the same month the Ripley and Knaphill Harriers met at Henley Park (see Plate 35) and other hunts were pictured there at different times. Lord Pirbright was both an expert fisherman and a capital shot, and he strictly 'preserved' the fishing and shooting on his lands.

A story concerning the Duke of Cambridge was told to SPB Mais when he came to Normandy in 1938 researching a radio broadcast on William Cobbett. The old duke came over for a big shoot when there was a great scarcity of pheasants and got more and more peevish until at last he blurted out loudly and tactlessly "there's none but poachers in Normandy!" Whereupon one of the beaters leapt forward to knock him off his horse, duke or no duke, and it took three people to hold him back. The shooting parties were colourful occasions long remembered by the local inhabitants who took part in them. Each of the noble guests was accompanied by an expert loader and a local man to carry the heavy bag of cartridges. The carrier was paid five shillings a day, and was generally selected by the gamekeeper based on 'favours' bestowed in the local pub. The 'beaters' were paid two shillings a day and normally wore white smocks so that they were clearly visible to guard against over-zealous marksmen. Some of the beaters were local boys to whom two shillings was a fortune. At lunchtime the helpers received bowls of hot stew, bread and cheese at the Henley Park kitchen while the gentlemen were being entertained to lunch in the house. To preserve some of the catch for the summer months, Lord Pirbright had a brick ice house built into the side of a small hill to the north-east of the house, and it was the job of the estate workers to cut ice from the river in the winter and pack it into the ice-house. The small hill is still there.

In the warmer months Henley Park lake often echoed to the gay laughter and revelry of midnight parties held in the summerhouse on the island in the lake. Four boats were always at the disposal of the guests to convey them across the water. He is said to have had 'his own private cricket ground' where he entertained some of the big cricket sides from time to time.

Lord Pirbright laid on elaborate celebrations at Henley Park on the occasion of the coronation of the Prince of Wales as King Edward VII in 1902, with athletic sports, a military band and a conjuring and gymnastic display, all held in the grounds between the mansion and Cobbett Hill Road (see Plate 41). Tea was provided for adults and children at 4pm and supper for the adults later. The celebrations management committee expressed the wish that all employers of labour should show their appreciation to Lord and Lady Pirbright by giving their employees a half day's holiday for the occasion. The Prince of Wales was a friend of theirs and Henley Park was one of the places he liked to visit, supposedly being elegant enough for royalty and discreet enough for him to entertain his lady friends. The story goes that at the end of one particular stay the Prince clapped Baron de Worms on the back and said "I have had a wonderful week - what would you like to be?" and he replied on the spur of the moment "Lord Pirbright".

He was created Baron Pirbright on 15 November 1895, but the title existed for less than eight years. Although it was an hereditary peerage it could only be transmitted in the male line and Lord Pirbright had only daughters, so it died with him in 1903.

Properties in Pirbright

Lord Pirbright also put much of his considerable wealth into buying and building houses. He believed that the provision of 'wholesome dwellings' with good sanitation would encourage people to return to the villages from the slums of industrial cities, which would bring prosperity to the countryside and combat the depression in agriculture. The cottages that he built locally were substantial and well-appointed. 'Lord Pirbright's Cottages' are a distinctive and familiar feature of Pirbright and parts of Normandy and his obituary stated that he 'has made Pirbright what it is'. These cottages, with their familiar crowned 'P' motifs on the walls or chimney stacks (see Plate 42), line many of the roads around Pirbright - along The Terrace on Guildford Road leading south from the green, taking up the length of The Gardens north of the green, a group at Fox Corner, the row of Stanford Cottages by the Royal Oak and several along Pirbright Road in Normandy. The cottages at Fox Corner were described in the 1910 valuation survey as having 'good sized rooms' with mains water and 'nice gardens'. Several of his developments included shops, with two in The Terrace and 'the Old Post House' at Fox Corner.

And there could easily have been many more - Lord Pirbright bought several other pieces of land which he may have intended to develop, including 15-acre Chandler's Field behind The Old Homestead at Willey Green, the 2-acre field at Stanford Farm behind Stanford Cottages, the 9-acre Nursery in Pirbright, Throat Moor in Pirbright and Stream House Farm. In 1896 he bought Vine Farm for £500 and The Glen for £425, both on Pirbright Road near Henley Park. These were all smallholdings rather than substantial farms and there is no indication that he planned to use them for agricultural purposes, but if he did intend to build housing estates on these properties he apparently died before his plans could be realised.

He bought or built several substantial villa properties as well, presumably as investments and to increase his presence and influence in the area. These included Connemara, formerly Suffolk House, on Pirbright Green, Pine House at Cooks Green and the four large semi-detached houses at Dawney's Hill in Pirbright, which were 5-bedroom villas 'in a fine position overlooking the common'. He built the substantial Gorselands in a two-acre plot on Newbridge Common as a lodge for his estate manager and before she died Lady Pirbright gave it to her former head gardener, John Bluck. In addition Lord Pirbright purchased the Manor House in Normandy, probably when it was offered for sale at the Normandy Manor estate sale in 1895. Possibly he was disillusioned when he found out that it had never been a real manor house and he advertised it for sale again in The Times in 1902, but it was still owned by Lady Pirbright when she died 12 years later.

Lord Pirbright also bought several old cottages and shops in Pirbright, including Baker's Cottage, a shop and bakehouse on the west side of the Green, a cottage on the south side of the green, part of which became Fulks butchers and onto which he built a large shop with an elaborate frontage facing the pond, still known as the Shop on the Green, and the nearby row of 'Henry Cottages', two of which became the Post Office and ultimately the Parish Shop.

His most incomprehensible purchase was the residue of a thousand-year lease of Normandy Pond, which he probably bought at the Normandy Manor estate sale in 1895, when the pond had an inlet and outlet and was stocked with several kinds of fish. He sold it in 1901 to the War Department (subsequently the Ministry of Defence) who owned all the surrounding common land as lords of the manor of Cleygate.

Involvement with Pirbright community

All this building activity not only changed the appearance of Pirbright but also the mix of its population. In the preceding ten years the population only increased slightly but from 1891 to 1901 it jumped by 450 and many of these people would have been Lord Pirbright's new tenants. The people who lived in his newly-built cottages were predominantly working men and women - labourers, plasterers, plumbers, bricklayers, carters, charwomen and a 'cemetery carman', as well as three tradesmen, four professionals and 11 'retired' people of whom seven were widows. The great majority of the occupants of these cottages were new to Pirbright; of the 51 householders listed in the census only 5 were born in Pirbright, 14 in Surrey and 32 came from various other counties. Many of them had been in Pirbright for less than five years, so it appears that the new cottages attracted people from outside the parish rather than local folk. A handful were from

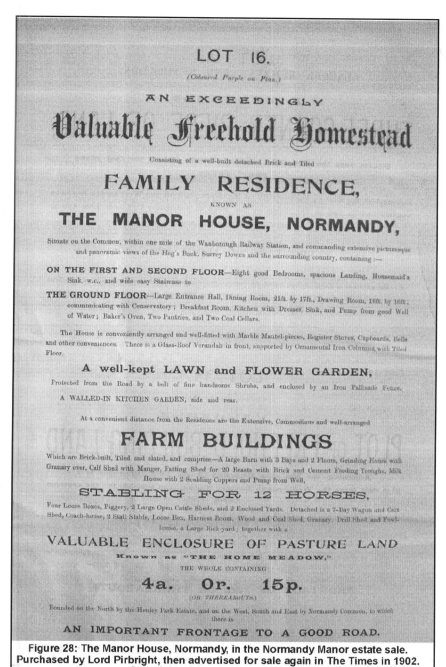

LOT 16.

(Coloured Purple on Plan.)

AN EXCEEDINGLY

Valuable Freehold Homestead

Consisting of a well-built detached Brick and Tiled

FAMILY RESIDENCE,

KNOWN AS

THE MANOR HOUSE, NORMANDY,

Situate on the Common, within one mile of the Wanborough Railway Station, and commanding extensive picturesque and panoramic views of the Hog's Back, Surrey Downs and the surrounding country, containing :—

ON THE FIRST AND SECOND FLOOR—Eight good Bedrooms, spacious Landing, Housemaid's Sink, w.c., and wide easy Staircase to

THE GROUND FLOOR—Large Entrance Hall, Dining Room, 21ft. by 17ft., Drawing Room, 16ft. by 16ft., communicating with Conservatory ; Breakfast Room, Kitchen with Dresser, Sink, and Pump from good Well of Water; Baker's Oven, Two Pantries, and Two Coal Cellars.

The House is conveniently arranged and well-fitted with Marble Mantel-pieces, Register Stoves, Cupboards, Bells and other conveniences. There is a Glass-Roof Verandah in front, supported by Ornamental Iron Columns, with Tiled Floor.

A well-kept LAWN and FLOWER GARDEN,

Protected from the Road by a belt of fine handsome Shrubs, and enclosed by an Iron Palisade Fence.

A WALLED-IN KITCHEN GARDEN, side and rear.

At a convenient distance from the Residence are the Extensive, Commodious and well-arranged

FARM BUILDINGS

Which are Brick-built, Tiled, and slated, and comprise—A large Barn with 3 Bays and 2 Floors, Grinding House with Granary over, Calf Shed with Manger, Fatting Shed for 20 Beasts with Brick and Cement Feeding Troughs, Milk House with 2 Scalding Coppers and Pump from Well,

STABLING FOR 12 HORSES,

Four Loose Boxes, Piggery, 2 Large Open Cattle Sheds, and 2 Enclosed Yards. Detached is a 7-Bay Wagon and Cart Shed, Coach-house, 2 Stall Stable, Loose Box, Harness Room, Wood and Coal Shed, Granary, Drill Shed and Fowl-house, a Large Rick-yard; together with a

VALUABLE ENCLOSURE OF PASTURE LAND

KNOWN AS "THE HOME MEADOW,"

THE WHOLE CONTAINING

4a. 0r. 15p.

(OR THEREABOUTS)

Bounded on the North by the Henley Park Estate, and on the West, South and East by Normandy Common, to which there is

AN IMPORTANT FRONTAGE TO A GOOD ROAD.

Figure 28: The Manor House, Normandy, in the Normandy Manor estate sale. Purchased by Lord Pirbright, then advertised for sale again in The Times in 1902. Copyright of Surrey History Centre.

London, perhaps in a small way fulfilling his dream of giving people a chance to leave the urban slums.

Lord and Lady Pirbright did much for the village of Pirbright and they were very popular with the people there. They gave a new organ to the church, repaired the belfry and had the bells re-hung in 1895 at a cost exceeding £500. For Queen Victoria's Diamond Jubilee in 1897 there was no need for a fundraising committee as there had been for her Golden Jubilee, because Lord Pirbright covered all the expense. The whole population of the village sat down to lunch in a huge marquee on the green and every adult received a silver medal struck for the occasion, while the children were given a 'less expensive medal'. The cricket team were given new caps in yellow and blue. There was an elaborate programme of sports in the afternoon, from a 50 yards infant race to the '100 yards old man's race' for the over 60s, as well as obstacle, egg and spoon and hurdle races and a ten-man a side tug of war between Pirbright and Bisley which Pirbright won. Tea, dancing and a fair with shooting galleries followed. On this occasion Lord Pirbright also presented the handsome drinking fountain (human and canine) which stands on the village green at the corner of the hall. Lady Pirbright was very keen on promoting education for poor children, hence the statue on the fountain is of a girl reading a book. The fountain's location was carefully chosen in two ways; firstly, it was placed where all the children passed on their way to school and additionally it was placed exactly on the corner of the freehold property on the green which Lord Pirbright owned.

When Pirbright Parish Council was formed in 1895 under the Local Government Act of 1894, Lord Pirbright who was present at its first meeting in person was unanimously elected as its chairman, although he did not expect that the Council would 'undertake any very serious responsibilities' at this early stage of the operation of the Act. He often paid personally to defray the expenses of the Council, for example providing equipment for the fire brigade.

The relationship between the new Parish Council and the 'old order' represented by the lord of the manor was an uneasy one. They came into conflict less than 18 months after the Council was formed, over who had the right to control the village green. The Council believed the Act of Parliament gave them complete control over the green as a public open space, but first Edward J Halsey as a trustee of the lord of the manor (Henry Joseph Halsey) and then Bircham and Co the Halseys' solicitors, wrote to the Council stating that it was not a village green but formed part of the 'waste' of the manor and as such the lord of the manor had control of it. The parties appealed to the Local Government Board but they in turn found themselves unable to make a decision in the matter and rather unhelpfully suggested that the Council should obtain a lease of the land from the War Department. This issue was still unresolved when the next dispute blew up, but here the Halseys made a mistake. They claimed that Lord Pirbright's fountain had been put up on the waste of the manor without a licence, but Lord Pirbright was able to triumphantly reply that the fountain was on his freehold property and Messrs Bircham had to express their regret that they had been misinformed. Chastened, the manorial trustees soon reached a compromise agreement about the village green and the matter died away.

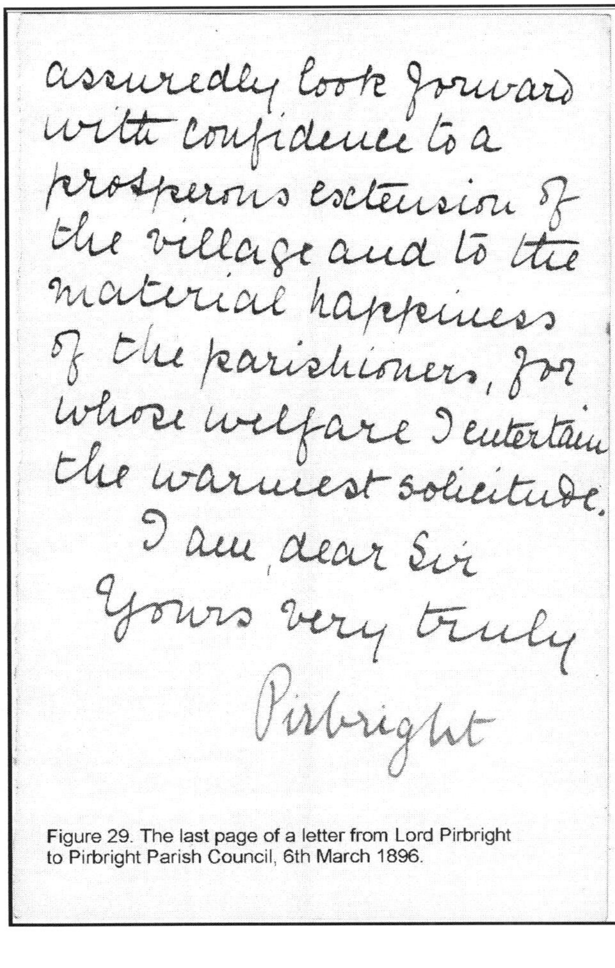
assuredly look forward with confidence to a prosperous extension of the village and to the material happiness of the parishioners, for whose welfare I entertain the warmest solicitude.

I am, dear Sir
Yours very truly
Pirbright

Figure 29. The last page of a letter from Lord Pirbright to Pirbright Parish Council, 6th March 1896.

On several occasions Lord and Lady Pirbright laid on entertainment and festivities for the villagers, and also performed many unostentatious acts of relief for the suffering and the poor. He was a favourite of the younger generation because he would throw pennies to the children as he drove past in the first motor car ever seen in the village. Further afield they donated cups and prizes on several occasions for annual athletic club meetings and were lavish supporters of hospitals and children's charities and performed many opening ceremonies. Lord Pirbright was vice president of the Royal Surrey County Hospital and a generous contributor to its funds. They took a leading part in arranging for 'comforts and necessaries' to be sent to the troops when the South African War broke out in 1899, and they were generous contributors to the various patriotic funds. They presented land at Bisley for homes for disabled soldiers and sailors, and they presented land in Pirbright for a new village school.

But Lord Pirbright's life displays a pattern of bitter and acrimonious disputes, and this came home to Pirbright over the apparently innocent subject of a children's Christmas party. Back in 1885, the management of the local school had been transferred from the care of the Church of England 'National Society' to a board constituted under the Government's Department of Education. Although the National Society technically retained ownership of the premises and the right to use it outside school hours, the old management board under the chairmanship of the local vicar became defunct and did not meet again, while the running of the school was taken over by a newly elected School Board. Nobody gave this a second thought until the Reverend Arthur Krauss took over as the vicar of Pirbright in September 1898.

Lord Pirbright had established the custom of an annual Christmas treat for the local children using the village school as its venue. So it appeared to be a formality when he wrote to the School Board in December 1898 requesting permission to use the school premises on Thursday the 29th for the annual children's treat, and at their meeting on the 19th the Board granted permission and recorded a vote of thanks to the Peer and his good lady wife for their kindness. However, Reverend Krauss then wrote to Lord Pirbright to the effect that the Board had no right to give permission to use the school as this was the prerogative of the school managers and that therefore permission must be withheld. If this action was intended to establish the new vicar's authority in the parish it backfired badly against him. Lord Pirbright did not negotiate or compromise - instead he notified the School Board who had no choice but to cancel the treat at very short notice. They circulated a pamphlet on Tuesday the 27th explaining that the treat was off due to the vicar's 'extraordinary action'. Reverend Krauss may have realised that he had gone too far and later that day he telegraphed the clerk of the board to say that, at some trouble to himself, he had contacted the other members of the old management board who had now given their consent, but they hoped that this breach of protocol 'must never occur again'. But it was too late, all the arrangements had been cancelled and the children did not get their treat.

This seems to have been a clash between two strong-willed, uncompromising figures, coincidentally both of German Jewish descent, but Lord Pirbright certainly won the hearts and minds of the residents of Pirbright and of the commentators of the time. Feelings ran high in the village - the church organist resigned, the choir and bell-ringers refused to appear at the church and the School Board was urged to take the matter to Court, but this idea was dropped. Meanwhile Krauss had to use the village constable as an escort to go from his home to the church. At 7pm on Saturday the 31st of December an angry public meeting was held in the club rooms at the Cricketers Inn at which the parishioners strongly condemned the vicar's 'hostile attitude'. There were representatives of the local and national press present to record the proceedings, so it is clear that this was not an impromptu gathering. The *Surrey Advertiser's* headline ran 'Vicar Censured by his Flock'. A few days later Lord Pirbright's first public statement on the matter came at a retirement presentation for Mr Searle, the village postmaster, which was also attended by the national press, who suddenly appeared to be taking a close interest in the affairs of an obscure Surrey village. Lord Pirbright used the occasion to fan the flames by saying that the vicar 'arrogated to himself an authority which he did not possess' and had undertaken 'personal action against himself and Lady Pirbright'. The press attempted to contact Reverend Krauss for his views but from behind a chained door he declined to be interviewed.

Although the people of Pirbright sided entirely with Lord Pirbright, there are some unsavoury aspects to his behaviour. He clearly stoked up the dispute rather than trying to calm things down, and he ensured that he received maximum publicity for his views by exposing the issue to the national and local press. There is, however, no correspondence on the matter in the Church of England Record Centre's files, so maybe the protagonists stopped short of taking the dispute to the highest authority. It is interesting to note that Lord Pirbright said that he had 'never met' the vicar, which is surprising if they had been sharing the same small village for three months. One gets the impression of them both standing on their dignity, waiting for the other to call.

At Mr Searle's retirement presentation Lord Pirbright also announced that, as a result of the vicar's action, he was 'building at once a large hall for the use of the inhabitants of the village who are, for the most part, my tenants'. This was something of an exaggeration because even at his peak he only owned 76 of the 260 or so dwellings in Pirbright at the time.

The hall cost £2,000 to build and it was opened amid great jubilation and festivities on 31 May 1899. The newspapers reported that 'everybody of importance' was present at this 'brilliant function' (see Figure 30), but apparently the vicar of Pirbright was absent. The opening of the new hall was the occasion of another theatrically-staged royal visit. The village presented a very gay and animated appearance on the day, with two imposing triumphal arches decorated with flags and evergreens, the road was lined by flagstaffs and elsewhere in the vicinity of the hall flags and bunting were freely displayed. The flags were Royal Standards and Union Jacks lent from Aldershot, and a detachment of the Royal Engineers assisted with the decorations. Many business premises and private houses were prettily embellished with, amongst others, fairy lamps, Venetian masts, streamers, Chinese lanterns and floral displays. At Brookwood railway station, where the royal party arrived, an elaborate scheme of decoration had been carried out by the Railway Company. The houses on the approach road were also lavishly embellished and the approach road was newly gravelled so that everything appeared 'spick and span'. The exit from the station was modified with the usual steps being replaced by a gentle ramp carpeted with crimson cloth, and lined with small fir trees specially cut for the purpose, leading to another miniature triumphal arch. Ten police constables were on duty in Pirbright throughout the day and Deputy Chief Constable Page was present for part of the time.

Lord Pirbright journeyed to Waterloo so that he could accompany Her Royal Highness Princess Christian of Schleswig-Holstein, third daughter of Queen Victoria, and the other guests in the royal coach on the special train that conveyed them to Brookwood. They were met by Lady Pirbright who presented a bouquet of choice exotic flowers to the Princess, then they drove to Henley Park in a procession of carriages, entering by the 'Guildford Lodge' at Cobbett Hill. Their progress was witnessed by large crowds at the station and the village green, where they were loudly cheered, and on their arrival at Henley Park mansion the string band of the Royal Lancashire Fusiliers played the national anthem.

The royal party was taken on a tour of the house to see the pictures and other art treasures, accompanied by reporters to record the lavish splendour of it all. The extensive report of the event in the *Surrey Advertiser* gives us a fascinating view into the interior of Henley Park mansion in one of its heydays which is worth repeating verbatim:

'The fine tapestries in the entrance hall were brought into relief by decorations of azaleas, mollis and other flowers of soft and pale yellow hues. Proceeding through the vestibule and anteroom, with its Blenheim, Rubens and grand example of Jordaens, the air was perfumed by hothouse flowers distributed everywhere in vases of choice Sevres, old Marcolini, Dresden, Berlin, Chelsea, Derby and Worcester china. Every flower and every plate seemed to be represented. Entering the Green Room decorated with roses, the guests were delighted at the aspect of the verandah, which was one blaze of colour from the gorgeous orchids of all kinds - but chiefly Cattleyas - which met the eye. The ballroom, with its exquisite Gobelin tapestries and unrivalled collection of Sevres china, was seemingly presided over by the marble bust of Lord Pirbright's ancestor who formed this collection of works of art. As in the verandah, the decoration of this apartment was formed of orchids, the mauve Cattleya harmonising artistically with the yellow tone of the furniture. It was, however, reserved for the dining room, which Lord Pirbright enlarged and heightened, to bear the palm of floral decoration. The luncheon tables, arranged to seat fifty persons, were one mass of pelargoniums of every shade and description, intermingled with the foliage of tiny calladiantha; whilst buttonholes of Malmaison carnations and gardenias were placed for each guest.'

As well as her Royal Highness the luncheon guests included Her Serene Highness the Princess Hanau, the Countess of Shrewsbury, Ladies Blythwood, Buller and Howard, the Hon William and Mrs Lowther, the Archdeacon of Surrey, Colonel and Mrs Tredcroft, the Hon Richard Moreton, the Hon Lady Filmer, Sir George Faudel Phillips, Sir Edward and Lady Carbutt, Sir Frederick Marshall, Colonel and Mrs Douglas, Baroness von und zu Egloffstein, Major Martin and several other notable figures of their day. The menu cards (one for each guest) were embellished with hand-painted sketches of Lord Pirbright's Hall, the Jubilee Fountain and other Pirbright views. During luncheon the band played charming music and Her Royal Highness was 'most graciously pleased' with everything she had seen. After lunch she was taken on a tour of the grounds and she planted a fine Wellingtonia Gigantea in the pleasure gardens to the south-east of the mansion - the tree used to bear a plaque recording the event, but this disappeared in the 1970s or 80s. Just before they left Henley Park, Lady Pirbright presented Her Royal Highness with two large down sofa pillows of rich amber satin, appliqued with flowers of Flanders point lace by her Guild of Needlework.

But all of this was just the prelude; now they proceeded back to Pirbright to open the hall itself.

As they arrived at the hall the school-children sang 'God Save the Queen' and Her Royal Highness was presented with more floral bouquets. The hall was packed with prominent residents and had been artistically decorated with flags and a variety of plants. Lord Pirbright presented

ROYAL VISIT TO PIRBRIGHT.

LORD PIRBRIGHT'S HALL OPENED.
A BRILLIANT FUNCTION.

Wednesday will long be remembered in Pirbright with delight and deep gratitude, for on that day the peer who chose for his title the name of the village he loves so well placed the parishioners under a lasting obligation. True, the gift to the parish of a Village Hall is only one of many thoughtful and generous acts for which Lord Pirbright during his residence at Henley Park has been responsible; but it is the most notable, as well as, we venture to think, that which appeals to the greatest number, and promises to yield the best results. When, a few years ago, his lordship presented to the Parish Church its very fine organ, repaired the old belfry, and rehung the bells, his munificence specially appealed to Churchpeople. The beautiful drinking-fountain, surmounted by the bronze statue of a reading girl, which stands on the Village Green to commemorate the Queen's Diamond Jubilee, is, while pleasing to the eye and artistic sense of all, more particularly utilised by children and travellers. The further celebration of that Jubilee by the entertaining to dinner and tea of the whole of the villagers was worthy of his lordship's generous nature, and will not easily be forgotten. But the project of which Wednesday saw the completion—or would inauguration be the better word?—is one which, besides including in its scope the whole of the inhabitants of the parish, bids fair to exert a permanent and very real educational influence upon them—an influence which must be ever-growing, and of which future generations will also feel the benefit. While Lord Pirbright retains control of the hall, he will place it freely at the disposal of the villagers for gatherings both grave and gay. First and foremost it will be used as a village club, with a well-stocked library and reading-room, and there is little doubt that as time goes on his lordship will find other and equally worthy uses to which it may conveniently be put.

DESCRIPTION OF THE BUILDING.

Before proceeding to describe the day's doings, a brief description of the building may not be out of place. Immediately adjoining the Village Green and the fountain above

each guest—were embellished with hand-painted sketches of "Lord Pirbright's Hall" and the Jubilee fountain, and other Pirbright views, and their wording was as follows:—

DEJEUNER.

Escalopes de Truite au Vin du Rhin.
Cendrillons de Soles a la Princesse
Poulets Printemps a la Chevalier.
Cotelettes d'Agneau aux petits Pois.
Cailles aux Cressons.
Boeuf roti froid a l'Anglaise.
Salade.
Asperges.
Suedoise de Fraises Celestine.
Bombe Glace Andalousé.

During luncheon charming music was discoursed by the band, with whose playing, and with everything she had been shown, her Royal Highness was most graciously pleased. Shortly before four o'clock, while the grounds were being inspected, a very fine Wellingtonia gigantea was planted by the Princess, to whom, before leaving Henley Park, Lady Pirbright presented, on behalf of her Guild of Needlework, two large down sofa pillows, of rich amber satin, with flowers of Flanders point lace appliqued all over them. For this gift H.R.H. expressed her thanks.

THE OPENING CEREMONY.

At four o'clock the general company started for the hall, Princess Christian following a few minutes later with Lord and Lady Pirbright. As the carriage containing H.R.H. entered the gates, the school-children, massed in front of the enclosure, sang "God Save the Queen," accompanied by the band, who had journeyed from Henley Park. The Princess was met at the entrance by the committee, headed by their chairman, Mr. Briant, and there presented by Miss Mabel Briant, daughter of the newly-elected Rural District Councillor, with a bouquet of flowers and a card illuminated by Miss Ada Long, on behalf of the children of Pirbright. Miss Briant was accompanied by eleven other little girls, all dressed in white, namely, the Misses G. Briant, I. Searle, E. and M. Slaughter, M. Wiggins, M. Goddard, E. Cheeseman, V. Ball, O. Mortimer, S. Mason, and E. Faggetter.

H.R.H. was then escorted by Lord and Lady Pirbright to the dais at the farther end of the hall, where the guests had already assembled. The body of the hall was packed, among those present being the Rev. C. A. Skelton, Dr. and Mrs. Templeton, Mr. and Mrs. Dodd, Mrs. Dunn, Rev. J. Spensley, Mr. G. J. Jacobs, Mr. A. F. Asher, Mr. J. H. Wiles, Mr. and Mrs G. H. White, Mr. F. H. Ball, Mr. R. Mason, Mr. W. R. Emery, Mr. A. Briant, Mr. and Mrs. Mollett,

giving three hearty cheers for Lord Pirbright and her ladyship, for their thoughtful kindness to you. In fact, kindness dwells in their hearts, and it comes out every day (applause).

Mr. A. J. E. Johnstone, in seconding the vote of thanks to Lord and Lady Pirbright, said he could not express the pleasure it gave him to be allowed to do this. Lord Pirbright had always given a helping hand to everything, and no matter what station of life a person was in, his lordship's hand was stretched out to assist him. The inhabitants of Pirbright would be to blame if they did not make good use of that hall, and he thought they could best repay his lordship for his generosity in providing it by using it as much as they possibly could (applause).—Cheers for Lord and Lady Pirbright were then lustily given.

In acknowledging the vote of thanks, Lord Pirbright thanked Sir Edward Carbutt for his kind expressions, and said he looked back on the days when he sat opposite him in the House of Commons, never disagreeing, except politically (laughter), as one of the most pleasant memories of his life; and he hoped in the higher House where he now sat that he might sometimes look forward to the exercise of those pugnacious proclivities he enjoyed in the House of Commons (renewed laughter). Referring to what Mr. Johnstone had said, his lordship said he hoped that hall would very, very often be used for the benefit and advantage of the people of Pirbright, and he re-echoed Mr. Johnstone's wish that parishioners would show their gratitude in that way (applause).

TEA ON THE TERRACE.

This concluded the speaking, and Her Royal Highness and the other guests then went on to the terrace, where they partook of tea. The children's sports, which had been in progress all the afternoon, prior to the opening ceremony, were resumed, and were witnessed by the guests with no little interest. Meanwhile more music was discoursed by the band, including German's ever-popular dances from "Henry VIII," and a selection from Caryll's "Runaway Girl." After tea the guests were photographed by Mr. W. Shawcross, of Guildford, and Miss Ada Long, his lordship's artist. At a quarter to six, some of the guests having already left in carriages for the railway station, Lord Pirbright approached the railings of the terrace, and called for three cheers for Princess Christian, which, needless to say, were given with abundant warmth. Her Royal Highness, accompanied by Lord and Lady Pirbright, was then driven to the station, the special train leaving at 6 o'clock on its journey back to town.

Tables had meanwhile been placed in the hall for tea, and after Her Royal Highness's de-

GUIL[D]
ARTISTIC PHOTOGR[APHY]
The "Daily News" says [that Mr. Robin]son's beautiful head or [por]tainly a triumph of th[e]
ROBINSON AND SO[N,]
GUILDFORD.—Advt.

H. BRAND, BUILDE[R]
WOODBRIDGE-ROAD, [Guildford.]
House Repairs and D[ecorations]

ESTABLISHED 6[0 Years.] 142, High-street, Guildf[ord.] smith, and Clothier. on gold and silver wat[ches] art, clothing, and [etc.] the address, 142, High-[street.]
TO THOSE INTER[ESTED]
MESSRS. A. W. WALL [&] WORKS, 160, HIGH-ST[REET] the people you should [know] where, because they gu[arantee] two years; moderate p[rices]
ARTISTIC PHOTOGR[APHY]
—Midgets, 3s. 6d.; O.[C.] per dozen; Enlargement[s] graphs copied.—DREW[E,] street, Guildford (esta[blished]) Advt.

CYCLES REPAIRED [by] workmen at moderate ch[arges]
WALL AND CO., MODE[L]
High-street, Guildford.—[Advt.]

BOROUGH [POLICE]
Monday.—Before the Ma[yor,] Alderman W. Swayne, [Alderman] Tayler, and J. Cahle.

A HORSE'S [TAIL.]
James Ede, 42, Churc[h-road,] furiously driving a horse [in a narrow] road, on May 16th.—[Defendant, in] going, he thought, at lea[st ... on] the wheels of the cart ca[tching] of Church-road, and his [horse] On going into Onslow-str[eet] pavement, one wheel b[roke] Brewery fence. As defen[dant] and smelt strongly of dr[ink at] police-station, and charg[ed him] whilst in charge of a ho[rse ...] wanted to see the doctor, [he was] of an hour afterwards, an[d was] sober then, but had charg[ed ... He] that the wheel touched [the] drunk.—George Welch, al[so] said the animal quite o[ut of] bolter, and had that char[acter] several people in the tow[n.—Mr.] Smith, of 2, Castle-stree[t, said] between five and six year[s and] ran away with people o[ccasionally ... did] not think anyone could h[old] The animal had belonged [to him] or a little more.—The M[ayor] for defendant's own safet[y ...]

Figure 30: 'Royal visit to Pirbright.... a Brilliant Function'.
Part of the Surrey Advertiser's description of the opening ceremony of Lord Pirbright's Hall in 1899. The report occupies three full columns with over 5650 words.

Princess Christian with a beautiful gold key with her arms on one side and his coronet and crest on the other, and the Princess declared the hall open, to the applause of the crowd. The Archdeacon asked a blessing on the hall, after which Lord Pirbright made a lengthy speech praising Queen Victoria and the British Empire, and finishing with three cheers for Her Majesty and Princess Christian. This was followed by further speeches thanking Lord Pirbright 'for putting his abilities at the disposal of his Sovereign and his wealth at the disposal of the people of Pirbright'.

After the speeches the guests partook of tea on the terrace of the hall while children's sports were organised on the green and the band played dance music. Then the guests were assembled for photographs, before they departed in carriages for the station to return to London. The Princess was in Pirbright and Henley Park for exactly five hours, arriving at 1 pm and departing at 6 pm, but the festivities continued. Tea was served in the hall to Lady Pirbright's Needlework Guild and the schoolteachers, then to the children who had a 'sumptuous repast'.

There was more music provided by the band of the Farm School from Bisley, and the children's sports continued until seven o'clock when the 'handsome' prizes, including cricket bats and stumps, writing desks and sets of tools, were distributed by Lady Pirbright. The momentous day concluded with a speech by Lady Pirbright, which was quite short because "when I married Lord Pirbright, we made the arrangement that he should do all the public speaking". There were further votes of thanks for Lord and Lady Pirbright's 'kindness to the working classes' and some closing remarks by Lord Pirbright, then the couple were sent off to Henley Park with three hearty cheers. The festivities continued into the evening as the large crowd enjoyed the fair and other amusements on the village green, while the organising committee were treated to dinner by his lordship at the White Hart.

There was just one sour note to the proceedings. Some of the attendees expressed surprise that the church bells had not been rung in honour of the royal visit. It transpired that the church had been locked up all day and the bell-ropes pulled up through the floor to prevent the bells being rung, so evidently Reverend Krauss was quite happy to continue his dispute with Lord Pirbright, even though this provoked a 'strike' by the bell-ringers who refused to toll the bells on the following Sunday.

On reflection it seems unlikely that Lord Pirbright could have initiated the whole village hall project in response to the dispute with the Reverend Krauss. There was originally a cottage on the green where Lord Pirbright's Hall now stands, which was occupied by Henry Collier from about 1860, until Mrs Elizabeth Collier, widow, sold it to Lord Pirbright in 1896, two years before the dispute flared up. The hall was completed and opened just five months after the acrimonious arguments at Christmas, so it seems likely that the planning must have been well advanced, if not the building actually in progress, by then. It seems that Lord Pirbright used the situation to gain more support and publicity, displaying the Rothschild ruthlessness by not resting until he had completely and publicly crushed his adversary. Both he and Lady Pirbright used the occasion of the opening of the hall to remind their audience and the wider newspaper-reading public that they had the support of the 'vast majority' of the inhabitants of Pirbright, and of the 'spite and envy' of their opponent.

It is interesting to note that the village hall that Lord Pirbright built in 1899 initially remained his own property, he did not actually donate it to the village until two years later. The hall was lighted outside and in by acetylene gas, the first installation of its kind in the district. There was an elaborate stained glass window in the south wall (see Plate 37), which was deliberately designed to be similar to the one in the church and carried Lord Pirbright's full armorial bearings and his strangely inappropriate motto, 'vinctus non victus' - to restrain but not to conquer. The window had to be removed when the hall was extended in about 1950, and although it was packed carefully into a crate and stored at Furze Hill, later it could not be found and has disappeared without trace.

In 1901 a new school was built in the village then in 1902 Balfour's Education Act replaced school boards by County Council education committees, so that the whole dispute became academic. Reverend Krauss remained the vicar of Pirbright for a quarter of a century, and his turn came to welcome royalty on the village green when King George V came to visit in 1918.

Estrangement from the Jewish faith

For many of his earlier years Lord Pirbright had taken a prominent interest in Jewish institutions and his first public appointment, in 1867, was as President of the Borough Jewish Schools. In 1872 he took over the presidency of the Anglo-Jewish Association and remained in this position for 14 years. He received considerable support from senior figures in the Jewish community in the advancement of his career, and he used his parliamentary position powerfully to further the Jewish cause.

However in 1886 he fell into dispute with the Jewish community and severed all his connections with the institutions that he had previously supported so strongly. This action was prompted by the marriage of his daughter Alice to a Christian, which would have been regarded merely as 'regrettable backsliding' if her father had expressed some regret or protest; but in fact he made no such expression and actually attended the ceremony in an Episcopal church. Perhaps it is hard for us today to understand what all the fuss was about, but passions ran deep on such matters among Jewish people until relatively recent times, due to centuries of fervent anti-Semitism from certain church bodies. He felt obliged to write to many members of the Anglo-Jewish Association justifying his position and he later requested that the correspondence be published, but the Association decided that it would only revive painful memories and declined his request. Nevertheless the Association expressed its desire that he should withdraw his resignation and 'forget their differences', but it appears that Lord Pirbright was not inclined to forgive and forget.

He believed that he had been slighted by the Jewish community again in 1901 when he was not invited to join the Jewish deputation which congratulated King Edward VII on his accession to the throne, and on this occasion he retired from the Council of the United Synagogue, of which he was a life member. Despite these disagreements, his subsequent burial at a Christian church came as a shock to them.

Death, burial, will

There are some clues that Lord Pirbright may have been unwell in his last few years, or at least lost some of his earlier zeal. His cottage-building activities appear to have ceased by 1900 despite the extra land that he owned, and in 1901 he handed over his village hall to the parish of Pirbright 'to commemorate the accession of HM King Edward VII'. However, there were seven conditions attached to his gift, the first being that the hall shall always be known as Lord Pirbright's Hall and by no other name.

In March 1901 Lord and Lady Pirbright were staying at the Metropole Hotel in Brighton where sea-bathing was regarded as a health-restoring activity. In the ensuite bathrooms there, patrons could choose from hot or cold fresh or sea water, which came from the newly-designed 'tapped water wells' (taps). Prices were from 3s 6d for a single room to £3 8s for a suite, with servants' meals at 6s per day. Lord and Lady Pirbright had their valet Walter Seward and lady's maid Mary McGinn with them, while Henley Park had only a skeleton staff resident, so Lord and Lady Pirbright may have been on an extended visit to Brighton and their return to Henley Park was not imminent. Of course, Brighton was a fashionable resort much frequented by Lord Pirbright's circle of royal friends and they may have been staying there for a social event, but there were no obvious society figures staying nearby or in the hotel with them. Note the third coincidental connection with Brighton - Mary Halsey was apparently living there when she died in 1819 and Charles Burnett the previous tenant was born there in the 1840s. Thanks to the favour of the Regent, Brighton was a 'society' playground and health resort for 'the idle, the rich and the fashionable' in the 19th century while Bath had rather faded from its 18th century prominence.

Lord Pirbright died on 9 January 1903 at the age of 62, at 42 Grosvenor Place. Like several of the important owners and occupiers of Henley Park, he actually died at his house in London.

Even now the dispute with Reverend Krauss of Pirbright was not over. Not satisfied with outliving his opponent, Krauss had to make a final gesture and apparently refused to let the church bell be tolled when news of Lord Pirbright's death reached the village. Predictably, this led to a hostile reaction by the inhabitants, initially by a crowd of children who 'booed' the vicar, then a crowd of youths who paraded in front of the vicarage beating tin trays, blowing mouth organs and generally 'making the night hideous with their noise'. Later that night events took a more sinister turn when the parsonage gates were thrown down and some damage done to the garden, and for the next few evenings about a dozen policemen guarded the vicar and his home as more serious attacks were threatened. As before, the vicar refused to say anything to the press on the matter. The parishioners appealed directly to the Bishop of the Diocese and probably as a result of this, the bell was tolled at the time of Lord Pirbright's burial on the 13th of January. On Monday the 19th the villagers gathered in the village hall to express their 'indignation and disgust' at the vicar's actions. The packed meeting heard the Chairman read a letter from Lady Pirbright protesting against any violent action but pointing out that 'what man might fail to avenge, God was sure to punish'. Nevertheless the meeting decided not to leave it to divine intervention and wrote to the vicar asking him to resign, copying their request to the Bishop. Whatever the response, Krauss did not resign and weathered the storm to remain in Pirbright, and was buried there in 1925.

Lord Pirbright's will was proved on the 7th of February and he left an estate worth £368,905 10s 11d, roughly £16 million at today's values, although many of his paintings would be almost priceless now. Lord Pirbright was apparently by far the wealthiest of any of the owners or tenants of Henley Park in the last 250 years. The will is surprisingly straightforward. Although it covers four pages this is mostly legalese - he left £500 to his secretary Peter McGinn, £20,000 to his nephew Dr George Landauer of Vienna, some rather complicated annuities to his daughters by his previous marriage and everything else to his wife Sarah Lady Pirbright, including all his many art treasures, which he did not itemise.

Lord Pirbright clearly identified much more closely with the village of Pirbright than he did with Wyke and Normandy even though his estate straddled both parishes, but he was buried at St Mark's Church, Wyke. He had apparently considered his own mortality and decided that he did not want to give Reverend Krauss the satisfaction of burying him, so even though he did not know the correct name of the church, the very first provision in his will was that he should be buried in 'Normandy Parish Churchyard'. Despite their earlier differences the Jewish community reserved a grave for him at the Willesden Cemetery of the United Synagogue, but it was with shock that they learned that he was to be given a Christian burial at Wyke. The funeral was not attended by any member of Lord Pirbright's family, although there were representatives of the king and members of the 'brilliant and worldly society' that he valued so much. The populace of Pirbright clearly loved him, but some of his less impressionable contemporaries felt that he 'unduly valued that brilliant and worldly society to the exclusion of higher things'.

Ironically, there is now nothing of Lord Pirbright's left at Henley Park, his grandiose extensions demolished, the gardens overgrown. However, everywhere you look around in Pirbright you can see his legacy there, and he still looks down on the parishioners from the portrait in his village hall. His tomb, to the north-east of the church at Wyke, is an elaborate marble chest tomb with inscription panels on the top and sides, and tablets on each side commemorating his descendants (see Plate 45). The tomb itself is now a Grade II listed structure, just like Henley Park, the mansion he occupied and for which he did so much.

Lady Pirbright

Lady Pirbright apparently retained the lease of Henley Park for a few years after Lord Pirbright's death, but probably never made it her home again. It was occupied in 1905 or 1906 by her relative Samuel Henry Faudel Phillips and by August 1906 Sir Owen and Lady Roberts had taken up residence.

She continued to play a role in the affairs of Pirbright, providing the annual treat for the children which moved from Christmastime to the summer, entertaining over 300 boys and girls to 'one of the happiest days of the year' with a substantial tea and sports matches. She attended the last event in 1914 in person although she was no longer living nearby.

In the early 1900s she sold some of the properties that Lord Pirbright had accumulated, mainly the smallholdings. In 1907 she sold The Old Homestead and Chandler's Field at Willey Green to James Collins of Bailes Farm, and the same year The Nursery and Throat Moor in Pirbright to Henry Joseph Halsey, the owner of Henley Park. In 1909 she sold Stream House Farm to Halsey for £460. Nevertheless, in the 1910 valuation survey she still owned many properties in the area, including 28 cottages, 41 houses, five shops, two bakehouses, glasshouses and land totalling 17 acres in Pirbright, with a freehold value of £20,148, and 13 cottages in Normandy, value £1,345. She continued to own many of them until her death, when she bequeathed the properties in Pirbright to her nephew Lionel Lawson Faudel Phillips and those in Normandy and Worplesdon to her grand nephew Philip Brydges Henriques, but sadly Philip Brydges was killed in action in 1915 and so those properties reverted to his father Sir Philip Henriques of Normandy Park. Most of the Pirbright properties were offered for sale by auction 'by direction of the executors' of her will in June 1916.

She had taken a deep interest in English politics and the house at Grosvenor Place, which one source describes as her house rather than Lord Pirbright's, was a rendezvous for the political leaders of the time. She was well-connected with European royalty and was a well-known figure in the diplomatic world. She had travelled abroad with her husband on his official duties and was fluent in several languages including French, Italian and German. She went to reside in Paris and from 1911 to 1914 was living at 11 Avenue D'Jena, in the fashionable west end between the Arc de Triomphe and the River Seine. One source says she died there, but she actually died at Claridges Hotel in London on 26 November 1914, age 76.

Lady Pirbright's will is far more detailed than her late husband's and she went to great lengths to dispose individually of each of the art treasures in her collection. For the pictures that she left to the National Gallery and the Louvre, she even went to the extent of specifying the wording of the plaque to be placed beneath them, and dictated that they must be kept on view there 'permanently'. However, it appears that the National Gallery did not accept this bequest and the whereabouts of the pictures now is unknown. The list of the specific possessions that she bequeathed, all of them obviously valuable, covers four pages. As an afterthought, in a codicil completed the same day as her will, she gave her dog 'Boy' to her maid Mary McGinn, 'confident he will have the proper care and attention'.

Even in her later years she apparently still enjoyed travelling, because she made her will at the Grand Hotel in Rome in April 1914 and it was witnessed by the hotel's General Manager and Assistant Manager. She travelled slowly back across Europe, writing codicils to her will as she went. In June she was in France and in September she had reached the Grand Hotel in Folkstone, but Folkstone could only offer the Hall Porter to act as a witness, rather a comedown from the General Manager furnished by the Grand Hotel in Rome. Later in September she reached Claridges in London, where she made the last two of the six codicils, bequeathing further specific items of jewellery. She finished her will by saying "I have made no special bequests to public charities because I have largely given during my life". She also directed that her wedding ring and small diamond and blue enamelled cross should be buried with her. She left an estate valued at £225,000.

She was buried on 30 November at Wyke, in the vault with her husband. According to local folklore in Normandy in the 1950s, Lady Pirbright was so disgusted with the behaviour of her husband's relatives when he died, that she ordered that the family silver should be interred with her in the family grave, so that they should not obtain it. When Prince Loewenstein, great grandson of Lord Pirbright, came to Pirbright in 1995 for the Parish Council centenary he told local residents that this fable was untrue, because they had opened the vault and looked.

Figure 31: Lord Pirbright's Properties.

Ref.	Name, location and contemporary description	Acquisition and disposal
1	Lord Pirbright's Hall, Pirbright Green	Purchased existing cottage c.1896, built Hall 1899, presented to Pirbright Parish Council in 1901
2	The Bungalow, The Green; 'Bijou Villa', cottage, yard and builder's shop, subsequently Cripps Garage	Purchased c.1895 from James Faggetter
3	Bakery Cottage, The Green; shop, bakehouse & stable leased by H Boylett from 1898	Purchased existing old house c.1898 from James Faggetter
4	Connemara, formerly Suffolk House, Little Green; leased by Dr WJ Fleming from 1905 for £70 p/a	Doctor's house built by James Faggetter 1880s, purchased c.1895
5	Vynes Cottage, Little Green; leased by Mrs Sarah Boylett and Andrew Cranstone 1901	Purchased existing old house c.1895 from James Faggetter
6	The Cottage, now partly Fulks butcher's	Purchased c.1899 from John Searle
7	The Shop on the Green; built shop with large new frontage 1897, leased by HW Briant from 1896 for £56 p/a, occupied by Moore and Rice	Purchased c.1896 from Henry Searle
8	1-3 Henry Cottages next to the shop; leased by Stonard, Bolton and Rose, rent £11 14s each	Purchased c.1896 from Henry Searle, demolished and rebuilt c.1899
9	Parish Shop, formerly 4-5 Henry Cottages then Post Office; leased by Boylett and Stonard	Purchased c.1897 from WF Tyler, extended c.1900
10	1-11 The Terrace, Guildford Road; two shops leased by E Cartwright and W Paris, and nine cottages	Purchased Cove House c.1896 from Charles Boylett; demolished and shops and cottages built 1897-98
11	Holly Grange, The Gardens, Pirbright; detached 3-bed villa leased by FH Ball for £30 p/a, occupied by Savage	Purchased by Lord Pirbright before 1899. House built c.1896
12	1-14 The Gardens, Pirbright; 14 semidetached 3-bed cottages in two styles, numbers 1-2 & 5-14 built c.1895	Purchased land and two existing cottages (nos 3 & 4) c.1895 from James Faggetter
13	15-16 The Gardens, Pirbright	Purchased existing cottages c.1895 from William Cobley
14	Hill House, Collingwood, Furzeholme and Broadview, Dawney's Hill, Pirbright; four 5-bed villas in two pairs, rent £32 per annum each	Purchased land c.1895 from William Wells, built villas c.1900
15	1 & 2 Pirbright View, Dawney's Hill, Pirbright; pair of 3-bed cottages rented by Carpenter and Stevens at £15 12s p/a	Purchased existing cottages called Sunfield and Sunfield Cottage c.1895 from William Wells

Figure 31: Lord Pirbright's Properties (continued).

Ref.	Name, location and contemporary description	Acquisition and disposal
16	Boro Hill & Victoria Cottages, School Lane; pair of old cottages rented by D Cheesman and A Stevens	Purchased c.1896 from Ruth Hillman. Sold 1916
17	Pine House, Cooks Green, Pirbright; detached 4-bed house with glasshouses, garden and almost 2 acres of land, occupied by E Bennett, rent £35 p/a	Purchased Bennet's Rose Nursery 1895 from John Cherryman. Sold prior to the 1916 auction
18	Gorselands, Aldershot Road, Pirbright; detached house built in 1897, leased by F Stovell in 1900	Lord P's first purchase; land from Henry Greenfield c.1894. Lady Pirbright gave to John Bluck, former Henley Park head gardener
19	Stanford Cottages, Aldershot Road, Pirbright; 8 cottages built c.1900, 2 later demolished and rebuilt	Purchased land c.1895 from Henry Greenfield and cottage c.1899 from WG Holt
20	Land near Stanford Common (behind Stanford Cottages); leased by Mr Page for £2 p/a and used for poultry and a small crop	Possibly purchased c.1895 from Henry Greenfield
21	Pirbright Cottages, Fox Corner; one grocers shop and PO leased by Moore, and 20 semidetached houses. Nos 5-8 purchased from John Faggetter, 1-4 and 9-18 built c.1896, shop built c.1897 and 19-22 built c.1898	Purchased existing houses c.1896 from John Faggetter, purchased land c.1896 from James Terry
22	The Nursery, Pirbright; cottage and Waterer's nursery lands, 9 acres	Purchased c.1895 from Henry Greenfield. Sold by Lady Pirbright to HJT Halsey in 1907
23	Inner and Outer Throat Moor, near Fellmoor, Pirbright; 5 acres of land	Purchased c.1895 from John Cherryman. Sold by Lady Pirbright to HJT Halsey for £145 in 1907
24	Stream House Farm, Aldershot Road, Pirbright; cottage, garden and 5 acres of meadow land	Purchased c.1895 from Henry Greenfield. Sold by Lady Pirbright to HJT Halsey for £460 in 1909
25	Pullens Farm, Ash Road, Pirbright, part of Cobbett Hill Farm; later sold for the Institute	Purchased old farm and land c.1897 from John Mason

Figure 31: Lord Pirbright's Properties (continued).

Ref.	Name, location and contemporary description	Acquisition and disposal
26	1-3 Pirbright Road, Normandy; cottages occupied by Colyer, Goodchild and Turner, rent approx £7 10s p/a	Lord P. demolished former Pear Tree Cottage and built a row of three 4-room cottages in 1896. After the death of Lady Pirbright, descended to Sir Philip Henriques
27	4-8 Pirbright Road, Normandy; semi-detached 2-bed cottages	Built in two styles between 1896 and 1900. Descended to Sir Philip Henriques
28	9-13 Pirbright Road, Normandy; two bungalows formerly Spring Cottages (now nos 10 & 11), and three semi-detached 2-bed cottages	Lord P purchased land and two bungalows by 1898 from Thomas Osgood. Built cottages by 1900. Descended to Sir Philip Henriques
29	Vine Farm, Pirbright Road, Normandy; 2½ acre smallholding copyhold of the manor of Cleygate	Purchased in 1896 from George Collyer and Kate Lee for £500. Descended to Sir Philip Henriques
30	The Glen, Pirbright Road, Normandy; 3½ acre smallholding copyhold of the manor of Cleygate	Purchased in 1896 from Thomas Osgood for £425. Descended to Sir Philip Henriques
31	The Manor House, Normandy Common; house and 4 acres of land	Probably purchased at Normandy Manor estate sale in 1895. Descended to Sir Philip Henriques
32	Normandy Pond; residue of a 1,000 year lease	Probably purchased at Normandy Manor estate sale 1895. Sold to the Secretary of State for War in 1901
33	The Old Homestead and Chandler's Field, Willey Green; messuage and 15 acres of land	Acquired by 1905. Lady Pirbright sold to James Collins in 1907

9. SIR OWEN AND LADY ROBERTS (1906-1925)

When Sir Owen and Lady Louisa Roberts moved into the mansion in 1906 it had been a gentleman's country residence for nearly 300 years, but the 20th century was to see the house take on two new and very different roles as a consequence of the world wars. The first of these took place during their tenancy, but for the first ten years there was very little change.

Sir Owen Roberts (see Plate 46) was in his seventies when he came to Henley Park and was just about to retire following a very distinguished career. He was born in 1835, the son of Owen and Catherine Roberts of Plâs Dinas in Caernarvonshire and not far from Glynllifon which two centuries earlier had been the ancestral home of Sir John Glynne. A full list of Sir Owen's achievements and offices is impressive. After excelling at Oxford he was called to the bar in 1863 and three years later was appointed Clerk to the Clothworkers' Company, a position he held until his retirement in 1907, being subsequently elected its Master. One of the great City Livery Companies originally founded to promote the craft of cloth finishing, the Company used its considerable wealth and influence in the 19th century to ensure that the less affluent should benefit, providing aid for the needy, promoting technical education and pioneering higher education for women, providing scholarships at the women's colleges of Oxford and Cambridge.

It was in recognition of his enormous services in the furtherance of technical education that Sir Owen received his knighthood in 1888. He was the driving force in the founding of the Yorkshire College at Leeds when superior scientific and technical education of continental workers began to threaten the local cloth trade, and University College Bristol, both of which were later raised to University status. He was the prime mover in founding the City of London Institute and as an exponent of the benefits of higher education for women, he was also one of the promoters of Somerville Hall, renamed Somerville College, Oxford. In addition he held many public offices and to name but a few, he served on the Technical Education Board of the London County Council and was later chairman of the London Polytechnic Council. He was a member of the Commission for the Reconstruction of the University of London, and a member of the governing board of the Imperial College of Science and Technology at South Kensington. In a different capacity he served as a JP for Surrey, was one of the Lord Lieutenants in the City of London for several years, and one of the Sheriffs of Caernarvonshire.

Sir Owen and Lady Roberts were active in the Women's Suffrage movement and large meetings in support were held at the house, so Henley Park again became a gathering place for 'dissenters' as it had been for the recusants in the 16th century. Sir Owen believed that women served the State as effectively as men, which drew applause from those at the meetings. He had raised the question of women's suffrage as early as the election of 1865 so "he supposed he might reckon himself as about the oldest supporter of women's suffrage in the county". Although older than his predecessor Lord Pirbright, Sir Owen appears more enlightened and more in tune with the great changes taking place in society.

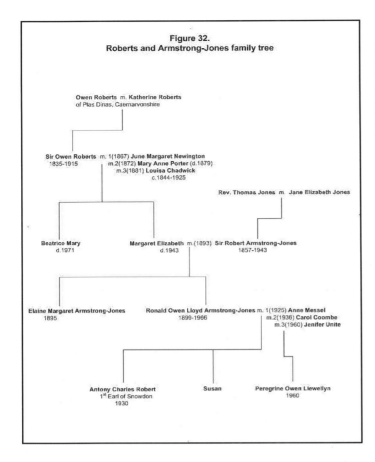

Figure 32.
Roberts and Armstrong-Jones family tree

Owen Roberts m. Katherine Roberts
of Plas Dinas, Caernarvonshire

Sir Owen Roberts   m. 1(1867) June Margaret Newington
1835-1915   m.2(1872) Mary Anne Porter (d.1879)
                    m.3(1881) Louisa Chadwick
                    c.1844-1925

Rev. Thomas Jones m. Jane Elizabeth Jones

Beatrice Mary   Margaret Elizabeth m.(1893) Sir Robert Armstrong-Jones
d.1971   d.1943   1857-1943

Elaine Margaret Armstrong-Jones   Ronald Owen Lloyd Armstrong-Jones m. 1(1925) Anne Messel
1895   1899-1966   m.2(1936) Carol Coombe
                                                                       m.3(1960) Jenifer Unite

Antony Charles Robert   Susan   Peregrine Owen Llewellyn
1st Earl of Snowdon   1960
1930

He married three times and Lady Louisa was his third wife whom he married in 1881. Sir Owen's eldest daughter by a previous marriage was Margaret and she married Dr (later Sir) Robert Armstrong-Jones and in due course inherited the family seat of Plâs Dinas. By the 21st century the house there had become a hotel, but the portraits of Sir Owen and his parents which hang on the walls provide a link to its past. Although retired, Sir Owen still had many connections with London so once again Henley Park's proximity to the capital must have been an important factor for him and Lady Roberts when they chose to make it their home.

It would seem that Sir Owen and Lady Roberts took over Lady Pirbright's lease of Henley Park directly from her, because it still had ten years to run and there is no record of a new lease or assignment. For the time being the annual rent remained £378. They occupied the mansion and about 338 acres of estate, orchard and garden, as well as about 134 acres of woodland with shooting rights. A game book from the period still in the possession of the Armstrong-Jones family records, for example, that one day in December 1910 Sir Owen with PG Henriques, ER Warne, Major Mangles, PM Evans, Robert Jones and 'WHD' dispatched 61 pheasants, five rabbits and two woodcock in Furze Field, Kiln Copse, Withy Bed and Anchor Copse. The previous month they had one of their best days, bagging 290 pheasants, five rabbits, a hare, three woodcock and 65 wild fowl, mostly duck, in Island, Grassypiece, Whipley, Anchor and Kiln Copses. However on 26 September 1908 Sir Owen did not shoot because 'his left gun barrel had a dinge in it'! On a lighter note the book records that on 2 January 1912 they returned in the afternoon for a children's party and one day in January 1908 they noticed a Bittern, thought to be extinct in England, rise from the edge of Tumbling Bay. Another day they 'put up a long tailed green parrot in a corn field on Longerhill Farm'.

Two thirds of the estate was in the parish of Ash and the rest in Pirbright. The lease also included Henley Park Farm consisting of 170 acres or so of dairy and mixed farm which was sub-let to Osman Chrismas, then later WG Harding, for an annual rent of £190. The house was described in 1913 in the National Valuation Survey (see Figure 33) as a brick built and tiled mansion containing dining, drawing and billiard rooms, an ante room, morning room, small dining room, study, gun room, cloak room, two staircases, a boudoir, 28 bed & dressing rooms, seven WCs, three bathrooms, a kitchen, servants' hall and butler's and housemaids' rooms. There was

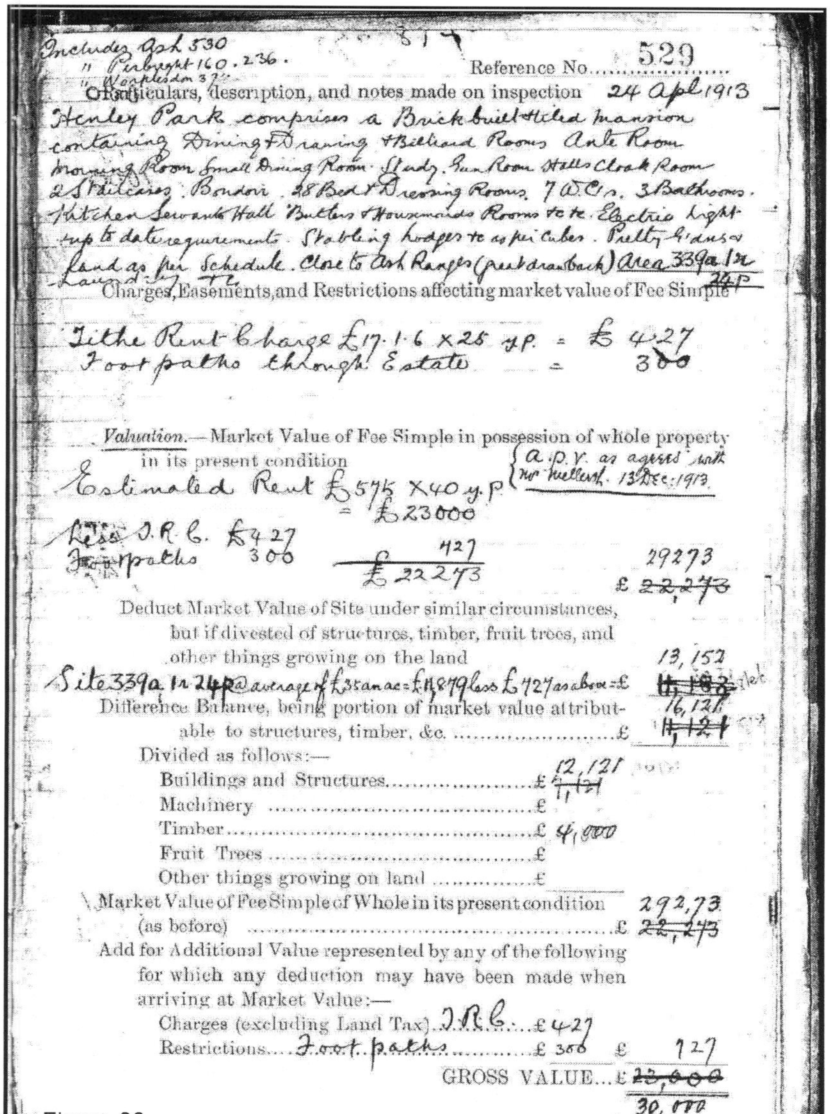
Includes Ash 530
" Pirbright 160.236.
" Worplesdon 37
Reference No. 529
Particulars, description, and notes made on inspection 24 Apl 1913
Henley Park comprises a Brick built & tiled mansion containing Dining & Drawing & Billiard Rooms Ante Room Morning Room Small Dining Room · Study. Gun Room Halls Cloak Room 2 Staircases. Boudoir. 28 Bed & Dressing Rooms. 7 W.C's. 3 Bathrooms. Kitchen Servants Hall Butlers & Housemaids Rooms &c &c. Electric light up to date requirements. Stabling Lodges &c as per cubes. Pretty G'dns & land as per Schedule. Close to Ash Ranges (great drawback) Area 339a 1r 24p
Charges, Easements, and Restrictions affecting market value of Fee Simple
Tithe Rent Charge £17.1.6 x 25 y.p. = £ 427
Foot paths through Estate = 300

Valuation.—Market Value of Fee Simple in possession of whole property in its present condition
{A.P.V. as agreed with Mr Mellersh. 13 Dec: 1913.
Estimated Rent £575 x 40 y.p. = £23000
Less T.R.C. £427
Footpaths 300
£ 427
£ 22273
£ ~~22,273~~ 29273
Deduct Market Value of Site under similar circumstances, but if divested of structures, timber, fruit trees, and other things growing on the land
Site 339a 1r 24p @ average of £35 an ac = £11,879 less £427 as above = £ ~~11,152~~ 13,152
Difference Balance, being portion of market value attributable to structures, timber, &c. .... £ ~~11,121~~ 16,121
Divided as follows:—
Buildings and Structures........ £ ~~11,121~~ 12,121
Machinery .... £
Timber........ £ 4,000
Fruit Trees .... £
Other things growing on land .... £
Market Value of Fee Simple of Whole in its present condition (as before) .... £ ~~22,273~~ 29,273
Add for Additional Value represented by any of the following for which any deduction may have been made when arriving at Market Value:—
Charges (excluding Land Tax) T.R.C. .... £ 427
Restrictions.... Foot paths .... £ 300 £ 727
GROSS VALUE... £ ~~23,000~~ 30,000

Figure 33.
Henley Park mansion described in the valuation survey, c.1913.

electric light and 'up to date requirements'. Outside were stabling and lodges as well as pretty gardens, but it was noted that the proximity to Ash firing ranges was 'a great drawback'.

The earliest known photographs of Henley Park were taken around the turn of the century by local shopkeepers who produced many postcards of the Normandy area (see Plates 48 to 51). The most prolific of these was John Horne, the founder and owner of Normandy Stores near the crossroads (most recently a shop for equipment for discos, DJ's and karioke). During his proprietorship from about 1907 to the First World War he photographed and published over 25 views of Normandy of which at least 11 were of Henley Park and its gardens. This series provides a wonderful impression of the mansion at its heyday. Several were reprinted by Friths of Reigate, the major publisher of picture postcards in England at a time before telephones were widespread, when cards were used for sending brief messages and thank-yous. Several were used as Christmas cards and are signed with Christmas and New Year greetings from Lord and Lady Roberts (see Figure 34).

Sir Owen and Lady Roberts did not have the grand social aspirations of Lord and Lady Pirbright, nor did they command the same fabulous wealth but they too, in a quieter and more unassuming manner, became great benefactors to the local community and it was Normandy and Wyke that benefited from their interest and generosity. They were well remembered for the great amount of work they did for the welfare of the school and the church. Each Easter and Christmas they entertained the choir from the village church to dinner. They instituted an annual summer treat for the children of Wyke Sunday School, but unlike Lord and Lady Pirbright they entertained

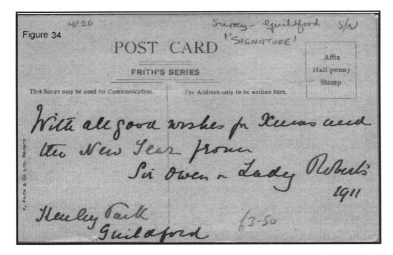
Figure 34

POST CARD

FRITH'S SERIES

This Space may be used for Communication.   The Address only to be written here.

Affix
Half penny
Stamp

With all good wishes for Xmas and the New Year from Sir Owen & Lady Roberts 1911

Henley Park Guildford

the children at Henley Park itself. On one occasion 70 to 100 children had 'an excellent tea' in the coach house and afterwards enjoyed themselves with games and races, for which Lady Roberts presented the prizes. She also gifted a hedge of rhododendrons to be planted on the boundaries when Wyke churchyard was extended for the first time.

Sir Owen Roberts died at Henley Park on 6 January 1915 at the age of 79. He was buried at Highgate Cemetery. His will was proved on the 4th of March, with probate to his wife Louisa, son-in-law Robert Armstrong-Jones and others. His effects were valued at £82,760 5s 4d.

There were two very significant events during Lady Roberts' tenancy, both of which had an important impact on Henley Park - they were the First World War and Henry Halsey's attempts to sell his estates. At the time of Sir Owen's death the First World War was in progress, and very soon after he died, she offered the house rent, rates and lighting free to the military authorities. Lord Pirbright had given land for wounded soldiers' houses after the South African War, one of Lady Pirbright's last acts was to be influential in converting the village hall at Pirbright into a convalescent home for the wartime wounded, but Lady Roberts went one better, giving up Henley Park itself for the war wounded. The later tenants of Henley Park seem to have had a lot of freedom to do what they liked with the place. We have seen how Lord Pirbright extended the building and gardens to make it more grandiose (possibly explaining the sharp increase in rent when the original lease expired). Now Lady Roberts was instrumental in turning it into a hospital. Presumably the trustees were consulted and approved these plans.

One of the duties of the British Red Cross Society was to plan for the creation, equipping and staffing of temporary hospitals in the home country in the event of an invasion. As the First World War unfolded it became evident that no invasion was imminent, but as the numbers of wounded rose these plans were adapted to create a number of Auxiliary Home Hospitals able to receive them. The outbreak of war brought more than 5,000 offers of hospital accommodation both from public bodies and private individuals. These were offered to the War Office, who delegated the task of selecting the suitable ones to the Red Cross. The buildings that were offered ranged from town halls and schools to private houses, garages and stables, many of which were entirely unsuitable for use as hospitals. The great majority of the buildings that were suitable, and which became hospitals, were larger private houses. The Earl and Countess of Onslow offered Clandon Park within three days of the outbreak of war and it was one of the first houses in Surrey to be opened as an auxiliary hospital. Amongst the others which followed was Henley Park.

The establishment of these hospitals was a local effort with minimal involvement from the Government or the Joint War Committee (the combined organisation of the Red Cross and the Order of St John, which existed for the duration of hostilities). Across the country, there was a great desire to do something to help, so that the difficulty perceived by the authorities was not to induce people to help so much as to 'direct and control their energies'. Thus once Henley Park had been chosen, there was little difficulty in organising local subscriptions and collections to meet the expenses of running it. The 1916 'Our Day' fundraising event raised £1,200 for the Pirbright Section of the Red Cross, and the same event in 1917 raised over £1,550. Furniture to equip the hospital was lent by householders in the neighbourhood and Lady Roberts herself lent 12 beds for the patients and a number for the staff. A Christmas fund-raising event at the hospital in 1917 raised £14 13s and prizes 'in kind' were awarded including a live pig, a turkey, fowls and rabbits. The hospital was staffed by Red Cross Voluntary Aid Detachments (VAD) and so, like most of the auxiliary hospitals, it maintained itself without management or significant financial support from the central authorities.

Although many members of the VADs wanted to become involved directly in war work and some did transfer to the front lines in France and Belgium to nurse the wounded there, there was generally continuity in the staffing of the auxiliary hospitals, which contributed to the 'homely' atmosphere that clung to these home-hospitals, and the patients' progress to recovery was facilitated by the pleasant atmosphere there. The auxiliary hospitals were staffed by a Commandant, a Quartermaster and a Women's VAD, assisted by local volunteers. Medical attendance was provided voluntarily by local doctors and the nursing team was in the charge of a Matron. The voluntary nursing work in the auxiliary hospitals was described after the war by the Director General of Army Medical Services as being of a very high standard and forming 'a splendid spectacle of patriotism'. The Pirbright Section of the Red Cross, which had two similar-sized hospitals at Henley Park and Beechcroft, had a Voluntary Aid Detachment of 34 people. When Henley Park hospital opened Mrs Shute was the Commandant, she was succeeded in October 1915 by Mrs AD Allen, then from February 1917 by Mrs Cruickshank. The honorary Medical Officer throughout the period was Dr Wilfred Fleming of Suffolk House, Pirbright, who was referred to as 'our highly esteemed present doctor, so popular for he is as good at sport as medicine'.

Henley Park hospital was managed by a 14-person local committee under the presidency of Lady Roberts and including Dr Fleming and Mrs Henriques of Normandy Park. Laurence Halsey, one of the trustees of the Henley Park estate and first cousin to the owner Henry Joseph Halsey, was the honorary auditor. In addition Lady Roberts and Doctor Fleming were on the management committee of the Woking Division of the British Red Cross Society, and Lady Roberts was president of the Wyke, Normandy and Wanborough Nursing Association.

Henley Park Auxiliary Hospital opened in June 1915 with beds for 50 patients. There were seven wards, the largest of which was in the former drawing room which easily accommodated 20 beds. The former dining room had eleven beds and between the two was the surgery with an operating table. There were five wards on the first floor, but the billiard room was retained for its original purpose to provide recreation for the soldiers. The wards were all named after British colonies overseas. The entrance hall was transformed into a dining room and also on the ground floor were rooms for the Commandant and Quartermaster and a sitting-room for the nursing staff, with a piano. Outside, the soldiers had the use of the grounds for recreation including the boating lake, and games were provided such as croquet and clock golf. By the end of 1917 huts had been set up for open-air treatment which increased the patient accommodation to 60 beds.

Several of the country houses that were converted into hospitals were charmingly situated, giving patients the benefit of the 'health-giving breezes that sweep over the Surrey uplands' and glorious views which were 'restful and refreshing to war-jangled nerves', while the gardens were themselves a delight to the sick and offered opportunities for healthy recreation and sports. Certainly Henley Park's impressive setting and well-kept grounds must have seemed a million miles from the awful muddy, bullet-ridden battlefields. Even the landscape with its rolling hills must have been blissfully different from the flat expanses of Flanders.

Every auxiliary hospital was attached to a military hospital which directed the movement of patients, so Henley Park received patients from the Cambridge Hospital in Aldershot. A very efficient transport system for the wounded was established and soldiers could be received into hospitals across the south of England within 24 hours of being carried off the field of battle in Flanders. The patients remained subject to military control throughout their stay, although the auxiliary hospitals were regarded as having milder discipline and more homely surroundings than their military counterparts. The War Office issued a set of Orders for Patients in Auxiliary Hospitals, which included instructions like - Patients marked 'up' will shave, wash and dress before breakfast; and - Patients will wear shoes in the building and boots in the grounds. Non-commissioned officers were directed to assist the nursing staff in maintaining good order and discipline. The patients who were sent to the auxiliary hospitals were usually those with the less serious wounds or ailments.

There were over 500 patients admitted to Henley Park Hospital in 1916, with an average stay of just over a month. 18 minor operations were carried out during the year. The hospital was well-utilised, with one of the highest occupancy rates of the Surrey auxiliary hospitals and the average cost of running the hospital was correspondingly high - 4s 2d per patient day, again one of the highest in Surrey. Clandon Park was by far the most expensive to run at over 6s per patient day. Henley Park's 1916 annual report commended the Matron, Miss F Abell, who was a 'thoroughly efficient head of the nursing arrangements'. There was also an anaesthetist, a consulting oculist and a dental surgeon. Miss Abell remained the Matron at Henley Park throughout, and she was awarded the Royal Red Cross second class.

Many excellent concerts were given to the nurses and men at Henley Park Hospital and elaborate celebrations were laid on at Christmas. The wards were colourfully decorated by the patients and they were awoken on Christmas morning by the nurses singing carols in the hall. Each patient found a 'Christmas stocking' on his bed, well filled with sweets, smokes, musical instruments and gadgets. There was a substantial mid-day meal complete with beer, then a concert in the afternoon, ending with a procession of nurses in fancy dress carrying a gigantic plum pudding on a stretcher. Inside the pudding was a young girl who distributed more presents, sweets and a cigar to each patient. On Boxing Day another concert and a whist drive were held.

In March 1917 the hospital began to specialise in the treatment of knee and joint cases. A gymnasium was fitted up and two masseurs were appointed. In 1918 the number of patients admitted had risen to 678 while the average stay had dropped to 26 days. The average cost per patient day had risen slightly to 4s 5d, but the costs at the other hospitals had risen more so that Henley Park was no longer one of the most expensive to run. By 1918 Henley Park was the only local auxiliary hospital where the authorities did not have to pay any rent, rates or taxes, because Lady Roberts was still paying these herself.

Number	NAME OF HOSPITAL.	Average Number of Beds available.	Number of Days open.	Average Number of Patients resident daily.	Number of Patients admitted during year.	Patient's average residence.	Rate of Army Allowance.	Total Army Allowance.	COST OF MAINTENANCE.							Average Cost of Maintenance per Patient per day.	Cost of Administration.
									Provisions.	Surgery and Dispensary.	Domestic.	Establishment.	Salaries and Wages.	Miscellaneous.	Total.		
	1	2	3	4	5	6	7	8	9	10	11	12	13	14	15	16	17
	Group II.—contd.						s. d.	£ s. d.	£ s. d.	£ s. d.	£ s. d.	£ s. d.	£ s. d.	£ s. d.	£ s. d.	s. d.	£ s. d.
25	Hibfield, Reigate	50	365	33	382	32.2	3 0	1,765 16 0	572 1 6	41 9 10	414 2 2	37 9 6	733 12 7	86 5 1	2,119 4 8	3 7.4	14 15 6
26	Blendown, West Byfleet	40	83	35.4	91	21.5	3 0	513 8 0	422 6 7	16 2 10	80 17 10	...	2 2 0	9 8 6	529 12 9	3 11	...
27	Caenshill, Weybridge	40	368	20.3	979	29.8	3 0	1,701 6 0	1,164 11 0	122 13 4	569 9 6	25 14 3	222 8 8	81 1 0	2,174 1 5	3 10.2	...
28	Llandaff, Weybridge	24	361	31.6	117	27.0	3 0	902 2 0	416 2 6	37 3 3	96 9 3	...	38 13 9	5 4 2	539 17 11	3 7.6	...
	Summary, Group II. Average Cost per Patient	750	373	601.5	5,255	30.6	...	27,474 9 4	20,392 4 7 / 2 1.44	1,654 8 8 / 2.10	7,442 15 4 / 8.39	765 16 6 / .96	5,172 3 3 / 6.46	1,184 13 6 / 1.47	36,644 1 9 / 3 3.71	3 9.71	82 9 6
	Group III.																
29	Windlesham Moor	51	365	32.6	474	30.4	3 0	2,211 19 0	2,624 6 6	177 18 5	442 9 10	24 17 9	239 13 2	205 8 2	2,235 12 10	3 9	...
30	Henley Park, nr. Guildford	51	365	45.0	509	23.4	3 0	2,081 0 0	2,134 16 2	118 11 4	920 9 11	1 19 8	352 10 10	49 1 2	3,577 5 7	4 2.4	3 11
31	Beechcroft, Woking	51	362	35.4	475	29.5	3 0	2,109 8 0	1,270 15 9	187 0 8	586 8 1	87 13 9	214 3 6	47 15 9	2,393 14 5	3 5.5	111 2 2
32	The Green, Richmond	100	368	64.3	628	38.2	3 0	1,784 2 0	2,268 3 0	280 7 7	991 11 2	91 1 7	337 1 8	22 18 0	4,076 3 7	3 2.3	...
33	Camberley	78	365	46.8	461	37.1	3 0	2,658 1 0	1,384 8 3	131 13 11	574 3 10	46 2 1	873 1 4	61 15 4	2,275 7 8	3 5.3	...
34	The Hill, Lower Bourne, Farnham	60	296	48.8	503	33.8	3 0	2,592 9 6	1,354 1 2	131 18 11	808 17 6	87 8 9	162 19 6	118 8 9	2,563 15 3	2 11.7	6
35	Bridicot Hall, Suttas	83	305	65.1	521	48.7	3 0	3,737 1 0	3,177 19 6	110 14 5	709 6 9	2 5 1	622 14 7	130 18 11	3,648 19 3	3 3.8	116 15
36	Kingston, Surbiton and District, New Malden	212	296	139.9	1,024	50.5	3 0	6,406 8 0	6,820 18 0	235 18 2	1,534 17 0	1,142 7 11	1,698 14 10	85 0 10	10,307 16 10	3 5	...
37	Thorncombe, Bramley	60	366	48.7	326	42.7	3 0	2,714 8 0	1,750 1 10	161 12 1	1,091 11 11	...	608 19 4	133 9 10	2,658 7 0	5 0.1	...
38	Clandon Park, Guildford	162	365	82.3	1,368	21.6	4 0	6,831 11 8	4,458 3 11	846 6 8	1,656 6 7	183 12 0	1,401 3 6	8 8 0	8,542 9 8	3 4	116 7
39	Waverley Abbey, Farnham	125	303	103.9	1,265	39.3	3/-(4/-)	6,120 9 0	4,144 11 0	440 14 0	1,765 6 8	217 1 6	829 0 2	330 6 0	7,426 19 3	3 10.9	37 11
40	St. George's Hill, Weybridge	70	360	53.5	493	39.1	3 0	2,957 12 0	2,291 8 2	115 7 11	892 3 6	...	324 14 4	29 11 1	2,884 4 11	3 9.1	...
41	Hilders, Haslemere	60	331	55	493	37.8	3 0	2,658 9 0	2,177 9 1	318 10 4	761 12 3	220 15 3	660 14 3	62 0 12	4,141 2 11	4 5.6	...
42	Royal Surrey County Hospital (Annexe), Guildford	131	366	65.6	713	32.1	1 6	3,468 7 0	3,296 5 2	438 8 0	573 19 11	50 5 1	957 14 5	302 2 3	4,337 18 0	3 5	...
43	Brooklands, Weybridge	164	266	35.7	669	65.3	3 0	4,675 3 0	3,306 5 0	206 8 3	1,173 15 4	121 11 9	823 0 7	153 1 8	5,584 0 6	3 5	...
	Summary, Group III. Average Cost per Patient	1,533	354	1,014.2	10,378	36.2	...	63,207 6 2	39,496 2 0 / 3 1.61	4,091 9 11 / 2.60	14,162 15 0 / 9.22	2,276 2 4 / 1.43	8,737 14 2 / 5.53	1,749 12 7 / 1.13	70,446 13 0 / 3 5.79	3 9.76	384 13
	Summary for County Average Cost per Patient	3,217	334	1,814	16,196	36.3	...	93,950 13 0	64,583 7 3 / 2 1.58	8,550 7 0 / 2.10	23,353 14 7 / 9.26	3,472 7 9 / 1.30	15,692 18 2 / 6.32	3,072 2 1 / 1.22	116,695 16 9 / 3 5.98	3 9.98	478 1

Figure 35: Accounts of Auxiliary Hospitals in 1916.
Henley Park is the second entry in 'Group III'.
© British Red Cross Museum and Archives.

At its peak in 1918 the hospital accommodated up to 75 patients, 60 in the house itself and the rest in 'open air treatment' in tents and huts in the grounds. Altogether, 1,876 patients had been treated there by the time the hospital closed on 15 January 1919. The evening before the hospital closed a final entertainment was laid on with a fancy dress competition, games and dancing. After all the lent beds and furniture had been returned there was a grand rummage sale to clear the remaining stock.

During the period that Henley Park was a hospital, Lady Roberts lived nearby in Fox Lodge which was owned by Lieutenant General HE Belfield, but she retained a small suite of rooms in the mansion at Henley Park as well. She returned to live at Henley Park in 1919. Although it was not immediately obvious the First World War had changed the world and Britain's place in it irrevocably. The days of the great empire that Lord Pirbright used to praise so much were numbered, and the gentleman's sporting and leisured way of life that had supported country houses like Henley Park was coming to an end. For the time being however, things seemed to return to how they had been and by the 1920s Henley Park's pre-war elegance and grandeur had been restored. The photographs in the sale catalogue of 1922, reproduced in Plates 55 to 58, show that the house was tastefully decorated and elaborately furnished. There were many decorative touches including vases of flowers and many paintings on the walls, including 18th century oils by TE Roedinger. The large noble drawing room (Plate 57) had desks, potted plants and seating for about 20 guests. There was a full-sized billiard table in the billiard room (Plate 58). The flower gardens and park had also been restored to their beautiful pre-war condition.

After she returned to Henley Park, Lady Roberts remained active in village life and became the first president of the newly-formed Women's Institute. The British Red Cross Society paid her £1,000 to reinstate her home after the war but she chose to spend it instead for the benefit of Normandy and as a memorial to the local men who served in the war, so she used the money to establish a village hall so that the WI and other village organisations would have a place to hold their meetings. Trustees were appointed and Arthur William Milton sold them half an acre at the north-west corner of his land 'formerly part of the Manor Nurseries in Normandy' for £50 (half its market value, being his personal contribution) and this was paid by Lady Roberts. The hut, which had formerly been an Army recreation hut at Bramshott, was purchased for £220 and it cost a further £513 6s to move it to Normandy and erect it on the site. The hall was opened in September 1921 and it was to remain Normandy's village hall and the centre of community life for 80 years (see Plate 54).

For several years she was president of the Normandy and District Horticultural Society, she provided financial support to establish the Boy Scouts' hut on a piece of land purchased from Longerend Farm and which still stands between Guildford Road and Normandy Pond, and she is said to have given substantial aid to repairing the fabric of Wyke Church and the school, including hosting a village fête in the grounds of Henley Park to raise funds.

Lady Roberts occupied Henley Park on a yearly tenancy after the original lease expired in 1917 but the rent had doubled to £750 a year, probably taking into account the extensions and improvements which had been made by Lord Pirbright. When Henry Joseph Halsey put Henley Park up for sale in June 1922 the mansion was offered with 'vacant possession' even though her tenancy was not due to expire until Michaelmas (29th September), yet despite the potential sale she felt confident enough to allow a fête to be held in the grounds the same month.

Although the greater part of the Halsey estate was sold in 1922, the mansion and grounds did not reach their reserve price at the auction and Lady Roberts continued to live at Henley Park with a retinue of servants. After a prolonged illness she died there on 4 February 1925 aged 81, almost exactly ten years after Sir Owen. Her funeral service took place at Wyke Church where she had been a regular attendant, and she was buried at Highgate Cemetery. Her will was proved on the 15th of April, with probate to Sir Robert Armstrong-Jones and others. Her effects were valued at £89,693 17s 7d, more than double the value of Henley Park.

Like most 'self-respecting' historic houses Henley Park has a ghost story and this one concerns the so-called Lady in Mauve who, it is claimed, appeared whenever the house was about to change hands. Towards the end of Lady Roberts' occupancy the apparition was seen walking along the second floor corridor by a friend. It was wringing its hands and appeared to be greatly distressed. The friend, thinking it was another guest for lunch, was very puzzled when she entered the dining room and found that the table was only laid for two. When she described the incident to her hostess, Lady Roberts seemingly unperturbed, replied "Oh, you must have seen the Henley Park ghost". No explanation has been offered as to the identity of the Lady in Mauve nor is it known whether she ever appeared again.

10. END OF THE HALSEY ERA   (1922-1926)

In 1922 almost all of the remainder of the Halsey Surrey estate including Henley Park and the mansion which had been in the ownership of the family for 138 years, was put on the market. Advertised as a beautiful residential and agricultural estate, it was offered for auction at the Lion Hotel, Guildford, on Thursday 8 June 1922 by Alfred Saville and Sons of Lincoln's Inn Fields, London, in association with FA and AW Mellersh of Godalming. Although its size by now had fallen to 1,335 acres it was still one of the largest property sales for some time to take place at Guildford. Its sale catalogue (see Figure 38) ran to 39 pages with detailed descriptions and included five photographs of the interior of the house and four of the grounds. There was no bid for the estate as a whole so it was then offered in 21 lots which are summarised in Figure 36. Henley Park with the mansion and its grounds formed part of Lot 1.

The mansion itself was described as stately, presenting a dignified appearance of great charm and restful beauty, with the creeper-clad east front and the warm tiled roof which can be seen in some of the photographs. On the ground floor there were six reception rooms and two business rooms, and in the west wing, which had been built by Lord Pirbright, was the Noble Drawing Room or Saloon. The fittings and decorations were described and included fireplaces with wrought iron furniture and fine old dog grates, beautifully carved Carrara marble mantlepieces and Delft side tiles. There were mahogany doors and enriched ceilings and friezes, while the ceiling in the Morning Room was decorated with an oil painting in the centre. On the first floor in the west wing over the Noble Drawing Room was a 'charming suite' which had been occupied by Edward Prince of Wales when he visited Henley Park. It comprised a boudoir with a ceiling decorated with paintings of cupids in Italian style, two bedrooms and a bathroom. There were six more principal bedrooms, dressing rooms and three more bathrooms on the first floor, and over the dining room a 'handsome' Billiard Room (Plate 58). The second floor was taken up with guest rooms, servants' bedrooms, a flower room, sewing room, workroom, bathroom and box room.

The principal stairs were an open-well staircase with quarter landings, lit by a tall arched window overlooking the west gardens. The secondary staircase was a dog-leg design, but in later pictures taken during the years of decline (see Plate 99) it had the same decoration as the main stairs, and so was probably used by members of the family and guests as an alternative access to the first floor.

The domestic quarters included a 'light and lofty' kitchen, a serving room, pantry, scullery, larders and a strong room, with more bedrooms for servants and a cistern above. In the basement were extensive wine, beer and coal cellars. There was central heating from a furnace and boilers in the basement, and electric light powered by an engine and dynamo in the outbuildings, where there were more servants' quarters.

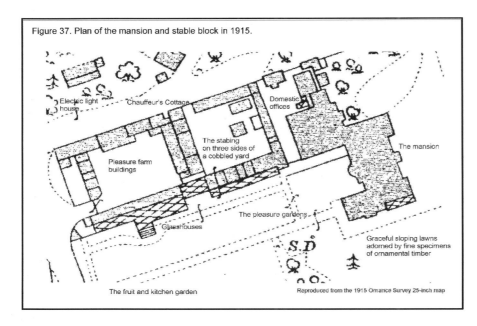

Figure 37. Plan of the mansion and stable block in 1915.

Electric light house · Chauffeur's Cottage · Domestic offices

The stabing on three sides of a cobbled yard

Pleasure farm buildings

The mansion

Glasshouses

The pleasure gardens

S.D

The fruit and kitchen garden

Graceful sloping lawns adorned by fine specimens of ornamental timber

Reproduced from the 1915 Ornance Survey 25-inch map

To the north-west of the mansion there was stabling in five stalls, six loose boxes, harness rooms, a hay loft, a granary and four grooms' rooms, as well as three coach houses and a garage. There was also a separate gun room and store and a Chauffeur's Cottage. There was still a home farm or 'Pleasure Farm' adjacent to the mansion and stables, with cow stalls for 14 cows, calf pen, calving box, five-stall cart-horse stable, harness room with forage room and loft over, double-bay barn, hog house, fatting stall with loft over, bull house, fowl house, piggeries and yard. This was quite separate from Henley Park Farm which was let to other tenants.

The Pleasure Gardens surrounding the house were delightfully laid out with graceful sloping lawns and fine specimens of ornamental timber, rhododendrons, azaleas, a choice collection of flowering shrubs and a beautiful rosary or rose garden. A gravelled path led down from the rose garden to a 2½-acre fish pond with a boathouse. Adjacent to the Pleasure Garden was the walled fruit and kitchen garden including a well-stocked 2-acre orchard with a large variety of wall, pyramid, espalier and bush fruit, and to the west was the Head Gardener's Cottage. There was an excellent range of glasshouses, palm house, vineries, peach and nectarine houses, greenhouses, forcing pits, cold frames, a double span carnation house and a rose house, as well as a stoke hole, packing and potting shed, mushroom house and fruit and onion rooms (see Plate 59).

Surrounding the mansion and pleasure grounds was the Finely Timbered Park of 79 acres with many delightful walks and drives and an 8-acre lake. A fine old avenue of specimen trees of exceptional size and beauty extended half a mile up to the front of the mansion from the Guildford Lodge entrance on Cobbett Hill Road. In addition there was an entrance and a lodge called Ash Lodge on the Pirbright Road. Also within the park was a 2½-acre pheasantry. The woods and plantations which extended to about 134 acres formed excellent covers and had been disposed over the estate with the intention of making it a 'capital shoot'. Great emphasis was made of the estate's sporting facilities which, with its 'social amenities and considerable historic associations' made it eminently suitable for 'the enjoyment of country life'.

The mansion, grounds and Henley Park Farm had been valued in 1913 at £29,273 for tax purposes but Lot 1 of the sale, which included Rails Farm as well, had a reserve price of £40,000. This was not met and the lot was withdrawn from the auction at £33,500. Some of the other lots (namely 6, 10-13 and 18) also failed to reach their reserve prices and were likewise withdrawn. The properties that were sold in 1922 raised £12,560.

Lot 1 was the most important lot to remain unsold and it is still not clear exactly what happened immediately following the auction. The mansion had been offered for sale with vacant possession but Lady Roberts continued to live there until her death in February 1925 and by June 1925 Edwin Ramsay Moodie and his family had taken possession of Henley Park. Rails Farm was sold separately in 1929 to Sir Laurence Edward Halsey KBE by the Halsey trustees and it was purchased some time later by Sir Robert Armstrong-Jones, Sir Owen Roberts' son-in-law[*]. The separate sale of Rails Farm ended the long association of Henley Park with Pirbright which had existed since 1677 when John Glynne bought the manor of Pirbright. Whipley Farm, on the other hand, had been offered separately as Lot 10 in the sale, but was acquired by Ramsay Moodie, possibly at the same time as he bought Henley Park.

So far all the properties which had been sold fell outside the bounds of the former royal park, the 428-acre park enclosed by Edward III in 1355 which had remained an integral unit under single ownership for more than 500 years. However in 1926 the park pale was 'breached' for the first time when Henry Joseph Halsey's trustees sold the eight acres in the south-west corner, which had formed Lot 6 in the estate sale, to Albert Henry Wiltshire and the land became a smallholding and nursery called Lynthorne. This lot also included an acre outside the park on which was an old house called 'Tatters' and the Normandy village smithy and the whole of it had been occupied for nearly 100 years by the Stedman family of blacksmiths and waggon builders. In the early 1900s it had been leased by Henry Joseph Halsey's trustees to Arthur Stedman at £23 per annum but in 1922 Arthur Stedman had recently died and by 1924 it was occupied by Albert Henry Wiltshire who probably used the former blacksmiths' shed as a paint shop for the family coach-building works on the other side of the road.

The only property owned by the Halseys which was not put up for sale was The Old School House in Pirbright, opposite the green. The family retained this house which was occupied by members of the Thompson family who apparently had a legal agreement stating that they could not be evicted 'while there was a Thompson descendant in the house'. In 1954 the freehold was conveyed to Edwina Countess de Kerdrel, Henry Joseph Halsey's eldest daughter, and it is said that she tried to remove the tenants so that she could use the house herself. The next year she agreed to let the occupants buy a plot of the garden and build a bungalow there and she took occupation of The Old School House at the age of 73. She tried unsuccessfully to have her son Michael Halsey de Kerdrel included on the Pirbright war memorial, claiming that "we have belonged to Pirbright for generations and she spent her youth at Henley Park". She lived at The Old School House for about five years and then finally sold the Halseys' last Surrey property in about 1960.

Soon after the 1922 estate sale Henry Joseph Halsey retired to the south of France where he continued to describe himself almost wistfully as 'formerly of Pirbright in Surrey'. He died on

---

[*] The Armstrong-Jones family lived at Stream House Farm which had formed Lot 14 in the 1922 sale and had been sold to a Mr Faggetter at the auction. In 1943 Sir Robert died and in 1945 his son Major Ronald Armstrong-Jones put his Pirbright properties up for sale by auction. He sold Rails Farm, with 84 acres, for £3,050 and Stream House Farm with 19 acres for £2,650.

31 May 1937 at Monte Carlo in his 80th year. He was cremated abroad and his ashes were deposited at Pirbright Church on the 16th of June, but there is no memorial in the church to the last Halsey to own Henley Park. His brief will drawn up in 1926 bequeathed 'all his real and personal estate' to a trustee for the benefit in equal shares of his younger daughters Linda Agnes and Brenda Iris.

The final document in the Halsey papers is a receipt dated 6 January 1939. Henry Joseph had deposited an envelope with his solicitors, Messrs Bircham and Co of London, containing four rings, being 'the property of Linda and Brenda Halsey'. Brenda called and collected the rings but left the empty envelope behind.

Figure 36: The Henley Park Estate Sale 1922.
Summary of Lots.

Lot	Description	Occupied by	Sold to
1	a) Mansion & grounds 224 acres in Normandy and 110 acres in Pirbright	Lady Roberts rent £750	*(Not sold at auction)*
	b) Henley Park Farm 168 acres in Normandy and 2 acres in Worplesdon	Mr WJ Harding rent £190	
	c) Rails Farm 80 acres in Pirbright	Messrs Rushen rent £85	
	d) A part of Whipley Farm 36 acres in Normandy	Mr Isaac Bolton rent £36	
	e) Woods & plantations 60 acres in Normandy and 75 acres in Pirbright	In hand (Halsey)	
2	Cottage (former laundry) with 4 acres in Pirbright [now called Stream House]	Lady Roberts sublet to Mr Charnock	Mr Charnock, the tenant, for £710
3	Smallborne Cottage, Stanford Common with ½ acre in Pirbright	Mr WG Harding rent £10 8s	Mr Humphrey Quin for £200
4	Longerend Farm 92 acres in Normandy	Mr EH North rent £85	Mr EH North, the tenant, for £2,000
5	Smallholding 3 acres in Normandy [now Normandy Hill Farm and Quinta Cottage]	Mr Lipscombe rent £25	Mr Quin for £500
6	Lynthorne (including the Smithy) 9 acres in Normandy	Exors of A Stedman rent £32	*(Not sold at auction)*
7	Cottage and garden, with ¼ acre in Normandy [former cottage on Guildford Road opposite shop which became the Motorcycle Shop]	Mr A Marshall rent £5	Mr FF Ramez for £180
8	Accommodation arable land, 4 acres in Normandy [on Guildford Road opposite shop which became the Motorcycle Shop]	Mr William Deedman rent £10	Mr Ramez for £150
9	Bailes Farm 100 acres in Worplesdon and 4 acres in Normandy	Mr Ewen Maclacklan rent £140	Mr EM Tenant for £2,800

Figure 36: The Henley Park Estate Sale 1922.
Summary of Lots (continued).

Lot	Description	Occupied by	Sold to
10	Whipley Farm 140 acres in Worplesdon and 4 acres in Normandy	Mr Isaac Bolton rent £134	*(Did not reach its reserve of £3,250 and was withdrawn)*
11	Whipley copse 14 acres in Worplesdon	In hand (Halsey)	*(Not sold at auction)*
12	The Duchies (2 cottages) and 1 acre in Pirbright	Mr Mark Boylett, Mr D Boulter gross rent £17 8s	*(Did not reach its reserve of £450 and was withdrawn)*
13	The Nursery 8 acres (formerly Waterer & Sons) and a cottage with ½ acre, in Pirbright	The Nursery in hand, Cottage Mr Cranston rent £11 14s	*(Not sold at auction)*
14	Fellmoors smallholding, Stanford Common, 5 acres in Pirbright [now Stream House Farm]	Mr Avenell rent £25	Mr EB Faggetter for £670
15	Stanford Farm 57 acres in Pirbright	Mr Alfred Fry rent £56 10s	Mr HB Baverstock for £1,200
16	Stanford Cottage ½ acre in Pirbright	Mr John Chandler rent £5 5s	Mr Avenell for £210
17	Manor Farm 110 acres in Pirbright	Messrs Rushen rent £70	Mr Ramez for £2,500
18	Parkland opposite Pirbright Lodge (offered as a building site) 7 acres	Mrs Poole rent £13	*(Not sold at auction)*
19	Halsey Cottage with ½ acre, in Normandy	Mr Jesse Deedman rent £5	Mr North for £340
20	Pusseys Copse (smallholding) 10 acres in Normandy	Mr Horton rent £9 2s	Mr Ramez for £440
21	Ground rents - Manor House & cottage with 4 acres in Pirbright	Mrs Armstrong rent £33	Mr Ramez for £660

Grand total for sale at auction: 1,334 acres (615 in Normandy, 463 in Pirbright, 256 in Worplesden)
with a total annual rental of £1,740 1s 6d
Total sale price of properties sold in 1922: £12,560.

Figure 38: 'Beautiful residential and agricultural estate'
page 1 of the 1922 estate sale catalogue.

SURREY

On High Ground, overlooking the Hogs Back, in the PARISHES OF NORMANDY, WORPLESDON and PIRBRIGHT, and about four miles from the County Town of Guildford.

PARTICULARS, PLANS, VIEWS AND CONDITIONS OF SALE

OF

The Beautiful

Residential and Agricultural Estate

DISTINGUISHED AS

Henley Park Estate

INCLUDING THE

STATELY MANSION

Erected early in the Eighteenth Century, but brought up to date with Modern Additions and Improvements, containing A NOBLE SUITE OF RECEPTION ROOMS, and a sufficient complement of Bed Room Accommodation, occupying an elevated position in a

FINELY TIMBERED PARK

WITH

Beautiful Pleasure Grounds, Gardens and Woodlands,

TOGETHER WITH

The Home Farm, Several Agricultural Holdings,
. and numerous Small Holdings and Cottages .

The Whole embracing an Area of about

1,335 Acres.

Which will be Sold by Auction by

ALFRED SAVILL & SONS

in conjunction with

F. A. & A. W. MELLERSH

At the Lion Hotel, Guildford,

On Thursday, the 8th day of June, 1922,

At THREE p.m. (unless previously Sold by Private Treaty).

Copies of the Particulars, with Plans and Conditions of Sale may be obtained of the Solicitors, Messrs. BIRCHAM & CO., 46, Parliament Street, Westminster, S.W. 1 ; or of the Auctioneers, Messrs. MELLERSH, Godalming, Surrey ; and Messrs. ALFRED SAVILL & SONS, 51a, Lincoln's Inn Fields, W.C. 2, and 7, Birchin Lane, E.C. 3.

Figure 39: Some other pages of the sale catalogue: page 10, a charming suite, page 22, Longerend Farm, page 27, Whipley Farm and page 36, the Manor House in Pirbright.

On the First Floor:

approached by an easy principal staircase and secondary staircase, the accommodation comprised:—

In the WEST WING over Drawing Room.

A CHARMING SUITE

comprising:

Boudoir, 16ft. 8in. by 16ft. 5in., with finely carved white marble mantel and ceiling decorated with paintings of Cupids in Italian style.

Bed Room adjoining, 24ft. by 16ft. with finely carved white marble mantel.

Bed Room, 21ft. 5in. by 16ft. 5in., with carved white marble mantel.

Bath Room, with porcelain enamel bath and lavatory basin, fireplace and W.C.

This Suite was occupied by the late King Edward when visiting Henley Park.

Adjoining is the

Blue Bath Room, with porcelain enamel bath and lavatory basin, communicating with the

Blue Bed Room, 21ft. 5in. by 20ft., with Dentil cornice and grey marble mantel.

Bird Dressing Room, with carved white marble mantel.

Bird Bed Room, 24ft. 9in. by 16ft. 5in., with Dentil cornice and carved marble mantel.

Bed Room over Business Room, 16ft. 4in. by 13ft. 2in., with marble and carved wood mantel.

Pompadour Dressing Room adjoining.

Bed Room over Study, 20ft. 7in. by 12ft., with grey white and black marble mantel.

The Red Bed Room, 13ft. 8in. by 16ft., with grey grained marble mantel.

The Red Bath Room, with fireplace and W.C. adjoining.

Bachelors' Bed Room.

HOUSEMAID'S CUPBOARD.

LINEN ROOM AND SERVANTS' W.C.

10

LOT 4

(Coloured *Green* on Plan).

The Attractive & Well-situated Holding

KNOWN AS

LONGEREND FARM

in the PARISH OF ASH AND NORMANDY. There is a Capital Farmhouse built of brick and tile, containing Sitting Room, Two Kitchens, Scullery, Larder and Cellar, and Four Bed Rooms over. The Buildings include Bullock Stalls, Three stall Stable, Barns, Root House, Cow Stalls, Two Cart Sheds, Piggeries and Yard.

The Water Supply is from a Well.

On Ordnance No. 330 is a BRICK, TIMBER AND TILED COTTAGE known as

LONGEREND COTTAGE

containing Four Rooms.

The Land has a Southerly slope and is in very good heart, and includes Three Pasture Fields adjoining Station Road, the whole extending to

92a. 1r. 35p.

as shown in the following SCHEDULE.

Parish.	Ord. No.	Description	Area.
Ash and Normandy	304	Arable	11·192
	306a	Ditto	2·929
	342	Ditto	9·667
	307	Ditto	4·751
	313a	Ditto	0·141
	360	House, Buildings, &c.	1·128
	361	Arable	4·974
	345	Ditto	2·423
	343	Pasture	4·195
	342	Arable	6·944
	359	Cottage and Garden	·367
	361	Pasture	5·920
	312	Ditto	5·135
	308	Ditto	3·580
	341	Ditto	9·013
	337	Ditto	1·931
	338	Ditto	2·431
	311	Pasture	4·371
	305b	Woodland	·132
	306c	Roadside Waste	1·005
Pt. 295		Garden	·141
			92·487 92 1 38

Pt. Ordnance No. 295 is let to Mr. Mullard at 30s. per annum, and No. 379a is in hand. The remainder is let to Mr. E. H. North on a Yearly (Michaelmas) Tenancy at a Rental of £85 a year.

The Property is understood to be free from Land Tax.

Tithe, apportioned value, £18 16s. 7d.

Small portions of this Lot are sold subject to the restrictions mentioned in Condition 14.

22

LOT 10

(Coloured *Brown* on Plan).

A Very Productive Corn and Stock Farm

KNOWN AS

WHIPLEY FARM

in the PARISHES OF WORPLESDON AND ASH AND NORMANDY well situate adjoining the main road and near the Village of Normandy.

The Commodious and Picturesque Farmhouse

dated 1733, contains Spacious Dining Hall, Two Sitting Rooms, Kitchen and Cellarage, Dairy and an Oak Staircase leading to Five Bed Rooms.

The Buildings

include Two Barns, Stabling for six horses, Lewin, Cow Stalls, Cart Shed, Granary, Piggery, and Two Yards.

On Ordnance No. 3b there is a Capital Cottage.

Together with productive Pasture, Arable and Woodland, extending in all to

143a. 2r. 17p.

as shown in the following SCHEDULE.

Parish.	Ord. No.	Description	Area.
Worplesdon	1128	Pasture	6·709
	1129	Ditto	9·906
	1127	Ditto	7·588
	1129	Ditto	6·915
	1153	Arable	23·728
	1132	Pond	·168
	1093	Pasture	4·986
	1107	Ditto	4·459
	1106	Ditto	7·890
	1096	Ditto	1·723
	1097	Arable	35·107
	1102	Pasture	4·295
	1131	Pond	·326
	1103	Plant., Buildings, &c.	2·418
	1121	Clayford Copse	2·089
Ash and Normandy	28	Pasture	4·285
	28	Cottage	·272
			142·607 143 2 17

Clayford Copse, Ordnance No. 1121 is in hand and the remainder is let together with other Lands forming part of Lot 1 to Mr. Isaac Bolton on a Michaelmas Tenancy subject to two years' notice to quit and the Rent apportioned in respect of this lot for the purpose of sale is £134 per annum.

The Purchaser of this Lot shall, if required, join with the Purchaser of Lot 1 (or if Lot 1 be not sold, with the Vendor), in giving the Tenant a valid notice to quit the entire Holding expiring at Michaelmas, 1924.

The Property is understood to be free from Land Tax. Company's Water is laid on and the Water Rate is paid by the Landlord.

OUTGOINGS:—

Tithe (apportioned value) £37 4 2 Worplesdon Parish.
                                    17 1 Ash and Normandy.
                           ————————
                           £33 1 2

27

LOT 21.

Valuable Freehold Ground Rents

OF

Per £33 Ann.

secured upon the RESIDENTIAL PROPERTY known as

"THE MANOR HOUSE"

(OF GREAT INTEREST),

situate at PIRBRIGHT, SURREY, containing old Beam Ceiling Entrance Hall; Beamed Ceiling Dining Room (formerly the Court House); Drawing Room with square lead light windows; Morning Room; Eight Bed Rooms; Box and Dressing Rooms; Domestic Offices and Cellarage; Coach-house; Stabling; Greenhouse; Coachman's Cottage; Pretty Old-world Gardens with lawns beautifully-timbered, Clipped Hedges, Flower and Kitchen Gardens, Orchard and a Fish Pond.

Of the Estimated Rental Value of

Per £300 Ann.

(including the Gardener's Cottage hereafter mentioned).

Let on Lease dated March 25th, 1896, to Mrs. Armstrong, for a term of 76 years (from March 25th, 1896), at a Ground Rent of £31 a year, with the reversion to the Rack Rental at the expiration of the Lease in 50 years.

ALSO

THE GARDENER'S COTTAGE,

situate in MILL LANE, PIRBRIGHT, SURREY, and adjacent to the Manor House, containing Sitting Room, Kitchen, Three Bed Rooms, Outbuildings and Garden.

Let on Lease dated March 25th, 1902, to Mrs. Armstrong, for a term of 72 years (from March 25th, 1902), at a Ground Rent of £2 a year, with the reversion to the property at the expiration of the Lease in 50 years.

The whole Property being in extent about

4a. 2r. 0p.

and is understood to be Tithe and Land Tax free.

36

11. Indian Summer; Ramsay Moodie (1925-1940)

Edwin Ramsay Moodie was the last private owner of the mansion and park at Henley. Although the great Halsey estate had now been broken up and the park pale was soon to be breached, the house was to enjoy one last period of occupation as a gentleman's country residence and in the Moodies' ownership it was a much loved family home.

Edwin Ramsay Moodie, who was usually known by his middle name Ramsay, was born in 1867 at Rock Ferry near Birkenhead, Cheshire, and attended the Grammar School at Beaumaris, Anglesey. His father was a captain on Cunard transatlantic liners and Ramsay himself travelled far and wide during his life, on business and pleasure. He was a director of the firm Watson and Co of Liverpool who traded in cotton, and in his position in charge of buying he regularly made extended visits to the southern United States, sometimes accompanied by his family. He became a very wealthy man and this enabled him to retire when still relatively young and live the life of a leisured gentleman. He had married his wife Helen Agatha in 1902 and they had three children, Dorothy (known as Deb), Robin (born in the United States during a cotton-buying trip) and Katherine. Before the family came to Henley Park their main home had been Moston Hall in Cheshire. Ramsay was a keen sportsman and liked shooting and fishing, and family tradition has it that he had always promised his wife, who did not like the north of England, that one day they would move to the south. Henley Park's situation and amenities must have suited both of them perfectly.

By the time they took up residence in 1925 their son Robin had commenced his naval career and was away at sea for most of the time but he always enjoyed spending his leave at home at Henley Park. His sisters were still living at home at the time the family moved south and after her marriage, Deb often remained at Henley Park together with her young children and their nannies, while her husband Leigh Windus returned to Argentina to run his farm there. Seventy years on, Deb's son and elder daughter who, although born elsewhere, were baptised at Wyke Church, have recalled the idyllic childhood they spent with their grandparents and the many servants who looked after them, including the diffident Miss Deedman who served at table and the terrifying Alice the cook! They remember the house being frequently filled with visitors and guests and their grandfather often hosting shooting parties. They have many photographs dating from this period, some of which are reproduced in this book, and these give an indication of the lavish care their grandparents spent in furnishing the house and maintaining the grounds as still befitted a gentleman's country home.

These photographs, together with those in the 1922 estate sale catalogue, make it possible to confirm the layout of the principal rooms on the ground floor as shown in Figure 26. The central porch (shown in Plate 62) and door on the east front led into the Entrance Hall (Plate 63). A comparison with the earlier photograph of this hall in the 1922 sale catalogue (Plate 55) shows that the Moodies made several changes here. The fireplace surround has been replaced and the walls repanelled, the ceiling smoothed out to remove the battens and the light fitting changed. The Moodies furnished the room in a more formal style with upright chairs against the walls and a small central table supporting flowers, unlike the easy chairs and writing desk which were there in Lady Roberts' time. There were also fewer pictures on the walls.

Adjoining the hall on either side were two small rooms which at the time of the sale in 1922 were known as the Secretary's Room and the Business Room. These were not illustrated in the catalogue and one of them may have become the Moodies' library pictured in Plate 64. The Study or Gun Room described in the sale catalogue was at the northern corner of the east front and adjoined the room to the right of the entrance hall, but there is no illustration of it. The Morning Room, with the oil painting in the centre of its ceiling and a large full-length mirror (Plate 66) was on the opposite southern corner of the east front and it had both an east and south aspect. It led into a glass loggia which was rebuilt to a different design by the Moodies. The Breakfast Room in 1922 was on the north-west corner at the back of the house and beyond that the kitchen wing. An interior hallway ran behind the east front rooms, and the bottom step of the principal staircase can be seen in the view of the hallway (Plate 69). The Dining Room (Plates 56, 67) was in the centre of the west front with doors leading to it from the entrance hall. This as previously mentioned had been extended by Lord Pirbright with a bay window and the Moodies apparently re-panelled it with dark wood panels, possibly mahogany. In the Noble Drawing Room or Saloon in the west wing (Plates 57, 68) the walls and the decorative ceiling remained unchanged by the Moodies, but the furnishing was radically different. Gone is the crammed ostentation of Lady Robert's padded armchairs, side tables and potted plants which must have left her guests little room to move, while the Moodies had a very open, almost 'minimalist' feel to the room.

The first and second floors were taken up with bedrooms, bathrooms and the servants' quarters and Mrs Moodie's grandchildren especially remember their grandmother's sewing room on the second floor. They also remember the fun and excitement of the fire evacuation practices, when they would all slide down a temporary chute from an upstairs window.

The gardens at Henley Park had always been an attractive feature. The Moodies not only continued this tradition but extended the gardens to the south by taking a rectangular 'bite' out of the fields of Henley Park Farm to create the 'Lily Garden', later called the 'Italian Garden' and this change is shown on the Ordnance Survey maps. There were two fountains in the Lily Garden (Plate 70) which were gravity-fed by mains water from the mansion - until recently there was an inspection cover just by the footpath that crosses the grounds. At the top of the steps above the Lily Garden was a sundial and there was a stone leaning against it with leaded lettering containing a poem about an English garden. In addition Mr Moodie hired steam tackle to dredge the river and boating lake from Chinese Bridge to Tumbling Bay, which must have silted up since Lord Pirbright's time.

The extent of the large stable block situated to the north-west of the mansion and enclosing two yards can be seen from the aerial photograph (Plate 71). The western yard was used as a farmyard, described in 1922 as the 'pleasure farm buildings' and the eastern yard was used for stabling the riding horses as well as garaging cars. The Moodies had a fleet of cars and two chauffeurs, and Plate 73 conveys the atmosphere as they departed on one of their motoring excursions. Mrs Moodie often holidayed in the south of France and was driven there in one of the family cars.

The main entrance to the mansion in the Moodies' time was from the Pirbright Road where there were two large ornate gateways with gilt wrought-iron gates, at approximately the same position as the main entrance to Vokes was for many years, with the three roadways shown on Plate 72 leading from it. The left one swept round to the front of the mansion, the right went round via the cottages where the workers lived and the middle one led to the stables. All three roadways were still there until Vokes' factory was built in the 1950s. In the 1930s a local resident used to go carol singing at the mansion and she thought it was very grand. She remembers that there were peacocks in the stable yard which used to make a most horrendous noise.

As well as the 13 acres of grounds around the house, Ramsay Moodie owned and occupied a total of 420 acres of parkland and woodland. This included the 135 acres of copse within the park which had always been held 'in hand' by the Halseys and another 110 acres including Henley Park Lake outside the former royal park. In addition he owned the 168-acre Henley Park Farm where he kept his herd of pedigree Guernsey cows. The farm was occupied by Thomas Harding in the late 1920s and then by G Dart who came from Tiverton in Devon and looked after the sheep and lambs on the farm. They had about 200 lambs in 1938. Mr Dart was succeeded as tenant farmer in the late 1930s by Robert Turner who, according to local hearsay, used to watch the farm workers from an upper window of the farm house with binoculars!

Ramsay Moodie also owned Whipley Farm which had formed Lot 10 in the 1922 sale but had not been sold at that time. He sold the farm in about 1935 to the then tenant Mr Hawkins but retained the fields in the south-eastern part of the royal park which had formerly been farmed as part of Whipley.

He increased the number of dwellings within the park. By 1927 there were six including the Stables Cottage later Garage Cottage or Chauffeur's lodge, attached to the stable block, and two lodges - the Pirbright Road Lodge which comprised two tenements and the White Lodge (at Cobbett Hill), one of which was described as the 'handyman's lodge' and the others were occupied by gardeners. The House in the Wall, next to the kitchen garden, was sometimes called 'Dolly and Parry's cottage' and was the head gardener's cottage with three bedrooms, and was occupied by Mr and Mrs W Parry. There was also the 'Steward's Bungalow', later Orchard Bungalow which was occupied by the estate manager Mr J Petrie, an agricultural expert from Fife in Scotland. It had a big room where the estate workers held meetings. In the early 1930s Ramsay Moodie commissioned a pair of semi-detached cottages for estate workers on the Pirbright Road, now called Orchard House and Orchard Cottage. They were designed by Colonel Lannoy John Coussmaker of neighbouring Westwood and the front entrances face towards Henley Park not to the road. He also gained planning permission in 1936 for a new pair of cottages at the other side of the estate opposite Whipley Farm, designed by Coussmaker and Armstrong, architects of Guildford, but these were never built and the planning permission lapsed.

Although the Moodies embraced many aspects of modern technology such as motor cars, the first telephone at Henley Park was apparently delegated to the estate manager and it was listed in the name of Mr Petrie from 1934 to 1939. Unlike the Coussmakers, who seem to have had the second telephone in Normandy with the number 'Normandy 2', the Moodies were not so quick off the mark and Henley Park's number was Worplesdon 91.

In the 1920s there was a plan to build council houses along the Pirbright Road, so in about 1927 Mr Moodie and Sir Philip Henriques of Normandy Park devised a scheme to prevent this. Mr Moodie bought 24 acres at the junction of Pirbright Road and Hunts Hill Road from Colborne Brothers the builders, and in 1928 he planted 5,000 Scots Pines there to prevent the plan being implemented. This land, now known as Longerend Plantation, was originally part of Longerend Farm which had been sold by the Halseys in 1922*. The plantation was still owned by the Moodie family 70 years later.

In 1938 the author and broadcaster SPB Mais came to Normandy researching a radio programme on the life of the politician and social reformer William Cobbett. He spoke to the 'squire' of Henley Park estate, Mr Moodie, his farm agent Mr Petrie and his gamekeeper Mr Clark (see Plate 75), who commented that Mr Moodie did not 'preserve' the pheasants like Lord Pirbright had done, which Mr Mais felt would have pleased William Cobbett who believed that all game should be common property. One of the gamekeeper's duties was to keep down the moles, and he had killed 95 of them on the estate in one month earlier that year. Mr Mais also interviewed Mr Hawkins the tenant of Whipley Farm, who observed rather cynically that there were very few Surrey-born farmers left in the area, and talked to Mr Mullard who had worked at Henley Park Farm all his life with the exception of the 1914-18 war. In the early 1800s when he lived in Normandy, William Cobbett had bemoaned the decline in farming that had occurred as a result of the enclosures, yet Mr Mullard did not seem unhappy with his lot and spoke of the improvements in agricultural life. He drove two fine Suffolk Punches when the ploughing was horse-powered (see Plate 76) and later he was driving the brand-new tractor. In 1926 he was getting £1 9s a week and by 1938 £2 a week and a rent-free house. He worked a 60 hour week, getting up at half past five to feed the horses, then after his own breakfast ploughing with the horses until noon, then an hour for lunch before continuing until 5pm. He felt that conditions were better than they used to be - "there's more variety in the food now we've got buses to go to market in Guildford or Farnham" - and he felt he had no cause for complaint. However, labourers in a service house were not allowed to keep pigs or poultry in case they took some of the feed for their own animals. Mr Mullard's son used to take the daily milk, cream and eggs up to the mansion before school.

The Moodies were not as evident in local affairs as the Roberts had been, although they did participate and are still remembered by many in Normandy. A year after they took up residence they opened the grounds for an historical pageant and fair in aid of St. George's Home for Children of Officers in need. Mr Moodie became a trustee of Normandy village hall and donated money to a trust fund for its improvement and maintenance. Mrs Moodie sponsored a cup for school gardens which was won in 1933 by Wanborough School, and local residents remember that the Moodies used to give children's parties with impressive fireworks. Mrs Moodie also performed charitable work, copying books into braille using a machine. On one occasion Mr Moodie was photographed at an event with the 'Old Contemptibles' and the British Legion at the

---

* The Colbornes sold the rest of Longerend Farm in 1927 to SN Jenkinson who planned an estate of more than 200 houses on it, but only two of them were ever built - Ragwort (now Gemswood Place) and Calshot (now Fairoaks) in Normandy Common Lane.

village hall, which may have been connected with his work in the First World War when, too old for active service, he drove ambulances in France.

Mr Moodie liked to spend a lot of his time away on his sporting activities, fishing in Norway or New Zealand, and during one of his absences in May 1934 there was a 'daring burglary' at Henley Park reported in the *Surrey Advertiser*. In the early hours of a Tuesday morning thieves got away with a haul of jewellery, objects d'art and valuables estimated at £1,000. Mrs Moodie and their daughter were sleeping in the house but they were not disturbed and it was not until the staff began their duties that it was found that the house had been broken into. The robbery was attributed to the 'Country House Robbery Gang' and Farnham police brought in Scotland Yard, but it is not known whether any of the property was ever recovered.

This affluent lifestyle might have continued for many more years but when war broke out in 1939 most of the staff and estate workers left to do war work and it became impractical to run such a large house and estate. Ramsay Moodie must have realised that the estate could be requisitioned for wartime purposes and he probably foresaw that the world would be very different after the war and the house and its lifestyle would not be sustainable. It is not clear whether the house was advertised for sale or whether one of the wartime ministries acted as a go-between, but Vokes Ltd bought the estate through Hewitt and Lee, land agents and auctioneers of High Street Guildford, and in October 1940 Mr CG Vokes called on Mr Moodie to discuss the terms of the purchase. It was apparently a private sale rather than at auction and by spring 1941 Vokes had taken possession of the estate. Although one corner of the former royal park had been sold separately, the rest of the park had remained intact in Mr Moodie's ownership up to the Second World War. However, the pace of the breakup was about to quicken with the acquisition by Vokes Ltd.

E Ramsay Moodie was about 73 when he sold Henley Park, but he still had great stamina and zest for adventure. He was, apparently, quite a character and in 1953 at the age of 85 he went with his grandson Robin Windus on a gruelling eight-week trip up the Amazon river to collect timber and brazil nuts. Ramsay was also a keen drinker of Port and he knew all the shippers, so they stopped at Porto on the way to sample the wares! After the war the family owned and lived at Ghyll Manor near Rusper in Sussex which was relatively smaller and more manageable than Henley Park, and he died there in 1954.

12. VOKES; WAR AND ITS AFTERMATH (1940-1953)

The Background of Vokes Ltd

Mr Cecil Gordon Vokes was very keen on new technology. He was also something of an entrepreneur, as we would describe him today.

He trained as an engineer and after the First World War went into business on his own with an overdraft of £100 guaranteed by his father. He founded Vokes Ltd in London in 1921 as an engineering and import-export company. They imported the first car windscreen wipers from the USA, but these were seen as a luxury item at the time - most people stopped and wiped the windscreen if it was dirty. Later, when car makers saw the value in this accessory and other manufacturers began to infringe Mr Vokes' patent he brought a successful legal action against them, but by then the market was over-supplied and Mr Vokes sought other fields of business. In the 1930s the company, now with its own manufacturing plant, became involved in filtration for cars and Mr Vokes used his own collection of Lagonda cars to test his filters. The 1935-36 war between Italy and Abyssinia (now Ethiopia) convinced Mr Vokes that mechanical warfare was the warfare of the future and that engines, if they were to be of any use, would need efficient air and oil filtration. When war broke out in Europe he proposed to the Air Ministry that filters should be fitted to all aircraft engines but this was initially regarded as unnecessary as the average life of an aircraft at that time was too short to justify it. The North Africa campaign altered this view when, with 'planes taking off in formation amidst a cloud of sand, engines were wearing out in 10 flying hours. Mr Vokes recalled a conference late at night with representatives of the War Ministry when they said "we do hope your filter is as good as you say or we have no hope of winning this war". According to Mr Vokes later, it was only when Vokes filters were fitted onto the Army's tanks in North Africa that "our boys could go the 2,000 miles to Tunisia". The logistic superiority given to the Allied forces by their efficient air and oil filters - not initially possessed by the Axis - was an important advantage in conducting the war. Another of Mr Vokes' inventions was a flame trap to hide the exhaust flames of night fighters.

By the time Vokes' main factory in Lower Richmond Road, Putney was destroyed by enemy bombing on 13 October 1940 their work was considered so vital that the Ministry of Aircraft Production urged them to find a place outside London, but within 30 miles of the capital, and get back into production as soon as possible, and the Ministry would subsidise the move to the tune of between £65,000 and £70,000. As Mr Vokes later put it, "as a result of enemy action we were ordered to take refuge in Normandy". By now Vokes were responsible for the manufacture of all military aircraft filters and were effectively consultants to Government departments on filtration issues.

Acquisition of Henley Park

Vokes are said to have established local representation in North Street, Guildford by 1939 and this local presence may have influenced their choice of location when they had to react rapidly to the events in Putney. Mr Vokes visited various properties in the western home counties and he made an offer to Sir Philip Henriques for Normandy Park. However, he judged Henley Park ideal for the company's purposes and in October 1940 he met Mr Moodie to discuss the purchase of the Henley Park estate. The company is reputed to have bought it for £50,000, complete with 600 acres of land and a number of houses, and the headquarters of Vokes Ltd was established at Henley Park in early spring of 1941. Vokes registered their title to Henley Park at the Land Registry on 14th March that year. The Ministry assisted them to built the factory, conforming to their ideas of the best layout to minimise the effect of an air attack - the workshops were dispersed over a wide area and were built at different angles so that a blast would affect few of them directly. By June 1941 big factory sheds were being built in the park under the trees, which provided good camouflage, and the offices were in the house. From the Pirbright Road passers-by could not tell there was a factory there because all the buildings were hidden amongst the trees - as Mr Vokes put it, they were "hidden away as much as possible to avoid further attentions from the enemy".

The layout of the site was described by a wartime employee as follows: "As you entered the site from the Pirbright Road you went through the woods and there was a police box on the right. Then on the left was a big building called 10X, made of brick and corrugated iron. After this on the left-hand side were buildings called Multi-V and 11X. On the opposite side were the prototype shop and the press shop. Behind that was the machine shop 12X and another one called 9X. There were lots of little Nissen huts scattered about all over the place, including a spray shop and a print shop." The layout is shown on a beautifully detailed hand-drawn map of the factory grounds produced in 1944 (see Figure 40) which mentions the 'head office and drawing office' in the mansion, canteen and kitchen in the north-west wing and rifle range, air raid shelter and ack-ack machine gun post in the grounds. This factory complex remained more or less unchanged until the post-war factory was started in the mid-1950s.

There were a lot of local objections to the company establishing itself at Henley Park, mainly from gentry and farmers who felt that the factory would attract all the local labour and they would have to pay a lot more to get people to work on their lands. A public meeting was organised and the discussion became very heated; John Milton, chairman of Normandy Cricket Club and Mr 'Bert' Osborne, a manager of Vokes, had a standup argument - Mr Milton called Mr Osborne "a cockney spiv" and Osborne called Milton "a country yokel". However, the emergency wartime powers overrode all objections, Vokes' factory was established, and subsequently Mr Milton and Mr Osborne became great friends and were both longtime members of the Cricket Club.

A national farming survey in 1941, presumably conducted to assess the nation's ability to be self-sufficient in food production, assessed the 67 acres immediately around the mansion as: mostly wood with six acres of potatoes and one acre of orchards, with no infestations of rabbits, moles, rats, mice, rooks, wood pigeons or insect pests, but heavy infestation of weeds (rushes and bracken).

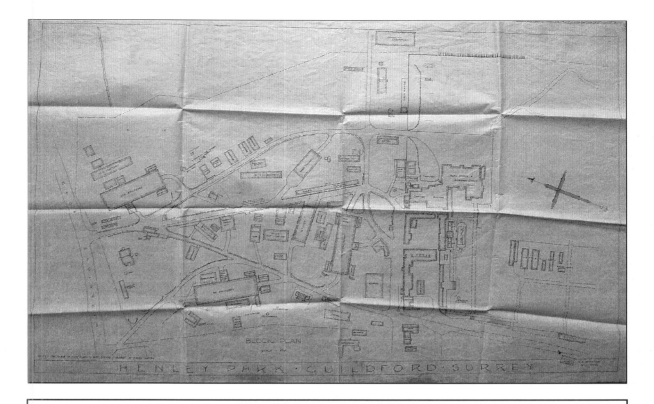

Figure 40:
Hand-drawn map of the factory grounds in 1944.

A detailed inventory in 1942 for insurance purposes valued the plant, machinery, vehicles, office equipment and furniture at Henley Park at £49,132 13s 8d, ranging from machines in 10X factory worth nearly £2,600 to the wicker wastepaper basket in Mr Vokes' office worth 3s 6d (see figure 41). Vokes' premises at Biddles in Martyr Road Guildford, Gray's Garage Guildford and at Alton were also valued, bringing the grand total to £75,853 14s 2d.

Because Vokes' war work was so sensitive, some of the public footpaths around the mansion were closed. Ash Parish Council debated the matter in November 1941 and Mr WJ Henry of Normandy Stores assured the Council that the 'round walk' on the cinder track past the gardener's cottage and back through the home walk to the war memorial was still open and was used by a good many people.

Wartime stories and Vokes' war work

During the war Vokes primarily designed and manufactured air and oil filters for aircraft and war vehicles to the order of Government departments. They operated under a veil of secrecy and it was not until Spring of 1946 that they were even allowed to disclose their whereabouts. One of 'Lord Haw-Haw's wartime propaganda broadcasts mentioned Vokes, he said that the Germans knew where it was.

Figure 41.
Page from the
1942 inventory.

ADMINISTRATION BUILDING.

Mr.C.G.VOKES' OFFICE.

6' leather top Partners' Desk with 12 drawers and 2 cupboards	60 - -
Revolving Tub Chair, leather	10 10 -
Elbow Chair, upholstered with cushion and spring seat	6 10 -
Carved oak Elbow Chair	5 10 -
Oak Standard Chair	4 10 -
2 carved oak Elbow Chairs, leather backs and seats	21 - -
Coat and Umbrella Stand	3 10 -
5'6" Walnut Cabinet, with three bevelled glass doors and ends, three drawers under	40 - -
4' Bookcase, ormolu mount, carved pillars	30 - -
21'6" x 14' Wilton Carpet fitted	45 - -
Window Cushion	10 -
Pair Curtains and fittings	6 - -
Ceiling Light with large opal bowl	3 - -
24" circular Mahogany Table, on carved legs, centre support	8 - -
3'6" Mahogany Show Case, with sliding doors, mirror back and glass sides	15 - -
Stained nest of three drawers under Showcase	5 - -
Oval Mirror in carved gilt frame	4 - -
Oxidised Coal Box	3 - -
" Curb	2 5 -
" Electric Stove	8 - -
Wicker wastepaper basket	3 6
Two-light Pendant with shade	1 15 -
TOTAL	£280 3 6

-46-

By February 1942, inside the mansion the former ballroom was described as a sea of drawing boards, the drawing room was the sales office, the long panelled dining hall was the planning office, the library was the head accountant's office, the lounge was the company secretary's abode and the morning room was the general office with the junior accountant's next door. Upstairs, the best bedrooms were converted to the Production office, Maintenance, Buying, Inspection, Mr Vokes' office and the former billiard room was Wages and Costs. Then there were extensive dormitories for the clerks and typists, cloakrooms, mess rooms and the canteen quarters. The outside buildings, some old some new, contained many more departments - electricians, stores, jig and tool designers, goods inwards, packing, transport, the employment office, police office and so on. There was a policeman permanently on duty at the main gates.

Vokes had a full-time billeting officer in 1941 and 1942, 20-year old Maureen Bolster, whose job was to find accommodation for the workers who were still being evacuated from London and drafted in from all over the country to work at Vokes. She rode around the district on her motorbike, a noisy, red Rudge Whitworth, cajoling people into taking just one more stranger into their homes and smoothing out the inevitable conflicts that arose between them and the local people around Normandy where they were billeted. In January 1942, when half the employees of another firm which had gone out of business were deployed to Vokes, the police were ready to issue compulsion forms on reluctant householders, in case Maureen's persuasive powers were not sufficient to convince them to take them in. Her office in the mansion was in the 'butler's pantry' with Major Blore, who was in charge of welfare at the factory.

The company expanded enormously to cope with the war work, and early in 1942 they acquired another former mansion in the area, Monkshatch on the Hog's Back at Compton, which formerly belonged to Lord Boston and which they intended to convert into a large hostel for the office and factory workers. However, by June 1942 there was a 'purge' and the Ministry of Labour transferred seventy employees including management and office staff to work elsewhere -

it appears that Vokes had little control over who worked for them and where, which caused considerable tension within the firm.

Vokes worked flat out during the war and achieved some impressive feats. When Tobruk was recaptured by the Germans, the Air Ministry required a number of Halifax bombers to be tropically equipped so that a heavy attack could be made. The company had first information about this on a Monday morning and the designs were completed by mid-day on Tuesday; air cleaners were produced from the designs and flight tested on Wednesday, then when they had passed the flight test the company was instructed to produce 256 of them by Saturday midnight; the employees worked non-stop and the complete batch was delivered by 11pm on the Saturday. On another occasion an invasion fleet of tank landing craft from America bound for Sicily became stuck in the middle of the Atlantic with clogged engines. The staff at Henley Park worked night and day for three weeks, sleeping by their machines in the workshops, producing 70,000 replacement fuel filters that were flown out and parachuted down to the fleet, which was then able to resume the invasion.

Figure 42.

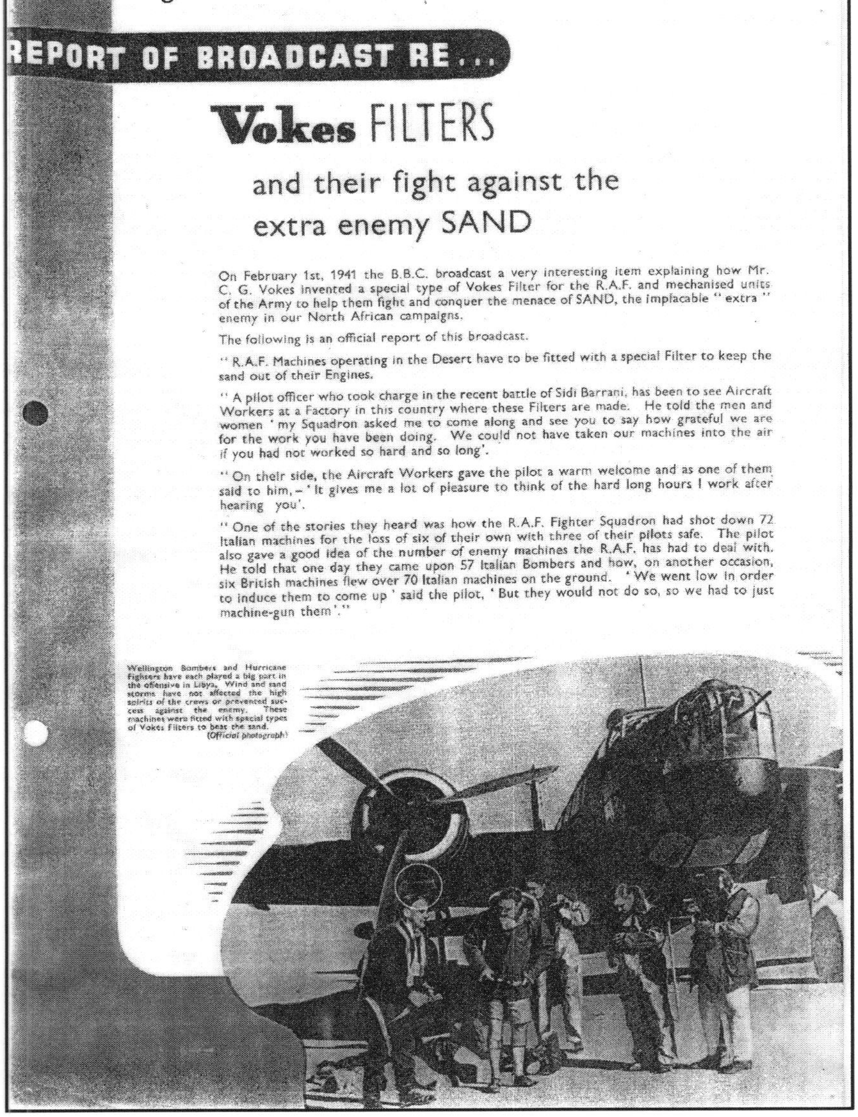

REPORT OF BROADCAST RE...

Vokes FILTERS

and their fight against the extra enemy SAND

On February 1st, 1941 the B.B.C. broadcast a very interesting item explaining how Mr. C. G. Vokes invented a special type of Vokes Filter for the R.A.F. and mechanised units of the Army to help them fight and conquer the menace of SAND, the implacable "extra" enemy in our North African campaigns.

The following is an official report of this broadcast.

"R.A.F. Machines operating in the Desert have to be fitted with a special Filter to keep the sand out of their Engines.

"A pilot officer who took charge in the recent battle of Sidi Barrani, has been to see Aircraft Workers at a Factory in this country where these Filters are made. He told the men and women 'my Squadron asked me to come along and see you to say how grateful we are for the work you have been doing. We could not have taken our machines into the air if you had not worked so hard and so long'.

"On their side, the Aircraft Workers gave the pilot a warm welcome and as one of them said to him, – 'It gives me a lot of pleasure to think of the hard long hours I work after hearing you'.

"One of the stories they heard was how the R.A.F. Fighter Squadron had shot down 72 Italian machines for the loss of six of their own with three of their pilots safe. The pilot also gave a good idea of the number of enemy machines the R.A.F. has had to deal with. He told that one day they came upon 57 Italian Bombers and how, on another occasion, six British machines flew over 70 Italian machines on the ground. 'We went low in order to induce them to come up' said the pilot, 'But they would not do so, so we had to just machine-gun them'."

Wellington Bombers and Hurricane Fighters have each played a big part in the offensive in Libya. Wind and sand storms have not affected the high spirits of the crews or prevented success against the enemy. These machines were fitted with special types of Vokes Filters to beat the sand.
(Official photograph)

A similar story is nicely described by pilot John Golley who was present at the time. In the long, dry summer of 1944, 245 squadron of Hawker Typhoons was based at Le Fresne Camilly in Normandy, providing air cover for the Allied advance in France, flying several operations each day from their wire-mesh airstrip. Takeoff from the strip generated clouds of fine dust which infiltrated the engines and the resultant abrasive action began to wear them out rapidly. Attempts to dampen the strip by spraying oil failed to cure the problem and the situation had become extremely serious, when 'a gentleman dressed in a lounge suit and carrying a large briefcase appeared on the scene'. He was, of course, CG Vokes and within 48 hours of him inspecting the problem, large filters were being stuffed into the air intakes, held in position by a special fitting designed by Hawker Aircraft. Mr Golley found it amusing that Mr Vokes had to travel from Normandy to Normandy, which would have looked odd in anyone's logbook.

In April 1942 the working hours at Vokes were increased from 54½ hours a week (7:30 am to 6:30 pm with an hour for lunch, and to midday on Saturdays), to nearly 64 hours a week (7:30 to 7:15 with ½ hour for lunch, 12:30 on Saturdays).

In the 1940s Vokes was awarded a large Admiralty contract but the conditions of the contract required them to increase security, and as part of this the Admiralty paid for six-foot chain link fencing around the site. The footpath that runs up the hill outside the former kitchen garden to the west of the mansion grounds was a roadway at this time, and continued straight up to a separate entrance on the Pirbright Road, about three yards from the boundary. This was known as 'Admiralty Gate' and was built for separate wartime military access. Vokes' security force originally comprised eight or nine people including gatekeepers, but over the next 50 years it was gradually reduced down to one man, Dave Rance, who lived in the 'Security Man's Cottage', formerly Orchard Bungalow.

Mr Vokes was officer in charge of Vokes' Home Guard platoon which was based at Henley Park. A photograph of the platoon (see Plate 81), probably taken at the time the Home Guard was disbanded, has a caption which reads: 'Presented to their O.C. Lieut C.G. Vokes, by the non commissioned officers and men of No. 4 Platoon E. Coy 1st Surrey Btn, Home Guard, to commemorate the happy years of service together.' There were 65 people in uniform in the Home Guard picture. One of the members was Tom Cousins, who has been described as 'a real country yokel, smoking a clay pipe'. One night when Tom was on guard duty he challenged Mr Osborne, who was duty officer. Mr Osborne replied with the appropriate password, but Tom kept on repeating the challenge until Mr Osborne heard him loading his gun, and rushed forward to restrain him. When Mr Osborne asked why he kept challenging him he replied that he though it must be the enemy, normally when he challenged people they replied "bollocks"!

A lot of the people who had previously worked at the factory in Putney transferred to Henley Park and they used to travel there from many different places. A man called Fred Hunt came to Henley Park all the way from Southend every day. Others would stay with local families during the week and go home at weekends and sometimes one of them would not return on a Monday morning if they had been caught by the blitz in London. There was a family sort of atmosphere at Vokes, they were all happy-go-lucky type of people. Former workers recollect a lady called Miss Clegg who went round the factory with a tea trolley selling rolls and buns.

Stan Sharp started work at Vokes in 1942. He was directed there from the Air Force for six months with 22 other people. Most of them went back after a while but Mr Vokes retained two people, Stan at Henley Park and one at Alton. Stan was 'renewed' for six months then another six months, and ended up spending his whole working life at Vokes until he retired in 1984. Mr Vokes liked Stan because he could fix anything. He was originally in charge of transport, then he was maintenance foreman and looked after all the machinery in the factory, including the manufacturing machinery, boilers and the water pumps up at the top lake. Some of Mr Vokes' Lagonda cars were in a bad condition and he expected Stan to repair them as well. One day an Army tank arrived on a trailer and Mr Vokes asked Stan to unload it - he had to work out how to drive it and after that, whenever it needed to be moved, Stan was called in as the expert. The tank was there to have filters fitted and experiment with, but it ended up going rusty, parked beside the drive up to the factory from Cobbett Hill. Mr Vokes was interested in all types of engines and at one time he kept a torpedo boat or landing craft in the stables. Sometimes Mr Vokes would call Stan and say "have you got ten minutes?" Even if Stan was busy he had to drop everything and Mr Vokes would say something like "can you drive me down to see my sister in Southampton?" Then Mr Vokes would drive all the way, he just liked to have Stan there to talk to!

Ellen Warby, who worked at Vokes from 1945 for 32 years, used to do rivetting, drilling, welding and assembly work in the old workshops. She remembers that they used to do piece work at 3d a filter, and everything had to be passed by the inspector. They used to manufacture all sorts of things, including filters for Triumph motor bikes, and when there was no work on one occasion they made metal tables and chairs. It got really hot inside the old workshops when the sun shone on the corrugated iron roofs, especially up on the balconies (see Plate 79). The noise from the machinery inside them was horrific.

Twenty-one-year old Gwen Searle from Pirbright worked in factory 9X during the war, rivetting the big casings that held the filters. The canteen was near the former stable block and on the night shifts it was difficult to find your way there from the factory through the pitch-dark, blacked-out grounds. She doesn't remember much security around the factory, and when there were practice attacks and 'Germans' came through the factory building, she and the other workers ignored them and got on with their jobs. They also ignored the air raid sirens and she didn't even know where the air raid shelter was.

Mr Vokes ran the company very much as a 'benevolent dictator' and was a father-figure to his staff. He has been described by former employees as a good employer who really appreciated people, and a very nice gentleman. When he asked the staff whether they wanted to form a Trade Union they replied "you are our Union". He was very generous and when a cure for Tuberculosis first became available in Switzerland he paid for several people to go there for months until they were cured. When the Ministry insisted that there must be a static water tank on the premises at Henley Park it was his idea to create it in the form of a swimming pool.

Vokes had a full-time gardener, Percy Netherton, who started working at Henley Park in 1945 after answering an advertisement in a gardeners' magazine. His original job was to produce food to feed the workers and the front (east) lawn, south lawn, kitchen garden and the field to the west were all cultivated for vegetables - there were 30 acres of potatoes and the front lawn was devoted to cabbages. During the war there were German prisoners of war working there to help him and also 'land girls' working alongside the male gardeners. In January 1947 there were seven gardeners and a total weekly wage bill of £28 14s 2d, but Mr Netherton was instructed as head gardener to reduce the cost by £7 as the company had to make economies due to the completion of contracts. He laid the area in front of the mansion to lawn again in 1948.

The lake in the grounds to the north of Pirbright Road was drained when the war started and remained empty throughout the hostilities, because it would have been a landmark for enemy bombers and was too close to Cobbett Hill wireless station. When the lake was drained people came with bathtubs to collect the fish and afterwards there were reputed to have been lots of garden fishponds in the area with huge fish in them! In 1945 John Mullard and his father went and found the stopcock in the undergrowth and closed it and a week later the lake was full again. Several bombs did fall by the wireless station, and one morning John and his father were cycling down Cobbett Hill when they found the fence blown across the road and a couple of big holes to the side. The man who lived in a very white house at the bottom of Cobbett Hill refused to repaint it, so the Army are said to have hung fir trees from the eaves all round it to disguise it.

The Hawkins of Whipley Farm believed that they were on the flight path of bombers returning to Germany because they suffered several incidents where bombs fell on the farm, shattering windows and killing livestock, and on one occasion they found an injured German airman on the driveway. On another occasion a trail of bombs fell across Normandy, exploding opposite Westwood, behind Mariners, in front of the Manor House and a fourth which did not explode landed in the field west of Henley Park Farm. It is possible that these bombing parties were trying to find Vokes.

The battle to stay at Henley Park

When the emergency powers were relaxed after the war the company became embroiled in a battle to be allowed to stay at Henley Park. In 1938 Guildford Rural District Council had zoned the area for residential use. During the war this was irrelevant, but when peace dawned they attempted to enforce the zoning. In fact, even in the thick of hostilities, there was a nod at planning regulations, because Vokes had to apply for token permission to erect each new factory building, and six times in 1943 the Council replied that they would 'reconsider the use of the buildings for industrial purposes after the cessation of hostilities'. The Council considered that this was sufficient notice and in 1945 they felt it was time for Vokes' factory to go.

In December 1945 a ministerial conference attended by representatives of Guildford RDC reviewed the case and decided that Vokes should leave and be 'cleared away'. They felt that the factory was undesirable on planning grounds and the surrounding villages should not be enlarged to accommodate the workers. Vokes wanted to expand from their current workforce of 700 to 1,500 workers but Guildford was regarded as too far away from Henley Park to house them all and anyway even it was too small. There was a great housing shortage in the area and all the local schools were full. The Ministry of Labour was ambivalent; they would have great difficulty in finding another 800 workers if Vokes expanded, but they would also have difficulty in relocating the 700 if it moved, so they would really rather it stayed the same size in the same place. Mr CG Vokes' characteristic response to this was to propose to build a 'model village' at Henley Park with the company's funds. The Council said that any proposals to build houses by private enterprise would be carefully considered, but they were clearly uneasy about the idea; in postwar socialist Britain, housing was the Government's responsibility.

Despite agreeing that Vokes should go, the Government departments felt that they still had a pressing need for Vokes filters and production should not be interrupted, so they gave the company five years to find an alternative site and move away gradually. Indeed, Sir Stafford Cripps' Board of Trade had just asked Vokes to construct a new laboratory for fundamental research on filtration to reduce the incidence of illness in mines and cotton mills, and they recommended that this should be constructed at Henley Park as quickly as possible, but Mr Vokes said it was bad business to expect the company to spend £25,000 to £30,000 to build a laboratory which would be pulled down in five years.

Mr Vokes saw it very differently from the authorities and argued passionately that Henley Park was the company's permanent home and Vokes was one of the most vital factories in the country. When his factory was destroyed in 1940 the Ministry of Aircraft Production had pressed him to find accommodation outside London and encouraged him to purchase Henley Park from Mr Moodie. At that time the Ministry gave him the impression that it would be Vokes' permanent home and he would not have bought it otherwise. If the land had been zoned for residential purposes as reported, Mr Vokes was unaware of it. His staff had purchased homes in the area and would suffer great hardship if the company moved. A petition from the whole workforce was read out at the Rural District Council meeting where the decision of the conference was reported, but it failed to sway them. The company predicted great hardship, huge financial wastage and unemployment if they were forced to move. The factory buildings could not simply be removed and re-erected, and some of the most vital buildings were actually the property of the Ministry of Aircraft Production. The firm had already had to discharge some hundreds of specially trained and skilled workpeople due to the uncertainty of the future. Vokes estimated that they had laid about ten miles of gas and electricity services around the site, and they had their own power supply laid down the Pirbright Road. Mr Vokes pointed out the 'virtual impossibility' of removing a factory such as this - for some of the plant and equipment it had taken six months to construct the foundations before the machinery could be installed.

At a public meeting in Normandy village hall Mr Vokes went further and suggested there was a 'dirty rotten conspiracy' and challenged the RDC to 'do their job properly'. The meeting was adjourned to the next week and the Council was asked to send a representative. The next week Mr Jocelyn Bray, chairman and Mr WE Sellings, clerk, presented the RDC's case to a crowded and lively meeting in the hall. The Council claimed that they did not make the decision, they simply supplied information to a Board of Trade enquiry and when the decision was made they were told to implement it. They denied Mr Vokes' 'wild and unjustified statements' and his 'dastardly charge' of a conspiracy. They said the councillors could not take up Mr Vokes' invitation to visit Henley Park while the matter was under consideration by Government departments and was sub-judice. Mr Vokes countered by saying he would not see people thrown out of work needlessly, that they had come to Henley Park 'under orders' and had initially been given a lease for 60 years by the Ministry of Aircraft Production which showed they intended the move to be permanent. He declared "we are the victims", but soon tempered this by asking the Council to ignore all the hard things he had said and look at the matter dispassionately.

The argument reached the national press and an article in the *Sunday Pictorial* was headed 'Get Out say the Gentry', accompanied by a photograph of Sir Philip Henriques (see Plate 82). Sir Philip told a reporter that "Mr Vokes is paying fantastically high wages - you can't get gardeners and if those workpeople stay there my plum trees will be in danger". The *Daily Worker*, taking the opposite view, called it the 'New Battle of Normandy'.

Aware of the uncertainty that had arisen around his grandfather Sir Owen Roberts' former home, Mr Ronald Armstrong-Jones wrote to the Council referring to 'the beautiful Elizabethan house' that had been his home. He also wrote to Mr Vokes asking for first refusal if Vokes should wish to sell the property and Mr Vokes agreed. Here we can only speculate what the history of the mansion and its remaining estate would have been if it had become the property of his son the Earl of Snowdon instead of remaining with Vokes.

Prior to the next meeting of the RDC in January 1946 Mr Vokes lobbied hard for them to reconsider their decision - he wrote a long letter to every councillor and sent telegrams to some of them, but in his enthusiasm he had overstepped the mark because this brought strong protests from two members, Mr WJ Henry of Normandy and Mr MWB May, who had refused to receive the telegram over the phone the previous night. Interestingly, at this time the Rural District Council's meetings were held in private because there was no standing order allowing the public to attend. Possibly because of the pressure that arose from the Vokes case, the Council finally voted at this meeting to open their meetings to the public as other authorities had done, and following the vote four representatives of Vokes Ltd were admitted to the Council chamber. However, all that the Council were prepared to do was to recommend that Vokes appeal to the Ministry and offered to help them with any 'technical difficulties' with the appeal.

There was no visible progress for some months until the matter erupted publicly again in April, at a meeting in Normandy village hall which was actually called to discuss the proposal that Normandy should become a part of the 'Greater Aldershot' conurbation. Somehow the discussion moved to Vokes and an argument broke out between members of the audience - Mr Vokes complained in a letter afterwards that the meeting had been 'packed' with people deliberately intending to attack his firm. The correspondence in the press rumbled on with disagreements over whether the electricity poles installed to supply Vokes with power were intended to be temporary or permanent, whether Vokes' workforce could be seen as 'local people' and whether the money invested in Vokes was the nation's or the company's. Mr AP Bevan of The Elms, Normandy, on whose land one of the disputed electricity poles stood, understood that 'huge sums of public money were expended in the conversion of the mansion' and suggested that it should 'again be converted to a home for disabled service men'. Mr Henry of the Council said he would feel more sympathetic if the factory had been put up at Mr Vokes' expense and not the public's, but Mr Vokes responded that there was far more of his company's money invested in Henley Park than there was of the nation's, and he said Mr Bevan should come to Henley Park and ascertain the facts, because the mansion had not been converted in any way, and this was supported by the Reverend CL Bell, vicar of Tongham, who wrote that the mansion remained unspoilt inside and out thanks to the good taste of Cecil Vokes. Mr Vokes waxed poetic in a letter to the *Aldershot News*, where he said it appeared that the worker who had 'provided the fighting man with his tools' was to be discarded now that his job was safely completed. Mr Vokes argued that any complaint that anyone had should be directed firstly at 'the enemy' for destroying his premises in Putney and secondly against the Government for 'bringing us here'; "we have only asked for the hospitality to which any victim of war is entitled".

In May 1946 the Building Restriction (War Time Contraventions) Act was passed to deal with wartime businesses set up on land scheduled for non-business purposes and by September Guildford RDC had been 'relieved of the decision' in the Vokes matter. However, it became clear that any determination would take some time, so in February 1947 the Council applied to the Ministry in the interim to revoke the closing orders for the footpaths through Henley Park. There was a considerable furore about reopening the footpaths because groups like the Ramblers Association wanted them all reinstated exactly as they appeared on the pre-war maps. For security reasons the Air Ministry insisted that the footpath that previously ran from Cobbett Hill across to the north of the mansion and stable block could not be reopened to the public so the company offered instead to substitute a new, more pleasant path to the south. To demonstrate the proposal they produced a series of 24 photographs at 40-yard intervals along the new route which ran through the fields below the formal and kitchen gardens, and mounted them concertina-style for display. However, the Council supported those who insisted on keeping exactly to the pre-war route, so the compromise was to create the path between the mansion and the gardens which exists today, and to maintain security the company had to erect chain-link fencing along the path and topped it with barbed wire. The closures were revoked early in 1947.

Permission to stay granted

At last, in June 1947 it was announced that Vokes had been given permission to retain their factory at Henley Park for 21 years - interestingly, this decision came from the Ministry of Health. Mr Vokes published a letter thanking friends, neighbours, 'certain councillors', business associates, trade unions and ministries for their support during the long negotiations, but pointed out that the 'cost of this holdup' had been considerable in loss of employment and delayed investment.

The factory at that time occupied some 123,852 square feet of space in small scattered units, of which 30,000 square feet had been provided by the Ministry of Aircraft Production. In 1951 the Board of Trade issued an Industrial Development Certificate for 210,000 square feet of space at Henley Park and confirmed that it regarded the MAP buildings as permanent. In 1953 a master layout plan for the site was approved in principle by the planning authorities, allowing for the development of the factory that we have known for the last 50 years. Eventually permission was granted for 'permanent use' of the factory buildings and in 1964 for permanent use of the mansion itself as offices, canteens, kitchens, social club, stores and a staff shop.

During the war the company did well, with capital of £50,000 and a turnover of £2 million. However, the extreme hard work affected Mr Vokes' health, which deteriorated during the late 1940s and so in 1950 he was 'eased out' and retired as Managing Director due to ill health. He died on 12 November 1961 at his home in Alton aged 70.

13. VOKES; PEACE AND ITS AFTERMATH (1954-1982)

By 1954 the 'new factory' had been built (see Plate 83). This is the factory and office block that we could see from the Pirbright Road until it was demolished in March 2012, although the original design had a rounded end which had to be squared off because it encroached too far into green belt land. The factory block was built across the three roads that used to spread out from the Pirbright Road gate, in the space between the dispersed wartime workshops and then gradually extended in stages replacing the old shops, many of which remained in place until the 1970s. However, a planning application in 1955 for four illuminated red neon 'Vokes' signs with two-foot high lettering placed on four angles of the water tower was not surprisingly rejected by the planning authorities as being 'too prominent in a rural landscape'.

In its heyday about 1,500 people worked at Vokes and they used to commute from all parts of the surrounding area. Vokes hired several coaches to bring people from Guildford, Woking and Aldershot, and they owned their own ex-Aldershot and District double-deck bus which brought people from Alton for the main day shift at Henley Park (see Plate 90). The small number of people who worked the night shifts had to have their own transport. In the 1950s very few people had cars and they used to come in on motorbikes and push-bikes; there was a big bicycle shed to accommodate them. Vokes extended the car park in the 1960s as more people switched to owning their own cars.

Former workers have recalled two occasions when the machinery at Vokes was silenced. There was one very cold winter, probably 1947, when they could not get enough coal to heat the factory so they had to close it completely. All the workers were laid off but they were promised their jobs back when the coal was delivered, and sure enough they were back within a week. On the death of King George VI in February 1952 Vokes shut down all the machinery in the factory as a sign of respect.

Technological innovation

Vokes had a lot of little sidelines. In the 1950s they invented a 'waggler' device for collecting the fine dust in cigarette factories for Wills, which had a big filter then a fine filter, and a shaking mechanism which caused the dust to fall to the bottom of the bag. At the other extreme they had a laboratory with a wind tunnel powered by a big Scott petrol engine connected to a fan and with a 'dust feed' to control the level of particles in the air, which they used to test aircraft intake filters. When Vokes made the window frames for Viscount aircraft in the 1950s, they had to keep the aluminium refrigerated so that it did not expand because of the very tight tolerances.

Mr Vokes is credited with being the first person to apply scientific principles to filtration. All Vokes products were tested rigorously but there were no standard tests in the early days so Mr Vokes employed a research engineer to work towards standardised methods for filter evaluation. For this he needed dust with a particular particle size to feed into filters to find out how long they took to block up and he found the ideal stuff at Henley Park. A small pit was dug just at the edge of the lawn in front of the mansion and the sand from this pit went on to become the basis for British Standard 1701 air cleaner test dust, which was for many years the basis of testing all types of air filter!

In the mid-1950s British European Airways (now part of BA) planned to introduce a helicopter shuttle service from Heathrow Airport to the South Bank in central London, to reduce dramatically the time to get from the airport to town for those who could afford it. There were objections because of the noise the helicopters would create, particularly from MP's as the route would pass close to the Houses of Parliament, so Vokes, who were also experts in sound muffling technology, were called in. CG Vokes' son Gordon Heatherton Vokes, known as 'Tony', was the company's Technical Manager and he designed a silencer for the helicopter which was an innovative piece of work. He was able to make use of the fact that helicopter engines run at a constant speed and the resulting silencer was very effective[*]. In tests it reduced the noise by over 20 decibels (from a 'shattering roar' to a 'nicely tuned sports car') and he has photographs of himself and his father being congratulated by John Profumo, parliamentary secretary for Transport and Civil Aviation, after the tests at Westland. The project was proceeding when the safety department from the London County Council intervened - because helicopters are less reliable than aircraft, they insisted that they should fly over water, in other words the river, through the built-up areas. Although this almost doubled the flying distance, BEA agreed. However, at that point another safety department, probably from the Thames Conservancy, intervened to enquire whether helicopters would float in water. They were informed that helicopters do not float, whereupon they insisted that the helicopters must be fitted with floats, in case one came down in the river. This resulted in significant new design work, including a re-work of the silencer to fit around the floats. All this extra equipment weighed over a ton and reduced the number of passengers and luggage that could be carried, but BEA calculated that it was still worth proceeding. The introduction of the service was drawing closer when suddenly the Port of London Authority intervened; if a helicopter came down in the water and floated about, they asked, could it steer itself? When they were informed that it could not, they insisted that it must be fitted with *an anchor*. At this point the project was abandoned!

Use of the mansion - the rooms and outbuildings

The various rooms of the mansion were used for different purposes at different times by Vokes, but in the 1950s a typical layout was as follows. On the ground floor at the front of the mansion, running from south to north (left to right) were the research manager's office in the glass conservatory, then Tony Vokes' office (the engineering manager) in the 'Morning Room' of the 1922 estate sale, which was known as the 'Tea Room' in his day. It still had the painting in the middle of the ceiling, much ornate plasterwork and the full-height, 8-foot wide mirror. Next was Mr 'Bert' Osborne's office (the general manager, later MD), then the entrance lobby and Jim

---

[*] It was a resonant chamber silencer, a cylindrical tube split into several Humboldts resonators, which absorb sound of their own natural frequency. It attaches to the exhaust and does not produce any backpressure; it weighed 85 lbs but the pilot reported that the performance of the helicopter was, if anything, improved!

Phillips' office (the company secretary). Behind this in the north-west corner of the ground floor was Ted Queening's office (a director) in the 'Breakfast Room' of the estate sale. The room behind this had heavy grilles on the window and a safe in the corner which is said to be where the former occupants kept their silver dinner services.

The glass conservatory on the south end of the mansion was subsequently replaced by a new glass office which was full of typists. The new office was not as tall as the conservatory had been and it had less windows. Nobody could get the conservatory quite right - the Moodies had rebuilt it during their period of ownership and by 1972 Vokes had removed it completely.

In Lord Pirbright's west wing, on the ground floor was Vokes' drawing office in the 'Noble Drawing Room' which still had the fully sprung ballroom floor (see Plate 85), and part of this wing was also the board room. By the 1970s the ballroom had become the staff canteen and kitchen and the drawing office had moved into the new factory. In the middle of the west façade was the directors' dining room in the 'Finely Proportioned Dining Room' of the estate sale, with the beautiful dark panelling apparently dating from the Moodies' renovations. The entrance to the dining room was at the back of the entrance lobby, directly opposite the front door. Once a year the Cricket Club had a 'ladies evening' in the dining room where the men waited on them. Later, the dining room became the workers' canteen with a serving counter on the right of the entrance. The fire authorities insisted that all the wood panelling was removed because it was a 'fire hazard'. In 1971 Vokes built a single-storey, flat roofed extension to the main building on the west side between the ballroom and the dining room, to provide an ante-room to the Directors' dining room. This did not last long and was demolished in the 1980s.

The main staircase, which had 16 stairs, was on the west side, on the left of the dining room and behind it was another office. The less elaborate 'back stairs' were on the right of the dining room. There were two large paintings on either side of the main staircase, reputed to be of Prince Rupert and his Lady, which were still there in the 1970s. These were purchased by CG Vokes who thought that they would look better than the blank spaces there!

In the far right hand corner of the dining room (the north-west corner) was another entrance into a pantry. The kitchen was further round, down some passages leading into the north-west wing, which appeared old to the casual observer but was described as 'ramshackle' by former employees. The kitchens were huge, with Aga-type stoves. The staff canteen was originally in these buildings to the north-west before it moved into the ballroom within the mansion. By the late 1970s the north-western buildings had 'deteriorated to a point where they are beyond redemption' and in 1978 permission to demolish them was granted, against objections by the Surrey Archaeological Society, who believed that sections of them were 'of some age' and in character with the main block.

On the first floor of the mansion Mr Vokes' flat was on the south side in the upstairs part of the Victorian wing. His collection of antique guns was displayed along the first floor gallery (see Plate 78) and in the room over the entrance hall, which was known as the 'Gun room'. Mr Vokes had probably the largest private collection of antique firearms in the country, which he bequeathed to what became the Hampshire County Museum Service, and the collection is now on display at Havant Museum. On the north side of the first floor were Mr Vokes' office and his secretary, Miss Polly Collen's office. On the west side, in what had been the Billiard Room, was the company's sales office.

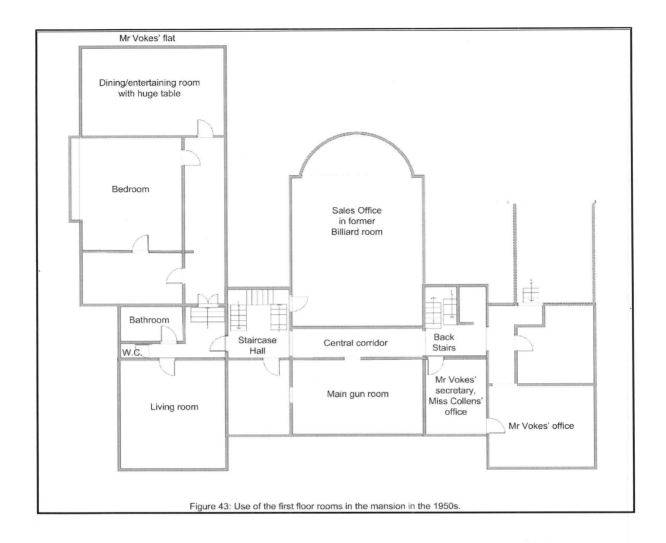

Figure 43: Use of the first floor rooms in the mansion in the 1950s.

Ted Queening started working at Vokes in 1947 and in 1948 he and his wife Margaret moved into a flat on the south side of the top floor of the mansion, with magnificent views out towards the Hog's Back. Margaret had been a 'code-breaker' at Bletchley Park during the war, a unique experience she still remembers fondly. The Queenings' flat was above Mr Vokes' gun collection and they slept directly above a big chest full of ammunition. Much of the mansion's structure was wooden and they were concerned about it catching fire, so they kept a 60-foot hawser with knots, to climb down in an emergency! They lived in the mansion until Mr Queening retired as a director of Vokes in about 1963. On the north side of the top floor was the gunsmith's workshop and Miss Collen's flat. Also on the top floor was a tank room with several very large water tanks. There was a door from the attic over the Billiard Room onto the flat lead roof and the Queenings used to have tea up there in the summer, 'walking on the leads' as Pepys described in his diary.

The Queenings said that it was a very friendly-feeling house, even though there were rats! It was centrally heated so it was always warm. In 1966 a group from the Ghost Club (founded in 1862) visited Henley Park and toured the mansion. They reported that they felt "more of a psychical nature associated with the mansion than they had experienced at Sutton Place".

In the 1960s the cellar of the mansion was full of lots of old books, pictures and oil paintings and when Vokes refurbished the canteen in the Victorian wing they intended to re-hang some of the pictures there. There were printing presses in the cellar which they used for producing publicity material, and there was a radiogram and musical equipment where music-while-you-work was 'piped' round the factory. Some of the books in the cellar were said to be gold-embossed, with information about the children of Queen Victoria. When the cellar was cleared out, probably in the 1970s, some of the staff, including Ellen Warby, were told to load the books into a skip and they were going to be burnt, but she believes that someone from Vokes' publicity department rescued them.

In Vokes' time the horse mounting block was still to the left of the front entrance of the mansion and the flagpole was still on top of the building. Mr Vokes had another flagpole put up on the edge of the front lawn to celebrate some occasion (see Plate 87).

The stable block to the north-west was used as offices and a despatch area, and at one time there was a chapel in it as well. In the 1950s Vokes' apprentices worked in the old stables and they found it very uncomfortable; there was only one coke oven and in the winter they had to work wearing duffel coats. The coach house still had big wooden gates and Mr Vokes used to keep his collection of about six Lagonda cars there. The stable block was demolished in the late 1960s because it was getting run down. According to Stan Sharp who lived in the house next to the stable block, Vokes had plans for a big new building on the site but permission for this was refused because it could be seen from the Hog's Back (although this may possibly refer to one of the later redevelopment plans). There used to be a first aid post in the stable block, underneath the bell tower. At one time there was a full-time nurse called Sister Sindon and when Vokes got rid of her there was a day's strike, and afterwards people had to go on first-aid courses.

Between the stable block and the north-west wing of the mansion was an archway (see Plate 94) which gave access from the western pleasure gardens to the stable block area and which is said to have had a bell hanging in it. The bell, which had been cast in 1701 by William Eldridge of Chertsey and was one of those removed from Pirbright Church by the Halseys, was donated to Guildford Museum by Vokes in 1963 and was subsequently transferred to Chertsey Museum in 1989. There was a preservation order on the archway and it was still in standing, in splendid isolation, in 1991, then when the mansion was redeveloped it was moved to a central position in a wall to the west of the mansion where it now stands.

At the edge of the front (east) lawn was a ha-ha (a deer leap) and the wall bounding the north-east part of the lawn still had a statue niche in it in the 1980s. On the corner nearby was a Red Oak, which was chopped down for the new roadway despite Mr Queening's pleadings. The palm house, vineries and peach and nectarine houses (see Plate 59) had disappeared by 1948. In Vokes' time the only way into the kitchen garden south-west of the mansion was through the double gates across the footpath, which were normally kept locked except between midday and 2pm on working days, so that employees could gain access to the garden which they used as allotments. There was a buried coal-fired boiler for heating the greenhouses in the kitchen garden, and a stoke hole, which was a brick building beyond the last greenhouse. The outer (west) wall of the garden had peas growing up it, there were strawberries by the opposite wall and apple and plum trees at the bottom. Mr Netherton the gardener had a machine for making flower pots out of compressed earth, and his son Peter used to enjoy using it when he got home from school!

The big water tower that loomed over the mansion until it too was demolished in April 2012 was fed by a pipe from the top lake on the other side of the Pirbright Road. There used to be a boat house next to the lake but it was dismantled during the war by troops who needed firewood, and now the pumping station is in roughly the same position. Vokes built the tower and the pumping station in the 1940s because the existing three-inch water main was not sufficient. When the woodland north of Pirbright Road was later sold to the Army, Vokes retained access to the lake to ensure the water supply. The sewage filter beds down the slope to the south-east of the mansion grounds were in use and looked after by a full-time maintenance man up to about 1967, when the site was connected to the main sewer.

The social club

In 1963 Vokes instigated a 'social revolution' by turning the stately mansion into the headquarters of the company's sports and social club. At the opening ceremony in April workers at the factory and their partners danced in the ballroom where stately hunt balls had been held in Lord Pirbright's day. Facilities included the ballroom, a licenced bar in the former dining room on the west side, a 'jive room' or 'twist room' for the younger employees which looked out to the west of the mansion, a table-tennis room, a children's room, a darts room which also had fruit machines, a billiards room and a room for golfing instruction. In addition the club had the swimming pool which had been installed during the war as a static water supply, as well as the stocked fishing lake, tennis courts located on part of what became the car park and football and cricket pitches. Mr Tom Scothorn, chairman of the club, who lived in the second-floor flat at the time it opened, hoped that families would come there on a Sunday afternoon and bring the children, but most of the activity actually took place at lunchtimes and on Fridays.

There were many social activities organised by members of the club (see Plate 89). In the 1950s the 'works outings' took people by bus for day trips to the south coast, usually Bognor or Littlehampton, and for people who couldn't afford a holiday these were their only chance to visit the seaside. As well as organising dances, Ellen Warby used to run a wine circle in the bar. The club had a band made up of Vokes employees who used to play on Fridays. They used to hold fêtes on the sports pitch. There was a gardening club in the 1960s and early '70s and they used the former kitchen gardens as allotments, as well as utilising some of the greenhouses which were still there. The pheasants, introduced by the long-departed landed gentry, were still in the grounds and in the 1960s Vokes had a shooting club to take advantage of them. Percy Oliver started a fishing club at the top lake and they tidied up the area for the fishermen. They let other angling societies use the lake, expecting a small number of people to use it, but on one occasion Essex Police brought a whole coach-load!

The company spent £8,000 on providing these facilities which, according to the *Surrey Advertiser*, any country club would envy. About 900 of the company's 1,200 employees belonged to the sports and social club but not all of its aspects were a success. Some people felt that it was like 'going back to work in their leisure time' and did not like going back through the factory gates out of working hours, and some of the facilities closed after about two years. However, the social club's bar and shop were popular and had an impressive turnover of £45,000 a year.

The last people to actually live in the mansion when it was a single unit were Eddie and Aileen Moore who ran the social club for many years. Eddie had been at Vokes since 1948 as a metal worker, foreman and an estimator in the sales office. At first he did not want to take the job as manager of the social club but Mr Osborne personally persuaded him to take it. They initially lived in the Queening's former flat on the top floor and then in Mr Vokes' former flat on the first floor, from about 1964 to 1974. In later years the bar was in the large first floor room over the dining room. The bar was very well used, it used to take up to £6,000 a week, but it was vulnerable because it was possible to jump from the flat-roofed extension up to the window of the bar, and they had seven burglaries there. There was a fire escape from the window of the bar which was a big canvas chute with an iron framework to the window, and a 'bell-rope' to slide down, but unfortunately the rope was ten feet short of the ground! Former employees of Vokes remember having several riotous parties in the Moores' flat. On Saturdays after cricket matches they used to go and drink in Vokes' bar, but many of those present were not members of the social club so the security man did not want to let them in and they had to persuade him that they were all going to the Moores' flat for a private event!

Who lived where in the park

There was a complete change of occupancy in the cottages and houses within the park in the 1940s, as Mr Moodie's stewards, gamekeepers and gardeners went their separate ways and Vokes' managers and directors moved in.

The 'House in the Wall' by the kitchen garden, which had been known as 'Dolly and Parry's cottage' when it was occupied by the Moodies' gardener, was initially occupied by Mr Culver and then by Mr Lew Moss, Vokes' catering manager. In the 1960s the McFarlanes lived there and then it was occupied by Len Warner, Vokes' plumber, until 1970 when he had to leave because it was too dilapidated. The cottage had nice arched windows looking out onto the kitchen gardens, but by the 1980s it was derelict and when Vokes sold the mansion there was effectively no access to the cottage except on foot and it was doomed. It was demolished a few years later by order of the Building Regulations authorities because it was dangerous and was so close to a public footpath.

In 1947 Stan and Edie Sharp were evicted from their home by their landlord 'Granny' James, who had previously owned the Westwood Lane Stores and Wanborough Stores, as well as other properties in the Normandy area. Mr Sharp asked Mr Vokes if they could live in the House in the Wall at Henley Park which was empty at the time. Mr Vokes had already promised it to Mr Culver, but part of the stable block had been a cottage called 'Garage Cottage', although it was now the employment office. He said the Sharps could live there if they moved everything out of it. Stan and Edie lived in the grounds of Vokes from 1947 for 33 years, first in the cottage in the stable block which they called Hilltop Cottage, then from 1962 in Orchard Bungalow where they lived until July 1980 when they moved to Pirbright Road. In the 1960s Hilltop Cottage was demolished with the rest of the stable block.

There was a sawmill in a separate building to the west of Hilltop Cottage, on the other side of the road which led down the hill to the House in the Wall. Just to the north of the stable block was another residence, a corrugated tin bungalow called 'White Bungalow'. It was occupied by the Wilson family from 1941 to 1955; Mr Wilson was one of the lorry drivers. It is said to have burned down in the 1950s, causing a dispute between the local fire brigade and

Vokes' own fire brigade (see Plate 92); both of them attended the blaze and were arguing about who should put it out!

Mr Netherton, the head gardener, and his family moved into one of the pair of cottages at the Pirbright Road entrance in December 1948. At that time it was called 'Gardener's Cottage' but by the time they moved out in 1961 it was number 1 Pirbright Cottages. Number 2 was occupied throughout the 1950s by John Goby, the works manager. These cottages, probably built in the 1890s by Lord Pirbright, were actually just outside the boundary of the former royal park, but the land had been the property of the owners of Henley Park for three hundred years and had become incorporated into the grounds. Both cottages were subsequently occupied by a succession of families until 1974 when Vokes applied for planning permission to demolish them and build a new house nearby. They were described in the application as 'vacant, old, inconvenient, in poor condition and of no architectural merit'. Nevertheless planning permission was refused, and a subsequent application in 1976 was also turned down, so Vokes demolished them anyway in the late 1970s, and now no trace of them remains.

Orchard Bungalow, north-west of the stable block and next to the former orchard, was built in the 1930s and had been the residence of Mr Moodie's estate manager. Vokes' company secretary Mr Phillips lived there until he retired in 1962, when the Sharps moved in. When they moved out in 1980 Dave Rance, who took over the maintenance work from Mr Sharp as well as being the security man, lived there until he bought a house in the north of England and moved out about 2002.

Orchard House, formerly number 1 Orchard Cottages (the western side of the pair of houses on Pirbright Road), was occupied in the 1940s by Mr Willis, the works manager, then by Mr Bert Osborne for many years until he retired in the 1960s. Orchard Cottage, formerly number 2 Orchard Cottages (the one on the east side), was occupied in the 1940s by Mr AA Smith, the general manager, then by Reginald Chaffrey, the chief designer, and then by the Stanley family who also moved out in the 1960s. Both houses were subsequently sold.

In the 1940s the old lodge at the Cobbett Hill entrance was known as the White Lodge and was occupied by the Maber family. In 1956 it became Cobbett Hill Lodge and was occupied by Fred Smith, the production controller. It was demolished about 1963 when Mr and Mrs Queening bought the site.

Further breakup of the Royal Park

According to details at the Land Registry, the land that Vokes purchased included most of the 428-acre royal park as well as 34 acres of additional woodland enclosed outside the north corner, and Standinghill Wood and Slyfield Wood on the other side of the Pirbright Road. The 34 acres of woodland had been purchased by the Halseys from the War Department in 1887, although they 'enclosed' it into Henley Park much earlier.

Anchor Moor, in the south-east corner of the royal park, had been sold separately by the Halseys in the 1920s when it was a smallholding, and by 2000 it was comprised of nine properties; a nursery, three houses and the 'ends' of the gardens of five houses on the Guildford Road. However, the fields in the south-east corner of the park, which had been farmed as part of Whipley Farm, were not included when Mr Moodie sold Whipley to the tenant, Mr Hawkins, and so were subsequently part of the property purchased by Vokes in 1941.

It was apparently a condition of the purchase by Vokes that the tenants should have the option to buy their land and this additionally helped to ease Vokes' cashflow situation, so soon after buying Henley Park Vokes sold much of the farmland. The principal sale was to Mr Robert Turner who bought Henley Park Farm in about 1942 or 1943, although Vokes retained a 'buffer' of land around the mansion grounds to enhance security, and they also retained the coppices and woodland because of their perceived value. However, Vokes subsequently realised that they did not have any land access to the plots at Kiln Copse and Withybed Copse and so they ceded them to Mr Turner, while retaining Anchor Copse.

The buffer of land that Vokes retained comprised a strip of the field to the west of the mansion grounds and part of the field to the south of the gardens (see map, Plate 120). Mr Turner rented these fields and farmed them as part of Henley Park Farm. In the 1970s a long court case about possession of these lands began and under the terms of the eventual settlement Vokes ceded 21 acres to the owners of Henley Park Farm, Mr and Mrs Atkins. The 21 acres comprised the field to the south of the mansion and Anchor Copse, but the land to the west was retained and became part of the plot that Vokes sold to developers.

The 46 acres of fields in the south-east corner of the park which was formerly part of Whipley Farm was also probably sold in the 1940s by Vokes, and by 1968 it was all owned by David Burrows of Mytchett. His application to build a farmhouse on the site was refused and over the next 30 years the land was gradually divided and sub-divided into 16 separately-owned plots, twelve of which became travelling showmen's winter quarters.

In early 1963, when Vokes moved the rest of the offices out of the mansion and turned it into the social club, Ted and Margaret Queening bought a plot of land from Vokes at the site of the old Cobbett Hill Lodge, which was still standing at the time. They measured out the boundaries of their site themselves and built a new house there which they named 'Deyrolles' after the creator of the mansion that they had lived in for the previous 16 years.

Vokes sold Orchard House and Orchard Cottage, the pair of semi-detached houses on Pirbright Road. They possibly sold them leasehold in about 1960, then finally sold the freeholds in March 1980. They also sold a nearby plot of land on Pirbright Road which became an electricity substation, and the Orchard House and Orchard Cottage properties have the right to lay an electricity supply from the substation across the intervening land.

Ultimately Vokes sold the mansion itself to developers, and by the year 2000 there were nearly 50 separate freehold properties within the area of the former royal park.

The decline starts; Vokes vacate the mansion

By the 1970s Vokes' fortunes had taken a turn for the worse. Like much of British industry they were plagued by labour disputes and there were strikes, redundancies, walkouts and lockouts at Henley Park. Production was brought to a standstill, sales slumped and there was little money available for the maintenance of the mansion and its grounds. In 1972 the Vokes Group was acquired by the Thomas Tilling Group, and in 1982 BTR plc took over Tillings. By 1986 Vokes employed 550 people at Henley Park, well under half its former size.

Opinions differ on Vokes' use of the mansion in the later years. Some recall that they moved out as early as the 1960s and the mansion was left empty, others believe that it was still in use as the company's dining room and social club and even offices as late as 1978. In 1964 a further planning application was approved, for permanent use of the mansion as offices, canteen, social club, stores and a staff shop and certainly the social club's bar and shop remained active there until the mid-1970s. However, in 1978 all use of the mansion ceased according to a later planning application, and by the end of the 1970s although the outside appeared sound, the mansion had been closed up and the floorboards and woodwork inside were beginning to rot badly. On a visit in 1978 members of the Surrey Archeological Society noted crumbling garden walls and piles of rubble in the surrounding area, which raised concerns about the deterioration of this 'highly important' listed building. Despite the deterioration, in the 1970s the drain pipe with the date 1751 on it was still on the outside of the south wall, commemorating Solomon Dayrolle's remodelling work more than two centuries earlier.

Mr Netherton worked as Vokes' gardener until 1963 but the pleasure gardens began to deteriorate much earlier, especially after Mr Vokes was obliged to stand down as MD and the number of gardeners was reduced. The gardeners were effectively excluded from the Tumbling Bay area from the early 1950s and for a time Mr Netherton used to mow the Moodies' Lily Garden (known by Vokes as the Italian Garden or the sunken garden) but he had to let it go when the new factory was built in the mid 1950s because he had to look after the new grounds. By 1948 the summerhouse by Tumbling Bay (Plate 44) had gone but rather strangely in its place was a huge pile of freshwater oyster shells. The waterfall itself dried up after Mr Vokes constructed a sluice to take the water away, following complaints that the adjacent field was waterlogged. In the 1950s Vokes took all the Virginia Creeper off the exterior of the mansion to repaint it, radically changing its appearance from that depicted in photographs over the previous 50 years.

Mr Netherton's son Peter remembers the beautiful smell of the Azalea Walk to Tumbling Bay, which he knew as the Chinese gardens. Peter always called the bridge below Tumbling Bay the 'Chinese Bridge' and thought of the bridge in the fields as 'Pack Horse Bridge' because of its shape. There was an old flat-bottomed boat on the lower lake (see Plate 51) and Peter and his friend Christopher Squier (the author's cousin) used to row around in it in the 1950s, as did many of Vokes' staff, although by then there was no sign of the nearby boathouse that was marked on pre-war maps.

By the 1970s the whole area had lost its 'cared-for' feel. There were vagrants living in the fields between the mansion and the Guildford Road and people didn't like to walk through on the footpaths after dark.

Vokes sell the mansion to developers

The 1978 planning consent already allowed for the north-west wing to be demolished and in February 1982 Vokes obtained outline planning permission to 'reduce the mansion to its original 18th Century size', in other words to demolish Lord Pirbright's grand extensions, and to provide 'prestige office accommodation' in a new office building of comparable size at the rear of the mansion. Rather than perform this work themselves, Vokes sold the property to developers. On 24 September 1982 Vokes sold the mansion, 26 acres of surrounding land and a new access road from Cobbett Hill for about £250,000 to Hampshire and City Estates (as agents of Britannia Arrow Holdings), who became the first of a series of property developers who owned the mansion for the next seventeen years.

The property that Vokes retained after selling the mansion, comprising 150 acres within the former royal park and 34 acres outside, remained intact for some time. In 1991 Vokes celebrated its 50th anniversary at Henley Park with an open day and fête, and at the turn of the 21st century Henley Park remained the center of the company's filtration technology research, manufacturing, administration and sales activities, employing 250 people.

14. DECAY AND RENEWAL; A CLOSE SHAVE (1982-2000)

'The south elevation wall shows considerable outward movement at first floor level and the second floor level is leaning inward; there are external cracks, it is structurally unsound and beyond repair. Bricks throughout the structure are very soft and crumble in the hand; it is in a seriously dangerous condition.' These words from a survey in 1997 demonstrate how close Henley Park mansion came to disappearing completely.

Before they sold the mansion, Vokes apparently commissioned detailed repair proposals from renovation specialists. When these firms surveyed the mansion in 1982 they found extensive wet and dry rot in the woodwork, deteriorating brickwork and widespread, heavy and active insect infestations of common furniture beetle and death watch beetle. Some ceilings on the ground floor had already collapsed, the dormers in the roof appeared to be 'close to collapse' and rainwater pipes and gutters were blocked and broken, causing damp conditions in the stairwell and elsewhere. The damp marks on the ceiling are evident in contemporary photographs (see Plate 99). Some tiles were already missing from the roof. The Victorian wing was found to be in particularly bad condition. The radical treatments they proposed included cutting out floor joists and beams, taking down doors and doorframes, hacking off plaster and lowering ground levels under floors to improve ventilation. In September 1982 Pritchard Building Preservation Ltd estimated that the cost of the renovation would be £96,246 plus VAT. The new owners must have taken this into consideration when they took on the task of redevelopment.

These surveys, backed up by contemporary planning officers' reports, show that the mansion had been neglected for some time and was already in very poor condition when Vokes sold it, but the decline was to continue as the saga of planning wrangles unfolded.

Hampshire and City Estates were the first of four main groups of developers who owned the mansion (see Figure 44) and they soon submitted new plans supposedly based on the outline permission that Vokes had gained a couple of years earlier. The plan that they put forward was for a new and much bigger three-storey office extension with glass-clad reflective walls, deliberately designed as an ultra-modern counterpoint to the ancient mansion, sited in a much more prominent position obliquely behind the mansion and linked to it (see Plate 104). This plan became infamous as the 'glass box' plan and caused much heated debate. The planning committee were taken by the architects, Michael Manser Associates, to a similar development which had been completed at Thorncroft Manor in Leatherhead and were reported to have been 'pleased with what they saw'. Nevertheless the scheme was heavily criticised as being too large and unsympathetic to the mansion and the site, and *Private Eye* magazine published a sarcastic attack on Michael Manser and his modernistic designs, illustrated by an impression of the Henley Park development. The application eventually went to appeal where it was approved in April 1984 because the planning committee felt it was the only way to save the house.

The developers soon dug some foundation trenches so that work on the scheme was deemed to have started, and so could be put into effect at any time in the future without further reference to the planning authorities. But work then stopped and nothing further happened until early 1986 when Hampshire and City Estates sold the property to Insight Securities of Binfield, Berkshire for £650,000.

Insight Securities lost no time in submitting an alternative development plan for courtyard-style offices and leisure facilities in place of the 'glass box', but without revoking the 'glass box' scheme. This could be seen as a missed opportunity because this plan was much more sympathetic to the mansion and site although the floor area of the development was increased, and it was received favourably, but planning permission was held in abeyance pending further negotiations and eventually lapsed. Over the next three years Insight Securities submitted alternative plans for housing and light industry use which also lapsed, but while the developers and the authorities remained locked in indecision the mansion deteriorated alarmingly.

The decline is charted in contemporary newspaper headlines. In 1987 there were 'fears about the state of the listed mansion', in 1991 it was 'crumbling into ruin', in 1994 'decaying' and by 1995 it had finally reached 'derelict' (see Plates 105 and 106). To add further insult to injury, in 1989 the site was 'invaded by hippies' who parked more than 70 vehicles on what had been the east lawn in front of the mansion for seven weeks, 'to the distress of neighbouring residents'.

During 1987 and 1988 Lord Pirbright's extensions on the south and west were demolished and all trace of his grand tenure of Henley Park effectively disappeared. This was allowed under the 1984 planning permission, although there were objections that the extension had 'been there long enough to become part of the mansion' and was probably helping to support the older building.

At this time all the internal fittings of the mansion, including fireplaces, panelling, floors, walls and ceilings were removed and one commentator reported that the fittings were all sold at auction. Insight Securities took away the fireplaces and internal fittings such as the circular painting in the ceiling of the Morning Room and Rentokil stripped out all the panelling and had to burn it because it was riddled with rot. While Insight Securities' contractors were stripping out the guttering in the roof gully at the front of the building they found sprockets which were part of the eaves of the roof structure from the earlier building at the core of Solomon Dayrolle's improvements. Local gypsies are said to have taken the huge timber floor joists and before long the mansion was not much more than a shell. One of the cellars under the demolished north-west wing was revealed when its roof collapsed (Plate 108). The front porch disappeared and the external windows and doors which had previously been boarded up were removed completely, leaving vacant empty spaces. Two of the glazing bars, retained by FM Modern Design, the architects for Insight Securities' developments, show the two styles of windows from the Halseys' redevelopments - one is a thick oak bar, the other a thin mahogany one.

By 1990 Insight Securities was trying to sell the property and another planning application was submitted by Stockton Corporation, a prospective purchaser, which included the coded threat that Insight Securities was 'close to insolvency' unless the sale went ahead. This plan was an innovative idea to use Henley Park as a design office and workshop for one of the Formula 1 motor racing teams, although it included a workshop in the kitchen garden area. The details of

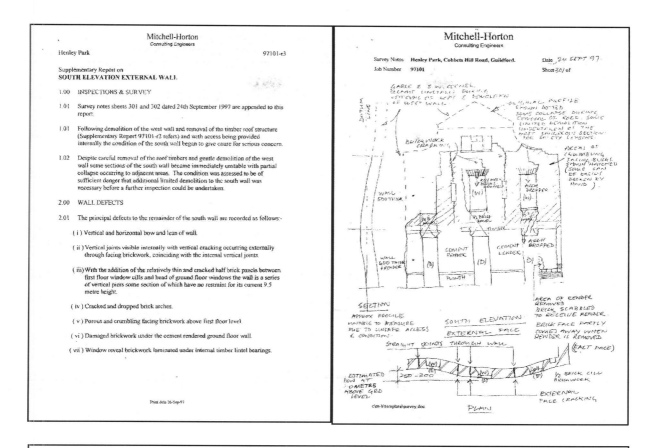

Figure 45: Excerpts from a 1997 surveyor's report
describing the dangerous state of the building.

this proposal were highly confidential as competitive motor racing teams would have liked to get hold of them. Nevertheless, nothing happened, the new plans were withdrawn, there were calls for Guildford Borough Council to use its listed building powers to save Henley Park but they deferred any decision and Insight Securities did indeed go into receivership.

This was probably the nadir of Henley Park's fortunes because by 1992 a new owner, Heritage Renovations Ltd, was in possession and they made a start on repairs by attempting to make the roof watertight. Scaffolding surrounded the building and they were described as 'going further than was required by the Council's emergency works order'. Nevertheless, this was only a holding measure and the condition, in fact the continued survival of the mansion remained in jeopardy for several more years. A survey in 1997 described vertical fractures in the external brickwork, failed ceiling joists, dropped floor beams and collapsed timber lintels inside and sagging and broken purlins in the roof structure. Henley Park reached the top of Guildford Borough Council's 'at risk' list of vulnerable listed buildings.

Heritage Renovations or their associated companies submitted a series of planning applications, all based on converting the mansion into five or six flats with additional residential development in the area to the west, comprising various combinations of houses and flats. Some of these proposed developments were quite attractive and architect's drawings produced in 1994 by Philip Design Associates show the houses grouped around a lake roughly where Vokes' swimming pool had been, with an ornamental bridge echoing the style of the bridge in the gardens below Tumbling Bay, which now lay broken in the undergrowth as the 'bay' silted up.

One after another these plans were narrowly rejected, apparently as an angry reaction against the developers who had allowed the mansion to deteriorate into such an awful state, until at last in April 1996 planning approval was given for one of these residential developments and the dreaded 'glass box' plan was revoked. Flushed with this success, Heritage Renovations promptly sold the property. On 20 November 1996 title absolute was transferred to Lochgate Ltd of Slough, Bucks, and their mortgagees Hencan Ltd of Ascot.

Although the condition of the mansion was extremely dangerous by now, with its walls threatening to collapse and the roof once again bare timbers, in fact its rescuers were at hand. There was just one more planning application to be debated first, because in April 1997 Lochgate submitted a variation of the approved Heritage Renovations plan. On 17 December 1997 Lochgate's plan was approved and the re-birth of Henley Park mansion could begin.

The renovation was executed by Hencan Country Homes Ltd, who had performed conversions of various traditional properties in prestigious locations over the last 15 years including their most recent development in Wanborough. Throughout 1998 work proceeded on the mansion (see Plates 112 and 113) and the extent of the renovation is described in the sales brochure:

'The complete refurbishment of the mansion included a whole new roof structure and a large portion of the brickwork has either been renewed, rebuilt or repointed under the guidance of a structural engineer. Basements have been reconstructed and fully waterproofed. All external windows have been replaced with purpose-made copies of the originals. New staircases, moulded skirtings and architraves are provided throughout.'

Many of the decorative internal touches were designed by Hencan's co-founder Heather Cantle. The complete replacement of the roof structure was specifically allowed in the planning application, subject to the retention of a single roof truss 'as record of the historical structure'.

By the end of the year work on the structure of the mansion was complete and the show house outside was finished and open to visitors. The selling agents, Browns of Guildford, issued a lavish brochure (see Plate 111) with descriptions of the 'superb development in a wonderful parkland setting featuring the conversion of an historic mansion building together with six detached family houses, three mews houses and two attached cottages'. Property writers in the press commented that it had been 'worth the wait'. The properties were offered for sale at premium prices ranging from £225,000 for the attached cottages to £535,000 for the detached houses, while three of the four apartments in the mansion were priced from £360,000 to £410,000. The fourth, the prestigious Thomas Sheriff Place with its huge south-facing rooms with magnificent views to the Hog's Back, was not priced in the brochure.

In 1999 the development work was completed and by August, 14 of the 15 properties had been sold to new owners. As the new century dawned, the mansion which had recently been an empty brick shell was owned by private individuals for the first time in 60 years. Over the next decade a community spirit developed and the residents came together for social events to celebrate occasions such as the Diamond Jubilee of Queen Elizabeth II, and once again families were enjoying living at Henley Park.

Figure 44:
Summary of Developers and Planning applications, 1980-2000.

Date	Application
1981, Mar	Vokes applied to reduce the mansion to its 'original 18th century size', restore its original appearance and create a new prestige office building of comparable volume at the rear of the mansion. The application was initially refused but subsequently approved in Feb 1982. Guildford Borough Council ref: 81P 0405.
1982-86	**Owners Britannia Arrow Holdings, subsidiary of Hampshire and City Estates Ltd of Winchester.**
1983, Oct	Hampshire and City Estates Ltd submitted new plans to restore the mansion and continue its office use, build a new and much bigger (3-storey) office extension with glass-clad walls, sited obliquely behind the mansion and linking to the house [the 'glass box']; also to demolish the Victorian extension along with the remaining outbuildings. Ref: 83P 0291.
1984, Feb	The 'glass box' plans were resubmitted, with an application for a new access road from Cobbett Hill, and all were approved in April. Ref: 84P 0117.
1986-91/92	**Owners Insight Securities of Binfield, Berkshire.**
1986, May	Insight Securities submitted new proposals for courtyard-style period self-contained office buildings (originally ten, later twelve), with leisure facilities and a small clubhouse for the occupiers, plus restoration of the mansion for office use. Ref: 86P 0624. Disposed of in 1991 under Article 27 of Town & Country Planning, which usually means application lapsed or was superseded.
1987, Mar	Insight Securities submitted a new planning application, this time for housing; 16 terraced houses, 32 lock-up garages, squash court and swimming pool, visitors' car parking and restoration of the mansion for office use. Ref: 87P 0555. Disposed of under Article 27 in 1991.
1989, Nov	New planning application for office or light industry use. Ref: 89P 1746. Disposed of under Article 27 in 1991.
1991, Jan	A new developer and prospective purchaser, **Stockton Corporation**, submitted new plans, for a research and development facility probably on behalf of a Formula 1 Motor Racing team. Ref: 91P 0061.
1992-96	**Owners Heritage Renovations Ltd, subsequently Hallpath Ltd.**
1993, May	Henley Park Ltd of Wimbledon submitted a planning application for 16 dwellings in three blocks. Ref: 93P 0582. Disposed of under Article 25 (possible referral to Secretary of State or an appeal.)

Date	Application
1994, Aug	Hallpath Ltd of Farnham applied for development of the site to include restoration and conversion of the mansion into 5 two-bedroom flats as well as 10 four-bedroom semi-detached houses and 4 two-bedroom flats in a separate building on the site of the old stable block. Ref: 94P 1032.
1995, July and Sept	Hallpath Ltd submitted two new alternative plans: Restoration of existing mansion to provide five flats, with construction of: (i) 6 four-bedroom detached houses, 4 two-bedroom flats with parking and 2 one-bedroom flats above lock-up garages for the mansion. Ref: 95P 0917. (ii) 36 low-cost homes in the grounds to the south. Ref: 95P 1218.
1996, Mar	Plan (ii) was rejected because it was considered an 'over-development' and an unwarranted intrusion in the green belt. Also Henley Park was considered an inappropriate location for social housing.
1996, Apr	Planning approval was given to restore and convert the mansion into six flats, plus to build 6 four-bedroom detached houses and 4 two-bedroom flats. Plan 84P 0117 for the glass box was to be revoked.
1996-2001	**Owners Lochgate Ltd, mortgagees Hencan Ltd.**
1997, Apr	Lochgate Ltd submitted a planning application for four houses (in the mansion), 2 four-bed and 4 five-bed houses and 5 three-bed mews houses and garaging. Ref: 97P 0488. (This was a revised version of 95P 0917.) Approved 17th December 1997. [This was the development that was actually implemented.]
1997, Aug	Lochgate Ltd applied for permission & listed building consent to dismantle the existing brick arch and re-erect it in the proposed wall central to the rear of the mansion. Ref: 97P 1224. Approved in November.
1997, Dec	A deed of planning obligation was executed between Guildford Borough Council, Lochgate Ltd of Slough (the owner), Lloyds bank plc (first mortgagee) and Hencan Ltd of Slough (second mortgagee). With ref to 97P 0488.
1998, Aug	Hencan Ltd of Ascot applied for permission to reduce and reshape cedar, oak, copper beech and redwood trees on the site. Ref: 98T 0130. Approved in Sept.

15. CONCLUSION

At first glance there is little left of the long history of Henley Park but the influence of its occupants extended far into the surrounding communities and if you look carefully, there are many reminders both within its park and scattered around the district.

The mansion that symbolises Henley Park remains, with its east façade looking much as it must have done 250 years ago when Solomon Dayrolle remodelled it, while the west façade has gone through many changes and now has yet another new shape. Some of its notable owners such as John de Molyns, Henry Halsey and the Tylneys, have been perpetuated in the names of the apartments and houses that now occupy the site.

The mansion was saved, but the former pleasure gardens to the south and west were not so lucky. The decorative trees by the footpath at the top of the former kitchen garden were incorporated into the 1994 architect's plan but they had all been cleared away by the time of the 1998 development. Although it was intended to have a residents' committee who would take over and maintain the area which had been the pleasure gardens, south lawn and kitchen gardens, in 2001 these were still owned by Lochgate and continue to be neglected. The palm house, nectarine house, carnation house and greenhouses are gone, the rockery and rosary are overgrown and the boating lake and Tumbling Bay have silted up. Almost the only reminder of the care and work that went into creating the lovely gardens are the remains of the Moodies' fountains which can be discovered hidden in the undergrowth in the 'Lily Garden' (Plate 109). Now even more isolated in the fields below the mansion, Chinese Bridge alone has been nicely restored and is still pleasing passers-by today.

As the former south lawn gradually becomes part of the forest, it is easy to forget that some of the trees nearby were planted by royalty. Its plaque has long gone but the cedar at the top of the lawn, planted by one of Queen Victoria's children, is still a fine specimen. However, the pine tree planted outside the front of the mansion by the Prince of Wales was never very healthy and it has disappeared.

The effect of the medieval royal emparkment is still felt today, with the rapid growth of housing in what we now call Normandy while the low-lying park has seen very little development and remains not very different from the landscape that King Edward would have recognised. A few modern buildings have encroached here and there around the edges and Vokes' former factory site stands out incongruously. A network of footpaths centred on the house criss-cross the park, a surviving testimony to the links which once existed between its occupants and the local community. Henley Park farmhouse and its old barn stand on the same spot that they have since the 1650s, although the barn now functions as a desirable residence rather than an agricultural workplace.

Unlike Guildford Park which was sold by the king two years earlier and was soon divided into several separate tenancies, the former royal park at Henley remained intact in single ownership for almost 300 years until 1926. Then over the second half of the 20th century it was divided and subdivided into nearly 50 separate freehold properties, including showmens' caravans' winter quarters and a fishing club (see figure 46). Nevertheless, traces of the original park embankment still survive in several places around its boundary - along the Guildford Road and across Dairymead at Willey Green, up Cobbett Hill and through the plantation to Vokes' former car park, set back some yards from the Pirbright Road west of Orchard House, and between Henley Park Farm and the adjoining fields (Plates 121 and 122) - to remind us of its illustrious past.

Outside the park Normandy Village Hall stood by the crossroads until 2001 as part of Lady Roberts' memorial to the men who served in the Great War, but after 80 years it had to be replaced and now there are houses on the site. Her window still graces Wyke Church, a large window in the east end of the church immediately above the altar which was given by her sister Miss Chadwick and designed by Mr Eden, a friend of the family, and on its dedication in 1926 it was described as 'considerably beautifying the church'. Nearby Lord Pirbright's elaborate tomb reminds us of his importance in the local community. Nothing remains of Lord Pirbright's grand works at the mansion itself but in the village of Pirbright he has left his mark everywhere you look, in the rows of cottages that he built and the hall that stands on the green. Portraits of him and Lady Pirbright, which probably once hung in the mansion, now hang in the hall that will always bear his name. Other portraits of former owners, occupiers and trustees are scattered around the home counties including Edward J Halsey in County Hall at Kingston, Sir John Glynn at Lincoln's Inn, London and Sir Owen Roberts in the holdings of the Clothworkers' Company, as well as the monarchs from Edward II to Charles I and their park keepers who managed the estate.

Within Pirbright parish church, the memorial plaques remain on the walls of the chancel honouring the Halsey family who were deeply involved with Pirbright for so long, while their tombstones remain in the burial ground which was reserved for their use more than a century ago. The family's former mausoleum now the vestry is still structurally the same, but the inscribed marble tablets commemorating Henry and his works have disappeared. The Advowson of Pirbright was retained by the Halseys until 1955 when Francis E Halsey, great grandson of the man who bought it, transferred it to the Lord Chancellor as representative of Her Majesty. The bell from Pirbright Church that hung for many years in the stable block at Henley Park is now in a museum in Chertsey, the town where it was cast. The fireplaces and fittings that were taken out of the mansion probably still exist, but they are rumoured to have been sold at auction and may now be scattered far and wide.

It used to be thought that the manor of Henley and its lordship had descended with the ownership of the estate. Less tangible than the other reminders but still a 'real property' in its own right, the lordship's supposed rights and privileges had been purchased by Henry Halsey in 1784 and the latest reference to it is in a tax assessment of 1885. If it did really still exist at this date, it presumably descended as did the manor of Pirbright. Although he sold all his lands, there is no reference to Henry Joseph Halsey selling his manorial lordships to Ramsay Moodie or anyone else. All the rights and privileges associated with being the lord of the manor were abolished by property acts in the early 20th century, and so the lordships might have been deliberately excluded from the estate sales to minimise the legal complexity of the transactions or they were simply overlooked. Henry Joseph did not specifically mention any lordships in his brief will of 1926. He bequeathed 'all his real and personal estate' to a trustee for the benefit of his younger daughters Linda Agnes and Brenda Iris, so they might automatically have inherited the lordship of Henley.

On the other hand it is more likely that the manor of Henley was quietly replaced by the manor of Cleygate in the 15th century. After the royal emparkment a large part of the manor was still inhabited by people who had been moved out by the king and also by people who already lived in Willey Green, Normandy and Flexford (to use the modern names). These people continued to transact property and trespass on the king's park and manorial procedure would be needed to control and document them. The name of the manor gradually changed from Henley to Cleygate (probably to distinguish the manor outside from the park 'inside'). The manor of Cleygate included all the land surrounding the royal park, and indeed most of the land in modern Normandy and parts of Worplesdon, quite a large area although thinly populated until recent times. It excluded only the royal park. The surviving manorial rolls of Cleygate start in the 1460s, but the manor of Henley/Cleygate existed and must have functioned in some form all the time up to the last Cleygate court record in 1936. So in fact the lord of Henley Manor today is the Ministry of Defence, whose predecessor bought Cleygate in 1876.

However, Henley Park still has to yield up the secret of one of its greatest periods, the site of the medieval royal manor house. It is likely that the royal manor house was located around the southern part of Vokes' factory and it seems no coincidence that the medieval manor, the 17th century Jacobean-style mansion and the 20th century factory buildings were established in turn on the highest point of this ridge which has probably been continuously occupied for over a thousand years. It may never be possible to prove this beyond reasonable doubt because the remains of the earlier buildings would have been heavily disturbed by the more recent building works, so unless archaeological exploration can find new evidence, the park will continue to guard its secret.

Figure 46: Break-up of the Royal Park.

Property	Description and location	Date	Fate
Anchor Moor	7½ acres in the south-west corner of the park, part of Lot 6 in the 1922 estate sale	1926	Sold to A Wiltshire.
		2005	Split up into a nursery, 3 houses and part of 5 gardens.
Henley Park Farm	215 acres on the west and south sides of the park	About 1942	Sold to the tenant, Robert Turner.
		21st century	The converted barns and possibly the farm cottages are separate freeholds.
Kiln Copse and Withybed Copse	Two copses within Henley Park Farm, having no separate land access		Originally retained by Vokes but subsequently ceded to Mr Turner of Henley Park Farm.
8-acre pasture	To the south of the mansion's gardens	1940s	Retained as a 'buffer' by Vokes when Henley Park Farm was sold.
		1990s	Vokes ceded to Mr & Mrs Atkins to hold with Henley Park Farm.
Anchor Copse	5 acres in the south of the park next to Guildford Road	1940s	Originally retained by Vokes when Henley Park Farm was sold.
		1990s	Vokes ceded to Mr & Mrs Atkins to hold with Henley Park Farm.
Deyrolles	1 acre on Cobbett Hill, formerly the White Lodge	1963	Vokes sold to Ted and Margaret Queening.
Electricity substation	Pirbright Road, west of Orchard House	1960s	Vokes apparently sold to the Electricity Board.
Orchard House	On Pirbright Road	1980	Vokes sold to the occupiers.
Orchard Cottage	On Pirbright Road	1980	Vokes sold to the occupiers.

Figure 46: Break-up of the Royal Park (continued).

Property	Description and location	Date	Fate
East Corner	46 acres, originally farmed with Whipley Farm	1940s	Apparently sold by Vokes.
		1968	All owned by David Burrows, whose application to build a farmhouse on it was refused.
	Cobbett Hill Meadow, 8 acres part of the East Corner at the junction of Guildford Road and Cobbett Hill.	1994	Purchased by Cove Angling Society who created a fishing lake.
	Whipley Moor, 7 acres part of the East Corner on Guildford Road	1995	Owned by Garry Whittle, used as a showman's caravan ground.
		2001	Twelve separately-owned freehold properties.
	Grassypiece coppice, part of the East Corner on Guildford Road	1970s-2000s	A separately-owned freehold smallholding.
	Anthony's Meadow and Drove Lane Moor, part of the East Corner	2001	Separately owned.
	Another part of Whipley Moor and another part of Cobbett Hill Meadow, 5 acres part of the East Corner	2001	Separately owned.
Henley Park mansion and gardens	26 acres including the mansion, gardens and meadow to the west	1982	Vokes sold to Hampshire and City Estates.
		1999	Hencan Limited developed and sold 15 separate freehold properties, plus the commonly-owned gardens and approach road.
	Meadow to the west of the mansion's formal gardens	1940s	Retained as a 'buffer' by Vokes when Henley Park Farm was sold.
		1982	Sold to Hampshire and City Estates with the mansion.
		1999	Part of 'Fox Hollow', one of the new properties developed by Hencan.
Vokes	150 acres of Vokes' factory and woodland	2001	Still owned by Vokes Ltd of London.

Figure 47: The Owners of Henley Park in the last one thousand years.

Approximate dates	Years	Owner
1066		Azor, a Saxon
Before 1086 to at least 1343	about 300	Chertsey Abbey
to 1324		William de Henley, leasehold from the Abbey
1324 to 1327	3	Kings Edward II and III, from the Abbey
1327 to 1337	10	William de Clinton, grant for life
1337 to 1340	3	John de Molyns, from the Abbey
1340 to 1345	5	King Edward III, from the Abbey
1345 to 1351	6	John de Molyns again
1351 to 1632	281	The Crown, from Edward III to Charles I (see Figure 5 for a list of park-keepers)
1632 to 1649	17	Arthur Squibb
1649 to 1703	54	The Glynn family; John, John and Dorothy
1703 to 1739	35	Richard Child, Earl Tylney and Dorothy Glynn his wife
1739 to 1784	45	Solomon Dayrolle
1784 to 1925	141	The Halsey family; Henry, Henry WRW and Henry JT
1925 to 1940	15	Edwin Ramsay Moodie
1940 to 1982	42	Vokes Ltd
1982 to 1999	17	Property developers (see Figure 44 for a list of developers)
1999 to date		Various separate owners

ACKNOWLEDGEMENTS

The original idea inspired by Pat Ashworth was to have a picture book, featuring the many pictures of Henley Park in the Normandy Historians' collection, with some historical description as captions. As we researched Henley Park's rich history this quickly grew into a full-blown book. So firstly with special thanks to Mrs Pat and the late Mark Ashworth, for sharing the monumental task of researching and editing the history of Henley Park for many years, until forced to retire due to personal circumstances.

The list of sources and bibliography overleaf will give an indication of the material consulted in many record offices and libraries and I am extremely grateful to the staff of all those establishments, in particular the Surrey History Centre at Woking and The National Archive at Kew, in both of which I have spent many, many hours over the last ten years and more.

This work could not have been produced without a multitude of people who provided their thoughts, advice, reminiscences, pictures, documents and help of various kinds. My sincere thanks go to everyone who has supported the Henley Park project in so many ways, including:
Mrs Ann Adey of Normandy, Jean Allan of Farnham, Peregrine Armstrong-Jones and Nina Holmes of Bentley's Entertainments, Mr Ashim at the National Library [of India], Calcutta, Mrs Elizabeth and the late Robin Atkins of Normandy, the late John Baker, artist and historian, Alan Capell of Normandy, Linda Crane and Rex Shorey of Vokes Ltd, Alan Crocker of Guildford, Derek George Crooke of Banstead, Roy Drysdale, photographer, Jonathan and Joan Foster of Pirbright Historians, Shirley Forster of Pirbright Historians, Wilf Fry of Pirbright, Emma Golding of The British Red Cross, Peter Harrod, postal historian, Mr M Hodgin, Verger and Parish clerk of St Giles in the Fields Church, London, Guy Holborn of Lincolns Inn Library, Joanna Hopkins of The Royal Society, David Inglesant, Audrey and the late Michael Jackman of Wrecclesham, Hannah Jefferey of Surrey Archaeological Society, Comte Anthony de Kerdrel, Jack Kinder of Normandy, Derek Love of Pirbright, David Low of Horsell, Dave and Tracy Mair of Normandy, Jonathan Manser of The Manser Practice, Hammersmith, Tom Miller of Philip Design Associates, Guildford, Paul Mitchell of Mitchell-Horton Ltd, Pirbright, Edward Moodie, Serena Hoult and Robin Windus, grandchildren of E Ramsay Moodie, the late Commander Robin HR Moodie, Eddie Moore of Woking, the late John Mullard of Ash, Ray Mullard, Peter Netherton of Pirbright, the late Hilda Noldart, Chris Pamplin formerly of Vokes Ltd, Robin Parr formerly of FM Modern Design Ltd of Eashing, Mrs Val Patrick of Aughton, Wilts, Dr Pennie Pemberton of Noel Butlin Archives Centre, Canberra, Australia, Christopher John Pettitt of Wyke, Pirbright Churchwardens, Pirbright Parish Council, Andy and Julian the proprietors of Plâs Dinas Country House hotel, Phil Potter of Pinewoods, Rob Poulton of Surrey County Archaeological Unit, Richard Prior, expert on deer, Mrs Margaret and the late Ted Queening of Cobbett Hill, David Rose, formerly of the Surrey Advertiser, Derrick Searle, caretaker of Lord Pirbright's Hall, Guy Selby-Lowndes, by email, the late Stan and Mrs Edie Sharp of Normandy, Dave Slaughter of Willey Green, AC Southern, the late Mrs Marguerite Suter of Pirbright, Robin Tapsfield, Gwen Tickner of Brighton, Peter Travaskis of Wyke, Dennis Turner of Reigate, Maggie Vaughan-Lewis formerly of Surrey History Centre, Roy Vickers of Ash, Gordon H 'Tony' Vokes of Guildford, Tony Waller of Camberley, Ellen Warby of Fairlands, Wyn Watkins of Pirbright, Dr Mrs L West of Whipley Manor, Marjorie Wheeler of Pirbright, Christopher Whittick of Lewes, Sussex, Linda Wilton of Sturminster Newton, Dorset, and all members of Normandy Historians past and present.

Finally, with special thanks to Sheila Squier for her support and tolerance of my preoccupation with Henley Park for the last twelve years.

My profound apologies to anyone I have inadvertently omitted.

SOURCES AND BIBLIOGRAPHY

Sources

Bath and North-East Somerset Record Office: City rate books.

British Library (BL): Lansdowne MSS (Chertsey Abbey cartularies); Dayrolle correspondence,
ref: Add MSS 15866-15885; Dayrolle references in other papers, ref Add MSS (various),
Stowe 243; Letters of Horace Walpole, edited by P Cunningham, ref: DSC W5/4139-4147.

British Library, Oriental and India Office (re: Henry Halsey in Calcutta).

British Library, Newspaper Library, Collindale: Surrey Times (re: funeral of HJT Halsey).

Burney Collection of 17th and 18th century newspapers at the British Library (online).

British Red Cross, National Headquarters Archivist, personal communication: Accounts of Auxiliary
Hospitals, 1916 and 1918; BRCS Surrey Branch, Annual Reports 1916 and 1917;
Reports of the Joint War Committee, HMSO 1921.

Browns Estate Agents, Guildford (sale brochure).

Cathedral and Church Buildings division of the Church of England (re: Pirbright Church).

Church of England Record Centre, 15 Galleywall Road, SE16 3PB.

City of London Archaeological Society web site 2004 (re: Sir Robert Burnett).

English Heritage, National Monuments Record, Swindon (re: the archway, 1991).

Essex Record Office, Chelmsford: Richard Child marriage settlement ref: D/DCw T13.

FM Modern Design Ltd of Eashing.

General Register Office birth, marriage and death certificates and indexes.

Guildford Borough Council; various planning applications.

Guildford Institute, Newspaper cuttings album, ref: Biog 1 p.69 (re: EJ Halsey).

Guildford Museum; Matthew Alexander, curator, and Nick Booth.

Hampshire Record Office, Winchester: Tylney deeds (various) including ref: 8M48/12.

Havant Museum (description of CG Vokes' gun collection).

Historic Environment Record (HER) at the Surrey History Centre (SHC), Woking.

History and Development of Vokes Ltd; typescript received from Roy Vickers of Ash.

Honourable Society of Lincolns Inn, London; Guy Holborn, librarian (re: Glynne portrait).

Hotel Metropole, Brighton, web site 2004.

Land Registry for Surrey, Boldon House, Wheatlands Way, Pity Me, Durham DH1 5GJ.

London Lives, an online searchable index.

London Metropolitan Archives: Middlesex Deeds Register (re: Halsey London properties);
Documents relating to Pirbright churchyard, ref: DW/OP/P.

McLeod Russel Holdings plc and Blake Lapthorn, solicitors (re: deeds).

Ministry of Defence, personal communication 1987 (re: Normandy Pond).

National Library [of India], Calcutta, Mr Ashim (re: Henry Halsey in Calcutta).

National Rifle Association, Bisley (re: Cowshot Farm).

Newspapers & periodicals: various editions of The Aldershot News, Jewish Chronicle,
News and Mail, Surrey Advertiser and County Times, Surrey Times, The Aeroplane,
War Illustrated and Woking Observer (quoted in The Day Before Yesterday).

Normandy Historians (NH), various including:
ref: MP7, Plan in a conveyance from the War Office to EJ Halsey, from Mr Hedges
ref: PW63, Invitation to Coronation celebrations at Henley Park, from the late Mrs D Page.

Ordnance Survey maps, various including 25-inch maps 1871, 1895 and 1915 at SHC.

Parish registers and marriage licences; various parishes at various locations, including Society of
Genealogists and the International Genealogical Index (online).

Pirbright Historians.

Pirbright parish church; Memorials and gravestone inscriptions.

Pirbright Parish Council: minute books and material in the hall.

Plâs Dinas Country House.

Somerset County Record Office, Taunton: Yeovil deeds, ref: DD/PR\9; Land Tax; Tithe Survey.

Surrey Archaeological Society (SyAC): ref: 140/4 Ash/1 (re: Ripley and Knaphill Harriers) and
    ref: 300/36/4 (letters from CG Vokes).

The Surrey History Service (SHS), records at the Surrey History Centre (SHC), Woking, including:
    Ash poor rate books 1891-1904, ref: 2618/1; Coussmaker family papers, ref: 7052;
    Declarations of the bounds of Worplesdon parish, ref: WOR/15/1; Deeds (various);
    Diaries of Edward Ryde, surveyor of Woking, ref: 1262; Electoral registers;
    Fords Farm Estate Sale Catalogue 1870, ref: 5238/4; Halsey family papers, ref: 1794;
    Henley Park Estate Sale Catalogue, 1922, ref: SP/368 or CC/99/8/1; Land tax, microfilm;
    Leases of shooting rights, ref: 1320/62/26-27; Loseley Manuscripts, ref: LM (various);
    Manor of Farnham Estate Sale Catalogues 1789, ref: 85/2/1(1)/32-33;
    Manor of Pirbright court records, refs: 1794 and 2924/1;
    Manor of the Rectory of Woking court records, ref: 2924/2;
    Normandy Manor Estate Sale Catalogues, June and November 1895, ref: SP/206;
    Old Woking poor rate books, ref: P52/6; Pirbright advowson and burial ground, ref: PI/9;
    Pirbright peat dispute papers, ref: 1209/26; Plans of pews at Ash Church, ref: AS/15/6-7;
    Rails Farm Estate Sale Catalogue 1945, refs: 1384/27/3 and 5280/5;
    Return of Owners of Land, 1873, open access; Tithing survey and apportionments, c.1840;
    Window tax, ref: QS 6/7; Worplesdon Place papers, ref: 6159/9/3.

Surreyproperty.com (re: Azor).

The British Deer Society.

The Clothworkers' Company.

The National Archive (TNA), records including: Various Accounts in Special Collections class SC6;
    Account for repairs to buildings in Henley Park 1515, ref: E36/262;
    Burials at Sandhurst Military Cemetery, ref: WO 156 450 (re: General Scovell);
    National Census returns, 1841-1901;
    Calendars and original Patent, Close, Fine, Pipe and Charter Rolls and Escheats;
    Close Roll ref: C54/189 (royal purchase); Letter Patent ref: C66/2600 (royal sale);
    Close Roll ref: C54/3553 (re: sale Squibb to Glynne, tenement called Marvines);
    Court of Chancery ref: C7/397/78 (papers relating to the Squibb dispute);
    Calendar of State Papers Domestic; Deeds enrolled at Chancery (various);
    Exchequer deeds, class E40 (re: land purchases 1355); Exchequer accounts, class E101;
    Lay Subsidy rolls (re: Stephen Squibb in Pirbright);
    Manor of Cleygate court records, ref: TS19; Manor of Southhenle court roll, ref: SC2/204/54;
    Manorial Documents Commission papers, ref: HMC 9/229;
    Manorial Documents Register, formerly at the Historical Documents Commission;
    National Farming Survey 1940-43, ref: MAF32/1044/39;
    National Valuation Survey field books 1910-15 for Ash, Pirbright & Worplesdon, ref: IR58.
    [Note: there is no relevant reference to Vokes in the catalogue of Ministry of War documents.]

The Royal Society, list of fellows (online).

The Ships List (online).

The Spickermans: A Palatine family (an online family history) (re: the Palatines).

Trade directories, at SHC and TNA.

Trustees of Normandy Village Hall, indenture of conveyance of land (copy at NH MSS151).

Westminster City Archive.

Whyte and Mackay, web site 2004 (re: Sir Robert Burnett).

Wills proved at the PCC, at TNA and online, and at the Principal Probate Registry, and indexes.

Wood Street Village History Society (re: farms).

Bibliography

Alumni Oxonienses, British History Online.

Ashworth P and Kinder J. Westwood, Normandy, the story of a Surrey Estate,
        Westwood Place Management, 1998 (re: Orchard House and Orchard Cottage).

Ashworth P and Squier J. John Norden's Survey of Henley Park 1607, in Surrey History vol XI, 2012.

Ashworth P and Squier J. Portrait of Sir John Glynne and his Family at Henley Park,
        in Surrey History vol XI, 2012.

Brayley EW. History of Surrey vol 1, Robert Best Ede, 1841.

Browning DC. Everyman's Dictionary of Quotations and Proverbs, 1965 (re: Chesterfield last words).

Bryson B. At Home, Doubleday, 2010.

Buildings of England, Sussex volume, edited by N Pevsner, 1965.

Burke's Dormant, Abeyant, Forfeited and Extinct Peerages of the British Empire, 1883.

Cawthorn Miss and Curtis H. Collections for a History of Pirbright, 1931,
        by courtesy of Mrs Margaret Queening and at SHC ref: 942.2 PIR S1x.

Chesterfield's Letters to His Son, by The Earl of Chesterfield; The Project Gutenberg eBook of
        the PG Edition, online transcript 2006.

Crocker A. Analysis of accounts for repairs to buildings in Guildford Park in 1514,
        in Surrey Archaeological Collections vol 90, 2003.

Crocker A. Keepers of Guildford Park, unpublished notes.

Curtis H. Early Incumbents of Pirbright, Worplesdon and Ash, 1924, at SHC and Worplesdon Hall.

Debrett's Peerage and Baronetage (various editions).

Dictionary of National Biography (DNB), Oxford University Press, hardcopy and online.

Driver JT. Sir Thomas St Leger, in Surrey Archaeological Collections vol 94, 2008.

Encyclopaedia Britannica 15th edition (re: Lord Chesterfield).

Flynn D. Sir William More of Loseley, in Surrey Archaeological Collections vol 91, 2004.

Gentleman's Magazine (several references, as indicated in DNB).

Halsey KD. Remembrances of Pirbright, at SHC ref: 2791.

Harvey J. Medieval Gardens, Batsford, 1981.

Hearnshaw FJC. The Place of Surrey in the History of England, Macmillan, 1936 (re: Norman Horde).

Henley Park, Historic Building Consultants report by AK Nyasai, Oct 1994.

History of the Kings Works, edited by HM Colvin, HMSO, 1963.

Hodge 'Billy'. The Parson, the Peer and the School Board, in Surrey History vol III no. 3, c.1986.

Howkins C. Royal Tapestry, Author, 1985.

Hurstfield J. Freedom, Corruption and Government in Elizabethan England, J Cape, 1973 (Wardship).

Jackson Rev HF. A Guide to St Peter's Church, Ash, 1981.

Janaway J. Surrey a County History, Countryside Books, 1994.

Kinder J. A History of the Family of Kinder, Author, 2009.

Kinder J. Frymlesworth, a discussion paper, 1994, NH ref: MSS73.

Kinder J. The geology of the region, 1993, NH ref: MSS66.

Kinder J. The Pirbright Tomb, 1992, NH ref: MSS56.

Lacey R and Danziger D. The Year 1000, Little Brown and Co, 1999.

London HS and Squibb GD. A Dorset King of Arms, in Proceedings of the Dorset Natural History
        and Archaeological Society vol 68, 1946.

Mais SPB. Britain Calling, Hutchinson, 1938.

Manning O and Bray W. The History and Antiquities of .... Surrey Vol 3, John Nicols & Son, 1814.

Milton G. Nathaniel's Nutmeg, Hodder and Stoughton, 1999.

Mitchell L. The Whig World, Hambledon, 2005.

Morton F. The Rothschilds, Penguin Books, 1964.

Munby L. How much is that worth?, Phillimore, 1996.

Nair PT. A History of Calcutta's Streets, Firma KLM Ltd Calcutta, 1987.

Nair PT. Hicky and his Gazette, S & T Book Stall Kolkata, 2001.

Newland W. Survey of Pirbright 1805-07, map hanging in Lord Pirbright's Hall.

Newland W. Survey of Pirbright 1805-07, accompanying schedule at SHC ref: 2124/1/4.

Norden J. Description of the Honor of Windsor, 1607, at BL ref: Harley MS 3749.

Notes & Queries Magazine, 1850 pp 219, 373, 476; 1886 ii p.425; 1924 July 5.

Notes on Normandy Village Hall, published by the management committee, 1932.

Notices and remains of the family of Tyrwhitt (unpublished), at BL ref: 9916.de.46.

Palmer RJ. Pirbright Papers, 1979, at SHC ref: 942.21 Pir.

Pepys diary (online) (re: Sir John Glynne).

Pirbright Historians. Pirbright Then and Now, The Pirbright Historians, 2012.

Rocque. Map of Surrey 1768, copy at SHC.

Royal Historical Society handbook no. 4, 1991 (regnal years).

Sambrook P. The Country House Servant, Sutton, 1999.

Sawyer PH. Anglo-Saxon charters, an annotated list and bibliography, Royal Historical Society, 1968.

Senex. Map of Surrey 1729, copy at SHC.

Shaw WA. Letters of Denization and Acts of Naturalisation 1603-1700, Huguenot Society, 1911.

Smith JE. Parliamentary representation of Surrey from 1290, Wightman, 1927.

Smith RAL. Bath, Batsford, 1944.

Stephens P. Surrey Heath under the Tudors and Stuarts, Surrey Heath Local History Club, 2002.

Surrey Archaeological Society Bulletin no. 411, Nov 2008 (re: Roman site).

Surrey County Archaeological Unit (SCAU). A preliminary archaeological assessment of the Henley Park development, 1996.

SCAU. An Archaeological assessment and evaluation at Henley Park, 1997.

SCAU. An Archaeological watching brief at Henley Park, 1997, copy at SyAC Library.

SCAU. Archaeological Assessment of land at Henley Business Park, 2004, at HER number 6942.

Surrey Record Society (SRS) volumes at SHC:
vol III, Surrey Musters; vol XI, early Taxation Returns; vol XII, Chertsey Abbey Cartularies; vol XVII, Surrey Hearth Tax; vol XXXIX, Surrey Probate Inventories.

Surrey Through the Century, Surrey County Council, 1989 (re: EJ Halsey).

Sykes L. Calcutta through British Eyes, Oxford University Press, 1992.

The A to Z of Regency London, London Topographical Society, 1985, at Westminster City Archive.

The Domesday Book, Surrey, edited by John Morris, Phillimore, 1975.

The Ill-fated House of Cowdray, British Isles Genealogy online, 2004.

The London Gazette online (various).

The Manor House, Normandy, DBRG report, from Mr & Mrs C Messer (re: Advert in the Times).

The Story of St Michael's Church, Pirbright (no author), at SHC ref: SP726.5 PIR.

Underwood G. Guildford Park, article in Surrey History, 2002.

Victoria History of the County of Surrey, 1994.

Vine PAL. London's Lost Route to Basingstoke, David and Charles, 1968.

Vokes Group Magazine, various editions 1965-68.

Vokes Ltd. The History of Henley Park, c.1971 (various details and reminiscences apparently from conversations with local residents and employees, also the 'Lady in Mauve' story).

Webb C. A Guide to Surrey Manorial Records, West Surrey FHS research aid 35, 1993.

Wells M. Entertaining Eric, Pan/Imperial War Museum, 1988.

Who's Who 2003 (re: John Profumo).

Who Was Who (various editions).

Wikipedia online encyclopaedia.

Worplesdon 2000, published by Worplesdon Parish Council (re: Sir LE Halsey).

Yool H. The Day Before Yesterday: The Story of Pirbright, 1973, at SHC ref: 942.2 PIR.

INDEX

192

194